MW00443936

More Praise for *The Practice of Professional Consulting*

"A timely, thorough, and thoughtful primer on the art and practice of consulting. Packed with practical tools and punctuated with the wisdom of experience, Verlander's book provides a great introduction to the profession, a detailed inventory of the skills of an effective consultant, and a solid foundation upon which to build a successful consulting practice."
Dr. Albert A. Vicere, president, Vicere Associates, Inc.; Executive Education Professor of Strategic Leadership, The Smeal College of Business, The Pennsylvania State University

"An invaluable, indispensable reference for independent consultants, scholars and firms of the consulting industry; Edward Verlander's *The Practice* of *Professional Consulting* unlocks the mysteries of the business by providing a clear, comprehensive guide to a practice often misunderstood by the masses."
Chengang Zhou, director and senior vice president, New Oriental Education & Technology Group, Beijing, China

"Developing a consultative mindset and accelerating professional (consulting) skills is critical to succeeding in business and growing a career. The skills described in this book are relevant not just for aspiring consultants, but for anyone interested in sharpening communication skills and improving their personal brand."
Bob Hannafin, Ph.D., former director at PricewaterhouseCoopers; dean, College of Education, Information, and Technology, Long Island University

"This engaging book provides a unique overview of the practice of professional consulting and what it takes for a successful and productive relationship with the ubiquitous consultant. In order to select a trusted advisor, from the onset the employer needs sufficient knowledge of the competencies required to coach, motivate, and navigate the consultant. Edward Verlander's book provides a fundamental knowledge of the basic principles for nonconsultant practitioners and should be especially useful for the medical and scientific communities who frequently rely on consultants without possessing essential knowledge to maximize their return on investment."
Martin R. Evans, Ph.D., MT (ASCP), director, Technical Affairs, manager, Environmental Sciences, Public Health Laboratory, NYC Department of Health and Mental Hygiene

"For young consultants who need to get a good start in this profession, for consultants who want to grow professionally, and for experienced consultants who seek new perspectives, Edward Verlander's book explains a proven consulting process. The book comes with a great set of tools for immediate use and explains new insights on consulting.

"Year after year, I have seen young and experienced consultants become enthusiastic, motivated, and eager to immediately apply Edward Verlander's ideas, tools, and techniques. Some felt awakened to a new level of professionalism; certainly everybody felt empowered for new successes. Chapter by chapter readers will ignite a better understanding of how to provide more business-oriented, more client-oriented, and therefore more successful consulting services."
Elmar Buschlinger, former CEO of several IT companies; entrepreneur and coach in IT-related businesses, Karlsruhe, Germany

"To build on the momentum of great ideas that are truly innovative, the business must move today with unprecedented velocity. Verlander's model of consulting describes the capabilities needed to develop ideas with a pace giving rise to product that is truly differentiated in the market. A strong read for anyone looking to take the consulting discipline to a new level."
Darrin Solomon, vice president, Product Management, CA Technologies, New York

THE PRACTICE OF PROFESSIONAL CONSULTING

THE PRACTICE OF PROFESSIONAL CONSULTING

Edward G. Verlander

JOSSEY-BASS
A Wiley Imprint
www.josseybass.com

Copyright © 2012 by John Wiley & Sons, Inc. All Rights Reserved.

Published by Pfeiffer
An Imprint of Wiley
One Montgomery Street, Suite 1200, San Francisco, CA 94104-4594
www.pfeiffer.com

No part of this publication may be reproduced, stored in a retrieval system, or transmitted in any form or by any means, electronic, mechanical, photocopying, recording, scanning, or otherwise, except as permitted under Section 107 or 108 of the 1976 United States Copyright Act, without either the prior written permission of the Publisher, or authorization through payment of the appropriate per-copy fee to the Copyright Clearance Center, Inc., 222 Rosewood Drive, Danvers, MA 01923, 978-750-8400, fax 978-646-8600, or on the web at www. copyright.com. Requests to the Publisher for permission should be addressed to the Permissions Department, John Wiley & Sons, Inc., 111 River Street, Hoboken, NJ 07030, 201-748-6011, fax 201-748-6008, or online at http://www.wiley.com/go/permissions.

Limit of Liability/Disclaimer of Warranty: While the publisher and author have used their best efforts in preparing this book, they make no representations or warranties with respect to the accuracy or completeness of the contents of this book and specifically disclaim any implied warranties of merchantability or fitness for a particular purpose. No warranty may be created or extended by sales representatives or written sales materials. The advice and strategies contained herein may not be suitable for your situation. You should consult with a professional where appropriate. Neither the publisher nor author shall be liable for any loss of profit or any other commercial damages, including but not limited to special, incidental, consequential, or other damages. Readers should be aware that Internet websites offered as citations and/or sources for further information may have changed or disappeared between the time this was written and when it is read.

For additional copies/bulk purchases of this book in the U.S. please contact 800-274-4434.

Pfeiffer books and products are available through most bookstores. To contact Pfeiffer directly call our Customer Care Department within the U.S. at 800-274-4434, outside the U.S. at 317-572-3985, fax 317-572-4002, or visit www.pfeiffer.com.

Pfeiffer publishes in a variety of print and electronic formats and by print-on-demand. Some material included with standard print versions of this book may not be included in e-books or in print-on-demand. If this book refers to media such as a CD or DVD that is not included in the version you purchased, you may download this material at **http://booksupport.wiley.com**. For more information about Wiley products, visit **www.wiley.com**.

Library of Congress Cataloging-in-Publication Data

Verlander, Edward George.
   The practice of professional consulting / Edward G. Verlander. – 1st ed.
      p. cm.
   Includes index.
   ISBN 978-1-118-24184-4 (cloth), ISBN 978-1-118-28605-0 (ebk), ISBN 978-1-118-28419-3 (ebk), ISBN 978-1-118-28311-0 (ebk) (hardback)
   1. Business consultants. 2. Consulting firms. I. Title.
   HD69.C6V475 2012
   001–dc23

                                                    2012012454

Acquiring Editor: Matthew Davis
Director of Development: Kathleen Dolan Davies
Developmental Editor: Byron Schneider

Production Editor: Justin Frahm
Editor: Kristi Hein
Editorial Assistant: Michael Zelenko
Manufacturing Supervisor: Becky Morgan

Printed in the United States of America
HB Printing   10   9   8   7   6   5   4   3   2   1

CONTENTS

PART TWO: APPLYING THE MODEL   53

Appendices

For Naresh and Maya

ABOUT THIS BOOK

Change is the lifeblood of consulting, just as organizations endure only through successful change. The reality of this mutual need lies at the heart of what consulting is all about. Consultants solve problems created by the powerful forces of change in an organization's environment, and in so doing, they themselves create change. Collectively, they drive a $300 billion, worldwide industry dedicated to improving the purposes of business organizations and how those purposes are achieved. To be in the midst of such a fascinating, global endeavor makes consulting an attractive, exciting, challenging, and rewarding career for the twenty-first century.

The Practice of Professional Consulting is a practical examination of what has been called "the world's newest profession." The book traverses the industry, the processes, tools, and skills used by consultants to produce solutions for their clients, and why it is a growing, attractive career. It discusses best practices used by leading consulting firms, specifies the capabilities needed in each stage of an engagement, and recommends ways to ensure that consultants solve client problems in a systematic, professional way. A core theme is learning what is needed to become a trusted consultant.

New information in this book includes:

- A model of the complete consulting cycle
- A diagnostic instrument for assessing consulting roles

- Ideas for how to develop political intelligence to navigate client organizations
- Tools for managing consulting meetings, risk assessment, and skills transfer
- Techniques for communications, emotional intelligence, presentations, and listening
- Tools for conducting effective needs assessment and problem framing
- Concepts of trust needed to become a trusted advisor
- Factors affecting the stature of consulting as a profession
- A general set of guidelines or competencies for effective consulting
- References and handy website sources

All of the ideas, tools, and competencies described in this book have been vetted by a wide range of consulting practitioners and thus represent their accumulated experience about successful consulting. They are gathered in this book for the first time.

Who should read *The Practice of Professional Consulting?*

○ *Anyone wishing to start a consulting business.* The book supplements other books on how to start and run a consulting business. Rather than taking a project management view, this book adds to the reader's understanding of how to deal with the rational and emotional, conceptual, and practical requirements of consulting. It presents, describes, and analyzes consulting as both a delicate interplay of human interactions and motivations and a cold application of expertise and logic, all applied to solve real problems for people and client organizations. The book is broad enough to be useful to anyone starting any kind of consulting business, yet specific in explaining typical client situations.

○ *New employees of consulting firms.* Any new employee in a consulting firm should read this book as a supplement to the firm's own formal training program. Consulting firms that provide in-classroom training as well as mentoring will find that this book accelerates development by providing new employees with a perspective of the rules, roles, values, methods, and techniques used across firms in the consulting industry.

○ *Instructors of training programs on consulting.* The book can be used to design and develop training programs on professional consulting or as a supplement to existing training, to give attendees more details and perspectives not covered in the training.

○ *Business school faculty.* The book can be used as the main text or supplementary text in a business school course on consulting (or related disciplines such as human resources, change management, or organization development). It is well-referenced and introduces students to standard industry practices. Importantly, it shows how to become a trusted consultant.

The Practice of Professional Consulting provides an easy way to understand the stages, roles, and tasks found in any type of consulting—management, information technology, human resources, strategy, or training—and it provides simple and easy-to-use techniques and templates for implementation. The book gives insight into how to think and behave as a consultant, practical advice about project teams, explanations of what clients expect of their consultants, and the personal qualities needed to be an outstanding, trusted consultant.

PREFACE

There has never been a better time to be a consultant. Like the medieval craft guilds that built the great cathedrals of Europe, consultants are the modern-day builders of business cathedrals, using data, information, and technology systems to develop business strategies that help businesses grow. Technology consultants design systems that enable companies to make money through the manipulation and selling of information. Strategy consultants conceive future plans; management consultants reengineer organizational structures, administrative systems, and workflows; and human resources consultants train employees on the skills to make it all work.

As was true for medieval craftsmen, the quality of the products and services produced by consultants—in terms of cost, efficiency, accessibility, usability, and effectiveness—depends on the quality of the people producing them. The quality of the people is tied directly to the level of their professionalism, technical knowledge, intellectual power, and interpersonal skills and the reach of their business perspective. These are the building blocks and mortar of today's business cathedrals. These critical success factors determine the quality of individual consultants and the quality of consulting firms.

I've said that change is the lifeblood of consulting—and we are in the midst of fundamental and widespread change at every level of human society. In government, business, not-for-profit organizations, schools at every level, churches, families, and individual lives, the scope of change is unprecedented in human history. In this context, leaders of every organization and institution are trying to answer the basic question: What should we be tomorrow that is different, more effective, and more efficient than we were yesterday? The very survival of an organization depends on the answer to that question and the corresponding actions taken to help it adapt. Failure to act can be disastrous. In recent years, we have seen the demise of very large, seemingly impregnable companies—such as Kodak, Circuit City, GM, Tribune, and Bethlehem Steel—that either could not or would not answer this question or were unable to make changes quickly enough to survive.

It is the role of consultants to help company leaders craft solutions to their strategic, operational, and human problems and then influence them on the scope, speed, and direction of the changes they need to make. In this role, consultants serve as agents of change by asking the right questions, identifying relevant issues, gathering and analyzing the facts, developing a plan of action, searching for solutions, and advising on their implementation. Consulting is the wellspring of change.

Consulting is also a strategic endeavor that enables people and organizations to better adapt to the changing conditions of their environment. The questions consultants face are often complex and challenging, involving matters at the very heart of an organization's vision and purpose. As such, consultants solve problems in organizational processes and workflows, governance structure, organizational culture, the skills and capabilities of people, management systems and administrative procedures, policies and practices, as well as business strategy. Consulting is therefore a vital and an incredibly important responsibility, with thousands of people in an organization often affected by the consultant's work.

Today, graduates from science and technical disciplines as well as the humanities go into consulting because it is a lucrative, exciting career, and consulting firms are looking for diverse backgrounds in their employees. Consulting is especially attractive to newly minted MBAs because it is a natural extension of MBA studies. Armed with a broad swath of theory, experience, and a systems view of the world, MBAs can apply their knowledge to many organizational problems. McKinsey, Booz, Bain, Deloitte, and Oliver Wyman, to mention just a few, annually hire hundreds of MBA graduates who can bring a combination of broad business knowledge, teamwork, energy, analytical skills, and excellent communications to the complex problems of their clients. Consulting is a well-paying career that provides many opportunities to travel, learn about many companies and industries, solve real-world problems, help people, and have a substantial impact in the world.

To be clear, this book is an introduction to consulting. It is not for consultants with many years of experience or for senior consultants in large consulting firms. Although the content may serve as a handy reminder to such people, most of the principles and practices will already be part of their professional repertoire. The target audience for the book encompasses four kinds of people: (1) individuals considering consulting as a career and wanting to know more about it, (2) new consultants who need a primer on building a consulting practice and business, (3) corporate professional development staff who need a text to accompany a related training course, and (4) university faculty who need a text to teach a course on consulting.

The book covers many consulting topics, some in more depth than others. But amid the myriad of principles, practices, values, tools, and techniques are several themes. The first theme is a unifying model of the cycle of consulting, from finding and winning business to managing client relations and deploying solutions. A second theme concerns the issue of professionalism in consulting. We offer a starting point for discussing the education, certification, and standards of practice needed to increase professionalism in consulting. It is ripe for a closer examination, and we hope this book makes a contribution to that end.

A third theme concerns the skills needed to build long-term client relationships. These are people skills or what McKinsey calls the "soft skills" of organizational effectiveness: shared values, style, skills, and staffing. Developing staff with strong people skills (not just technical ability) is a key differentiator for professional service firms, and as such, we highlight the many opportunities to demonstrate such skills throughout the consulting cycle. Finally, a fourth theme is the journey of becoming a trusted advisor. As an introduction to the field of professional consulting, in this book we point the way, discuss the building blocks, and suggest the success factors for achieving that important goal—of turning an apprentice consultant into a trusted advisor.

ACKNOWLEDGMENTS

This book has taken over five years to write and draws on the author's twenty-five busy years of international consulting experience. It is an obvious thing to say, yet true, that it could not have been written without the support and help of many people. It also true that over such a long period of time, the names of all the many people who helped to shape my thinking and practice cannot be remembered; but their teachings remain.

I would like to mention a number of consultants, professors, researchers, and leaders who have given their generous insights, advice, and support to me over the years (even if they did not know they were teaching me at the time): Robert Arning of KPMG; Michael Grimstad of Bain; Rachel Miller of Deloitte; Erin Zola of Russell Reynolds; and William Blanchard, Francis Bonsignore, Hagen Buchwald, Warner Burke, Deborah Cornwall, Ram Charan, Paul Croke, John Dinkelspiel, Don Dinsel, Ferdinand Fournies, Michael Golden, Don Hambrick, Bob Hargadon, Manual London, James MacHulbert, Ian MacMillan, Victoria Marsick, Peter Mathias, Jack Mezirow, Paul McKinnon, Elizabeth Nelson Cliff, Gerald Prior, Hastings Read, Paul Robertson, Hoke Simpson, Andrew Souerwine, Marian Verlander, Kirby Warren, and Geritt Wolf.

Special thanks must go to my colleague Elmar Buschlinger. As an entrepreneur and now an advisor to CEOs, Elmar has provided many years of useful counseling and new ideas with a combined high-touch and high-tech approach to consulting. Elmar has given his support and assistance generously. Never ceasing to test the validity of my work, he encouraged new ways of examining the challenges of growing a business and continues to be a champion of the ideas and tools contained in this book. I could not have finished this book without his enthusiastic urging, practical business knowledge, creativity, and great sense of humor.

I would also like to thank my MBA students at Long Island University and Stony Brook University for the critical thinking they applied to the essential elements of this book during our many graduate courses on business consulting. I also give my heartfelt thanks to Patricia McCabe for her useful improvements to this text, correcting the earliest draft with great care and a gentle hand. For their editorial advice, I would also like to acknowledge and thank Bryon Schneider and his colleagues at Jossey-Bass, who knew exactly how to effectively handle this sensitive author. Many thanks.

Finally, there is my friend, colleague, and international consultant, Sarah Qian Wang, without whom this work would not be here. Her ideas, attention to detail, creativity, and ability to manage this fickle author have been a blessing. Thank you, Qian Wang.

In the meantime, as everyone else says at this point, all errors, mistakes, omissions and commission, misrepresentations, and silly comments are entirely mine. The honor of your forgiveness is requested.

Edward G. Verlander
Setauket Bay, New York, May 2012

THE PRACTICE OF PROFESSIONAL CONSULTING

PART ONE

SETTING THE STAGE

CHAPTER ONE

THE NATURE OF CONSULTING

Consulting has become an important source of employment and professional satisfaction for tens of thousands of people in the United States and around the world. Despite the industry downturn in 2009, according to the U.S. Office of Personnel Management and the Association of Management Consulting Firms, major consulting firms continue to expand their global reach as well as their areas of consulting practice. It would appear that this $350 billion global industry will remain an attractive career for many years to come (Top-consultant, 2011; U.S. Department of Labor, 2006). Consulting is a large and vital industry. A hundred years' growth in the consulting industry indicates that clients have valued the services provided by consultants. Indeed, consultants have been a powerful force in shaping and influencing the very market they have pursued. Yet with its size and scope, the consulting industry could benefit from some close examination if it is to enjoy a second hundred years in the face of technologies that are changing the way information and advice are delivered.

This chapter lays out the nature of the industry as well as some of its major issues and challenges:

- Scope of the industry
- Types of consulting
- Concept of the trusted advisor

- Consultant qualifications
- Professionalism in the industry

Thus the chapter sets up and summarizes the main themes of this book: the values, knowledge, skills, and professional behavior needed by new consultants to the industry.

It's an Industry

Thousands of business consulting firms, ranging in size from one-person operations to perhaps a dozen people, have emerged over the last twenty-five years across the United States and around the world. Their consulting ranges from executive coaching and leadership development to advising on how to build and run a corporate learning academy; from corporate social responsibility and crisis management to sustainability, security, and integrating technology systems; from business turnarounds to personal financial planning. Consultants in "think tanks" such as the Brookings Institute, Rand Corporation, Cato Institute, American Enterprise Institute, Heritage Foundation, and the Hudson Institute conduct research and offer advice on a comprehensive range of international and domestic issues. In addition to the global consulting companies and research institutions, many self-appointed individuals travel the world offering advice on a wide range of business and personal effectiveness problems. Finally, since the 1950s, the industry has also included professors from university business schools who have consulted to business and industry on a plethora of management and executive education topics (Verlander, 1986). Christopher McKenna (1995), a historian of consulting at Oxford University, explains that management consulting has been around for more than a hundred years. First there were the big consulting firms, such as Arthur D. Little (founded in 1886), Booz, Allen & Hamilton (1914), A. T. Kearney (1926), McKinsey (1926), The Boston Consulting Group (1963), Capgemini (1967), and Bain & Company (1973), followed by a tidal wave of small, specialized boutique firms that hired MBAs and trained them in their methods and procedures to be first-class strategy and business consultants. The big accounting firms had developed their own management consulting units early in the twentieth century and believed—until recently—that using their audit and tax client base they could leverage those relationships to build management consulting and information technology (IT) consulting practices. But in the 1980s and 1990s this produced internal management conflicts, as the revenue from consulting in those firms started to exceed the audit revenue, and conflicts of interest, as the Enron, WorldCom, and Tyco scandals put their independence into question. According to McKenna:

> In 1998, the Big Five (accounting firms) employed more than 65,000 consultants and billed more than $12 billion annually. By 2002, four of the five largest consulting firms had new names and new owners: Anderson Consulting had become Accenture; Ernst &Young Consulting was bought up by Cap Gemini, PricewaterhouseCoopers Consulting was sold to IBM, and finally KPMG Consulting became a publically traded company and renamed itself BearingPoint. In the end, only Deloitte Consulting . . . remained attached to a leading international accounting firm. (McKenna, 2006, p. 238)

Perhaps the most recent large shift in business models for technology companies is that of IBM. From its origins as the leading manufacturer of IT hardware, the company now produces most of its revenue from consulting services (2007 pretax earnings: software 40 percent, services 37 percent, hardware/financing 23 percent). IBM competes with Electronic Data Systems (EDS, acquired by Hewlett Packard in 2008), and Microsoft, which has operated its own consulting services division since 1995.

Since the 1970s there has been a rise in the number of consulting companies devoted to and specializing in such areas of consulting as human resources benefits, organization development and training, and what might more broadly be called change management consulting—helping clients to build learning organizations, employee development systems, and leadership development strategies. Many management consulting firms have a practice in technology consulting, as it is such a rapidly growing area of business development and profits.

As Table 1.1 shows, however, management consulting firms generally specialize in something other than technology and have built their reputations and fortunes in the strategy and organizational change areas of practice. They have built formidable, high-quality client bases in health care, government, business, and education, and include Oliver Wyman (formerly Mercer Delta), Mercer Consulting, A.T. Kearney, The Forum Corporation, AchieveGlobal, Dale Carnegie Corporation, HayMcBer, FranklinCovey, and the now defunct Harbridge House. All of the traditional accounting firms (McKinsey started as one)—such as KPMG, PricewaterhouseCoopers (PwC), and Ernst & Young—divested their consulting practices, except Deloitte & Touche (which recently dropped Touche from its brand name), which continues to offer a range of management

TABLE 1.1 LEADING CONSULTING FIRMS

Firm Name	Start Date	Revenue	Number Employed	Traditional Focus
Accenture	2001	$25 billion[1] (2011)	244,000	Information Technology
Arthur D. Little Inc. Acquired by Altran in 2011	1886	Unknown	1,000	Strategy and Technology Innovation
AT Kearney Purchased back from EDS in 2006	1926	$79 million (2008)[2]	2,700	Management
Bain & Co.	1973	$2 billion (2007)[3]	5,000	Business Strategy Operations
Boston Consulting Group	1963	$3 billion (2009)[4]	4,800	Business Strategy Management
Booz Allen & Hamilton	1914	$5.5 billion (2011)	25,000	Management Technology
Booz & Co.	2008	$1 billion (2009)[2]	3,300	Business Strategy Management
Capgemini Merged with E&Y in 2005; sold NA business to Accenture, 2005	1967	$12 billion (2008)	91,000	Strategy and Transformation HR, Supply Chain Marketing/Sales
Deloitte Consulting	2000	$6.3 billion (2009)[5]	15,000	Human Capital Strategy and Ops Technology
HP Enterprise Business	2008	$53 billion (2009)[6]		Information Technology (Acquired Electronic Data Systems in 2008)
IBM Global Svc Group		$60 billion (2008)	100,000	Management Information Technology
Monitor	1983	$300 million (2001)[7]	1,500	Strategy Management
McKinsey & Co.	1926	$6 billion (2009)[8]	17,000	Business Strategy Management
Oliver Wyman Subsidiary of MMC		$4.6 billion (2009)	3,400	Management Strategy and Economic Analysis Operations
PricewaterhouseCoopers (PwC)	1998	$7.5 billion (2011)	38,000	Management Process Finance—Sarbanes-Oxley

Source:
1. Plunkett Research, Ltd.
2. FT.com January 26, 2011
3. Slideshare.net
4. BCG website, March 8, 2010
5. www.careers-in-business.com/consulting/mc.htm
6. HP 2010 Annual Report, p. 38
7. *Boston Business Journal*, July 23, 2001
8. *Forbes* October 28, 2009 estimate

consulting services. KPMG's divestiture became BearingPoint, which in 2009 liquidated and ceased its operations.

The particular field of management consulting grew, by some estimates, over 20 percent during the 1980s and 1990s. Unlike other parts of the broader professional services industry, it tends to be cyclical and linked to overall economic conditions. Although figures vary, it is clear that the consulting industry declined along with the general North American and global economy. For example, according to Plunkett Research (2009), the consulting industry shrank during the 2001–2003 period but has been growing slowly since. Ibisworld (2012) reported that the consulting industry declined by 2.6 percent in 2009 and fell another 3.5 percent in 2010. And according to the *Economist*, during the Great Recession of 2008–2009 the consulting industry experienced a severe reduction in client work, with a corresponding trimming of fees, cuts, or contract delays. In 2009 the global consulting industry shrank by 9.2 percent, the worst year since 1982 ("Advice for Consultants," 2011). Add to this the fact that Marsh & McLennan reported a 10-percent drop in consulting revenues; McKinsey and BCG held back bonuses; McKinsey and Bain suffered a slight drop in revenues; Marakon was bought by CRA International; Katzenbach, after shrinking in 2009, was saved by Booz; accounting firms with consulting practices—PricewaterhouseCoopers and Ernst & Young—had a 7-percent drop in revenues; and Towers Perrin and Watson Wyatt merged, as human resource consulting was hard hit.

In Britain, human resources consulting fell by 20 percent ("Laid Off Lawyers," 2010) but recently in Germany, Munich-based strategy consultants Roland Berger (2009 revenues of €616 million) declined to merge with Deloitte Touche Tohmatsu consulting services (which had 2009 consulting revenues of $7.5B), preferring to remain independent. In 2002 PwC sold its management consulting practice to IBM. Interestingly, Deloittte remains the only one of the "big four" accounting firms to retain its strategy consulting arm in the wake of the Enron scandals a decade ago ("Roland Berger," 2010).

Adapting to their economic realities, global consulting firms shifted their strategies to include the emerging Brazilian, Russian, Indian, and Chinese economies, as the United States and European markets came under downward pressure. However, this decline has been relatively short-lived, as small, nimble firms have found ways to compete, and as the growth rates in Table 1.2 show, the world's top consulting firms have bounced back. Reflecting the resilience of the industry, firms in 2010 started to declare a turnaround and an expansion in their traditional

TABLE 1.2 TOP TEN LARGEST GLOBAL CONSULTING FIRMS BY REVENUE*

2010 Rank	Consulting Firms	2009–10 Growth (%)
1	Deloitte	7.8
2	PwC	10.9
3	Ernst & Young	5.2
4	KPMG	8.3
5	Accenture	6.8
6	IBM	5.2
7	McKinsey & Co.	8.8
8	MMC (Mercer & Oliver Wyman)	3.9
9	Booz Allen Hamilton	5.2
10	Towers Watson	−3.8**

*Management, financial, & IT Revenue.
**Reflects merger between Towers Perrin and Watson Wyatt.
Source: Financial Times Special Report, November 17, 2011.

markets. Industry revenues were $345 billion in 2010 and $366 billion in 2011, and are estimated to improve further, to $391 billion in 2012 (Plunkett, 2012; "Roland Berger Calls Off Tie-up Bid," 2011).

Types of Consulting

Services in the consulting industry are expanding because clients have many problems and needs. For example, companies hire consultants to advise them on how to manage organizational change, produce a business strategy, facilitate group process, formulate policy, and build information technology solutions. Consultants provide advice and implement their solutions in such areas as executive coaching, reengineering work processes, training, and strategy development. To conduct their work, consultants need specialized training in areas such as research methods, interpersonal communications, analytical techniques, and group process, as well as technical and business expertise. Consultants also need a certain amount of expertise in a client's business, industry, organizational functions, and managerial processes.

   ○ *Executive Coaching.* At the individual level, consultants work with employees and managers to help them become more effective in their roles and responsibilities. The specific descriptor "executive" is a bit misleading, as this coaching is used with all levels of management. The focused nature of the coaching, conducted over three to six months on a few very specific areas of employee improvement, makes this form of consulting an attractive investment for companies. Although done since the early 1980s, over the last fifteen years executive coaching consulting has come of age and is now a burgeoning practice.

- *Organization Consulting.* At the organizational level, managers hire consultants to solve a wide range of problems that they themselves may lack the expertise (or time) to solve. An important form of this consulting is known as "organization development" (OD), wherein consultants bring skills and experience in managing change. Such consultants have the specialized knowledge needed to help clients solve a particular human or technical problem, or they use their research capabilities (known as "action research") to help management solve problems themselves, with the consultant acting as a facilitator rather than an expert advisor.

- *Strategy Consulting.* This service uses many analytical techniques but basically requires consultants to study a company's *strengths, weaknesses,* business *opportunities,* and industry *threats* (SWOT). Consultants develop hypotheses and use fact-based, issue-driven processes to produce business strategies for company management to consider, adopt, or reject.

- *Policy Consulting.* Consultants are hired to bring broad knowledge and experience at the societal level when government or private organizations need to ensure that they have the latest, broadest, and deepest thinking to address a complex social issue.

- *Change Management Consulting.* This is probably the largest area of consulting, but in reality, every type of consulting drives change in some way, according to the specialties associated with each type of consulting, from strategy to IT. Within the change management specialty we find both process and application consulting: organization redesign, culture change, employee education, change in skills for large groups of employees, competencies needed for cross-functional projects that improve teamwork and decision making, productivity enhancement of a company's value chain, or alignment of an organization with its corporate goals. Such consulting often uses meetings and conferences designed to provide a deeper perspective on a current organizational need, or training programs that increase skill levels among a particular population.

- *Process Consulting.* In this form of consulting, consultants are used to facilitate team meetings to improve interpersonal communications and to help employees and managers understand *how* they can make decisions with higher levels of collaboration and commitment.

- *Technology Consulting.* This is another large area of consulting, in which information technology (IT) experts design, develop, and deliver

IT systems, databases, software products, customized applications, and enterprise-wide solutions, as well as integrated legacy systems.

Interestingly, IT is one area in which many individuals, although playing a consulting role, do not consider themselves consultants. They call themselves "software engineers," "programmers," or "application developers." They think that a consultant is someone else or another person's role; something that other people do who have the word "consultant" in their job title. This is a mistake. We argue that such professionals are consultants whose consulting roles just happen to be narrow rather than broad in the scope of consulting practice.

Scope of Consulting

It is clear that consulting comes in many forms, and to understand the nature of consulting it is helpful to consider the practice of consulting in a broader context. In IT consulting, for example, consider two dimensions: business scope and advisory level, assessed on the basis of low to high and narrow to broad, respectively. Figure 1.1 shows a number of technical roles classified as "consulting" in relationship to the level of work being done on the two dimensions.

FIGURE 1.1 TECHNICAL CONSULTANTS BY SCOPE AND ADVISORY LEVELS

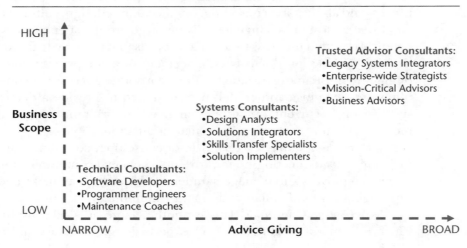

All levels and roles are part of consulting, differentiated in this case by the level of advice given and the size of the business problem being addressed. The point is, every role requires consulting knowledge and skills, including roles—such as software developer—that appear to have no consulting requirements. It all depends on how we define consulting. This will be discussed in more detail in subsequent chapters, but for now, it is important to understand that someone who is hired as "pair of hands," even on a daily basis to code programs, is still in a consulting role. As is true in all types of consulting, the IT person in this case is using expertise, applying important consulting skills, offering advice, and producing deliverables. It is merely consulting at the lowest level of scope and application.

Thinking as a Consultant

Are consultants unique in any respect? Is their thinking different from that of managers? The core job of both managers and consultants is problem solving, and in that regard they both use fact-based, rational decision making in their work, supported by analytical techniques and systematic project management procedures. Both recognize that human emotions play a big role in final decisions, and both bring previously acquired knowledge to new problems.

On the other hand, consultants are different from managers and are unique in certain respects. Consultants think about being in service to others and what is in the best interest of the client, not maximizing personal gain. Consultants recommend solutions and wait for client managers to decide what they want to pursue. OD consultants *only* help clients decide for themselves; they never decide for the client. Consultants think contextually, always considering the bigger picture when examining problems. Consultants want long-term relationships but empower themselves, knowing they can say "no" to an assignment and walk away. Consultants think about other people's problems, not their own. Finally, because consulting constantly deals with new, unique situations, consultants must think about how to accelerate their learning and quickly adapt themselves to new circumstances.

Work of Consultants

The daily work of consultants varies considerably depending on the type of consulting. However, all consultants engage in similar tasks and procedures. The common features found in all types of consulting are:

- Conducting needs analysis
- Preparing proposals
- Interviewing stakeholders
- Conducting focus groups
- Facilitating workshops
- Making presentations
- Writing analytical reports
- Being on-site with clients
- Identifying issues
- Framing problems
- Validating hypotheses
- Making recommendations
- Helping clients implement
- Managing projects
- Leading teams
- Managing client relationships

Trusted Consultant and Advisor

Regardless of the type or scope of consulting, there is a common theme and one critical requirement—trust. All consultants must work, communicate, make decisions, and function in a way that increases trust between themselves and their clients. Trust is *the* critical ingredient for winning business, successfully deploying solutions, and building long-term client relationships. Trust lies at the heart of being a successful, professional consultant and is a key ingredient in the trend of "relationship consulting," in which the goal is to develop long-term relationships with clients to monitor, discuss, and implement innovative ideas (Careers-in-Business, 2011).

Every profession functions on an implicit assumption of trust; it is central to professionalism and professional practice. The professional operates with the highest degree of credibility, honesty, integrity, confidentiality, and reliability. In consulting, the same requirements and standards pertain.

Maister, Green, and Galford (2000) conclude that as trust grows, clients spend less time worrying about the cost of the consulting than they do about the value they are receiving. Figure 1.2 represents the consulting relationships on two dimensions—breadth of work and level of intimacy—and

FIGURE 1.2 CHANGES IN CLIENT-CONSULTANT FOCUS WITH TRUST

Source: Adapted with the permission of Free Press, a Division of Simon & Schuster, Inc., from The Trusted Advisor by David H. Maister, Charles H. Green, Robert M. Galford. Copyright 2000. All rights reserved.

shows how the focus of involvement changes over time. The focus on level one is narrow and technical, where the consultant tailors a product or service to specific client needs. Level two includes the previous level, but the focus shifts to wider business needs and problems in the client's business function. As the relationship grows to level three the consultant is asked for advice on how the function should be run and participates in internal decision making. Success at this level puts the consultant in position for much bigger scope of work and is trusted to the degree that the client reveals sensitive political and personal information for the consultant to consider, as advice is provided.

Over time, as the consultant increases the range and scope of services provided, solves more problems, develops a wider network of relationships, and acquires a deeper understanding of the client's business, the consultant becomes more valuable to the client (the word "client" refers to the manager who hired the consultant).

As the consultant's business value and trust increase, clients will reward the consultant with more business opportunities, directly and through referrals. Consequently, an important ingredient in becoming a professional consultant is to acquire the reputation of trustworthiness. This is obviously a virtue for its own sake, but also of practical importance to building a consulting business. As yourself: "Am I conscious of the requirement of becoming a trusted advisor?"

Consultant Qualifications

Subsequent chapters describe in detail the entire consulting process in terms of four phases of work, four consulting roles, twelve competencies, and forty-eight practices. Taken together, they form a comprehensive picture of the competent consultant. At this point, however, it is necessary to understand that to use the consulting process described in this book (for *any* kind of consulting application), four qualifications and kinds of expertise are needed: technical, process, people, and business.

○ *Educational and Technical Qualifications.* A minimum requirement to be a consultant is usually a bachelor's degree that provides a breadth and depth of knowledge and technical skills in the subject studied, and an aptitude for learning (there are rare exceptions; some very successful individuals—such as Bill Gates, Richard Branson, Michael Dell, and Steve Jobs—lacked a college degree but nevertheless fundamentally changed an industry and revolutionized our thinking). In leading consulting firms, a graduate degree, professional degree, work experience, and demonstrated expertise are usually required. If such firms hire recent graduates, even MBAs, the firms then train and develop their consultants in the firm's own analytical techniques, processes, and methods. Interestingly, the "hard" technical skills gained early in a consulting career are believed to be the primary reason that clients hire a particular consultant. However, as will be shown, this is a misnomer. Although technical skills are an essential first requirement, a person's technical expertise is most significant only at the lowest level of consulting, when relationships are new and the scope of work is small. As the client-consultant relationship grows and matures, the so-called "soft skills" are critical for success. These skills include values, trustworthiness, emotional intelligence, perspective, judgment, and communications (see "People Qualifications," shortly).

○ *Process Qualifications.* New consultants must develop effective and efficient ways of working. All clients, consulting firms, and individual consultants develop and refine specific steps, methods, and procedures for getting work completed. Even consultants that conduct "process improvement" consulting have specific processes and methods to do such consulting. In a broad sense, consultants must have aptitudes and expertise in a wide range of processes. These typically include methods for developing business, defining the problem, and writing and presenting proposals. They include ways to launch projects and build a team with the right roles and responsibilities, as well as methods for designing, developing, and producing deliverables. Process expertise must also include methods to test deliverables so that solutions meet the client's expectations. As needed, process expertise may also include knowing how to ensure the full deployment (implementation) of the solution in the client's organization. Finally, consultants must have process aptitudes and expertise in working effectively with people in large, complex, changing organizations.

    ◦ *People Qualifications.* Consulting is a people business. All forms of consulting must be done with and through people. Therefore, regardless of the area of consulting application, consultants must be able to work with people effectively. Throughout the entire consulting process, good consultants must use human relations expertise to build strong long-term interpersonal relationships. Areas of "people aptitude" include a high level of emotional intelligence, teamwork, political savvy, negotiation skills, conflict resolution, performance management, all forms of formal and informal communications, influence, and client networking. Consultants need to learn how to balance their technical expertise with interpersonal acumen, to act always professionally and with just the right amount of camaraderie, and always to do the right thing for clients by acting with the highest levels of trust, integrity, and ethical standards.

    ◦ *Business Skills Qualifications.* Consultants must take a businesslike attitude in their role and work. All consultants need to make money (pro bono work excepted) and need to ensure that they strike the right balance between solving the client's problem and keeping an eye on billing and future revenue. Throughout the entire consulting process there are numerous business matters to take care of, such as billing clients, renegotiating scope and fees, documenting, accounting, and identifying new opportunities. This last area is the bane of independent consultants, as they often neglect to do enough marketing of their services while they are engaged in billable client work. When a project is finished, where will the next piece of work come from? To some extent, consultants must always be "marketing administrators" taking care of business—current and future.

    In subsequent chapters we will discuss specific consulting roles and competencies that show how the mix of these technical, process, business, and people skills combine to make one more professional—a person who performs consulting with a set of particular standards, attitudes, demeanor, and capabilities.

What Is Professional Consulting?

In the course of work, any professional usually offers advice based on education, expertise, and judgment formed over many years of experience. The advice is normally directed toward some kind of solution that the patient or client wants and needs, and the solution itself is the "deliverable." In other words, when a doctor gives professional advice it is supposed to keep the patient healthy; the deliverable is health. To provide that advice, the professional follows a set of standard procedures for examination, analysis, diagnosis, and recommendations. For example, when the doctor conducts an annual check-up, the doctor follows a precise method, uses specific and specialized tools, and develops data to compare against standards. This method is used in every normal physical and is a standard procedure doctors learn in medical school. Because all professionals—such as lawyers, engineers, and dentists—learn and use standards, it seems reasonable that a similar requirement should be applied to consultants. Therefore, a generic, working definition of professional consulting and one we use in subsequent chapters is as follows:

A professional consultant is one who can be trusted to use standard consulting methods and procedures, who gives advice and produces solutions on behalf of clients.

As mentioned earlier, a key word in this definition is "trust." To stress its seriousness, we will return to this important issue throughout the book. A professional is one who is *trusted* to produce a solution to a problem using standard procedures, data analysis, and judgment. Professional judgment is based on knowledge, expertise, and tested experience. An important related concept is that a consultant's professional goal is to develop a trusted relationship with a client that is sustainable over the long-term *career* of the client. This means that if the client is promoted or moves to a different organization, the client would still call on the consultant for advice because of the strength of the relationship, as the consultant has been proven to be a reliable, credible, and trusted personal advisor.

Developing relationships of trust and a professional reputation takes time and energy. In general, people tend to trust others who have the background, education, licensing, and experience to be in a profession. In life and business, we generally assume a professional person is someone who has integrity and honor, will not betray confidences, and will continuously learn and improve, pursue more training, solve problems, keep all records confidential, and be fair in charging a fee commensurate with generally accepted fees of similar professionals. Customers trust professionals to perform at the highest level of their capability. These values, attributes, and behaviors are so important to building a successful consulting practice that we will return to them many times in future chapters.

Finally, whether or not consulting is currently considered a profession by the general public and clients, the fact is that few consultants are licensed and many are not trusted in the same way that people automatically trust their family doctor or local clergy. We believe this needs to change—and the rest of this book describes the values, attitudes, methods, and behavior needed to make this change. As a start, ask yourself the following questions:

- Do I consider myself to be a professional?
- Do I use defined methods and repeatable procedures in my work?
- Do I exercise personal discipline in my work?
- Do people ask me for advice? Why? Why not?
- Can I be relied on to produce a solution—a deliverable?
- Do people trust me? How do I know?

If the answer is "definitely yes" to each of those questions, you are well-suited to consulting and already demonstrating a level of accomplishment as a professional. If, on the other hand, your answer to any of them is *not* "definitely yes," then you will find even greater benefit from what we provide in the pages that follow: a complete set of practical steps, specific ideas, principles, tools, techniques, frameworks, and methods that you can use to become more professional.

For readers who are already consultants with five-plus years of experience, this book will revisit basic consulting principles and ask you to think more deeply and critically about your consulting. It will offer some new ways to assess yourself and the quality of your consulting, and it will be an important reminder of those principles and practices you learned a while ago but perhaps have not practiced as fully as you might.

Conclusion

In this chapter we have provided an overview of industry trends, the scope of the consulting industry—including the different types of consulting practiced in the field, the importance and benefits of becoming a trusted advisor, the four main areas of qualifications needed by all consultants, and the general topic of professionalism in the industry—and summarized a number of the challenges it faces.

The next chapter digs deeper into what consultants do and the benefits they bring to clients, including how they add value, and what clients are *really* looking for from their consultants. In Chapter Three we describe a general model of consulting applicable to any kind of consulting practice. Those new to consulting will learn about the complete process, comprising four stages and consulting roles, sixteen specific tasks for all consultants, and four outcomes that are essential to exceeding client expectations.

The rest of the book provides details about the model as well as essential tools, techniques, and templates needed for its professional execution. Throughout, the reader is encouraged to ask three questions:

1. Am I professional?
2. How far along am I in my journey of becoming a trusted consultant?
3. What personal development do I need?

The answers to these questions—in relation to the principles, concepts, and skills covered in the chapters that follow—will provide insight into how to make progress in the journey of becoming a truly great, trusted consultant.

CHAPTER TWO

WHY COMPANIES HIRE CONSULTANTS

In this chapter, we take up the issue of why clients need consultants, the kinds of outcomes clients expect them to produce, the reason companies need those outcomes, and how consulting lies at the heart of helping clients achieve strategic success.

Why Consultants Are Needed

As a very experienced consultant from one of the oldest U.S. consulting firms put it, the traditional rationale management used for hiring consultants included the following:

- Capability rigor—to augment staff's skills and knowledge
- Resource deficits—to augment staff numbers
- Political cover—to provide scapegoats for unpopular or controversial decisions
- Objectivity—to obtain views free of political, functional, or other bias
- Bureaucracy—to get a decision made

These organizational benefits are still the reasons consultants are needed today. In addition to these organizational benefits, we can add reasons having to do with the nature of leading and managing in the twenty-first century. In this regard, the central feature of business life today is the speed, intensity, direction, and complexity of change. Chief executive officers (CEOs) now lead in a global business environment amid technological advancements that simultaneously extend and uproot company business models. Consultants are needed to help management solve the myriad of strategic and operational problems thrown up by this reality. It is not that strategic and operational challenges are new areas of consulting so much as the sheer magnitude of the forces and complexity of the problems that is new.

Business models have changed, and supply chains have become worldwide as companies continue their relentless pursuit of low-cost manufacturing, and suppliers continue to multiply around the world. On the one hand, companies look for ways to lower the cost of producing their goods and services in the face of fierce competition; on the other hand, customers now shop around the world on the Internet to get the most satisfying price/quality relationship they can find, instead of being limited to local suppliers.

In addition to external factors affecting performance, since the 1990s managers have had to deal with many internal issues. These include managing culture change; updating and integrating information technology; reducing errors and waste; improving the efficiency of organizational procedures, workflows, and systems; and responding to an increasingly diverse workforce. Retention strategies have become more important in order to find, attract, and retain the best possible talent—people who can make changes quickly enough to ensure sustained profitability. It has become essential to find people with the right knowledge and skills to do the work, attracting them with opportunities for growth and promotion, and retaining them with good management, state of the art organizational infrastructure, and excellent leadership.

Consultants can help CEOs grapple with these challenging internal and external issues by clarifying ambiguity, reducing complexity to its essence, and helping them recognize that all companies can and must find solutions that are faster, bigger, better, and/or cheaper (FBBC). These solutions are usually driven from the inside out in ways that enable a company to outperform competitors in the marketplace. Working with consultants, companies may try to achieve all four outcomes or a subset in some combination that gives them an edge.

Figure 2.1 visually depicts the dynamics of team-based learning organizations where vertical and/or horizontal FBBC solutions break down

FIGURE 2.1. TEAM-BASED LEARNING ORGANIZATIONS

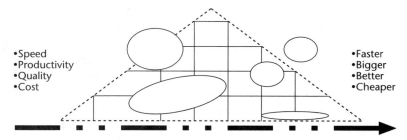

Nimble, adaptive, team-based learning organizations
with distributed leadership and empowered cultures

•Speed
•Productivity
•Quality
•Cost

•Faster
•Bigger
•Better
•Cheaper

barriers between suppliers and customers and the company, and break down barriers between organizational functions and levels of management. Such solutions drive teamwork, innovation, and distributed leadership. In a sense, consultants produce solutions that improve an organization's internal coordination and control to ensure stability, and at the same time power change, learning, and transformation to ensure adaptability and strategic success.

Faster, Bigger, Better, Cheaper Outcomes

Consultants work at both the big picture, strategic level and the micro level by "simplifying complexity"; that is, consultants help clients to sift through the complex mass of data and issues to identify what McKinsey calls the "critical few" issues or problems against which actions can be taken to make progress. In this context, all clients are searching for ways to improve the profitability of their business model and organizational effectiveness in ways that improve their *speed, productivity, quality,* and *cost.* In essence, this is what consultants are hired to do for their clients and how they add value. This is the reason to hire a consultant.

Faster

All organizations want to be faster in what they do. Why? In a global business environment, where competition is intense and can come from any corner of the globe, companies must be able to beat the competition to market. The speed of introduction of new products and services means that for a period of time a company can dominate the space, charge premium prices, and possibly shift customers' buying habits. However, in a world of benchmarking, product deconstruction, and best practices research, competitors can quickly learn, adapt, and produce products that compete with the market leader. Such competition may come from both large and small companies. If the market is perceived to be a growing one with significant profit potential, many companies and entrepreneurs around the world will be assessing how to exploit the opportunity.

The information explosion has created a situation in which knowledge about markets and customer needs is virtually instantaneous. Companies that use this information and can quickly adapt themselves to producing new and innovative products that may win in the marketplace.

Note, for example, that Apple introduced its iPod in 2005 for $900 and by 2008 sold its G3 model, with much greater functionality, features, and capability, for $300. Slower companies find themselves falling farther and farther behind with a shrinking market share. Speed is the key to success. The following are some of the areas in which speed can make a strategic difference—sometimes the difference between success or failure, winner or loser:

- Product innovations
- Time to market with new products and services
- Decision making up, down, and across the hierarchy
- Processing and handling of administrative forms
- Information flow throughout the organization
- Response time to customer questions and problems
- Production and publishing of reports
- Movement of materials through the supply chain
- Service improvements

Most speed has to do with how an organization works internally and how quickly it interfaces with its external environment. Increasingly, this means consultants (internal and external) have worked to change people's behavior and to use information technology to reduce time wasted in process and procedures. Consultants have redefined jobs and roles, helped to reshape the social architecture of organizations, and helped managers rethink how power and influence are used to motivate people and how to keep machines running at their optimum capacity.

Bigger

All companies are interested in growth; however, in recent years one exception has emerged: companies are *not* interested in growing their number of employees and are more likely to seek ways to reduce them. Workforce reductions result from automation (employee replacement), IT productivity solutions (employee redundancy), and a severe drop in profits (employee layoffs as a cost-cutting measure). It is usually the cost of salaries and benefits that form the largest portion of a company's fixed costs. Such costs often constitute about 60 percent to 70 percent of an organization's operating expenses. If revenues and profits decline due to economic cycles, industry competitiveness, or poor products, the only way to reduce compensation cost is to lay people off. Normal employee attrition usually takes too long in a fast-paced, globally competitive market in which customers simply want lower prices immediately. Therefore, unless a company is already experiencing growth in revenue, market share, customer demand, profits, and cash flow management (when hiring is necessary to keep up with the growth), the company will usually keep a tight grip on its headcount.

Aside from this, all companies generally want to be bigger in terms of profits, earnings per share, return on net assets, market share, product scope, and service coverage. Consultants play a central role in helping organizations achieve those "bigger" ends.

Better

The Japanese in the 1980s taught U.S. businesses that it is possible to give customers better quality *and* lower prices at the same time. It only requires management to take a fresh look at the entire scope of processes used to make and sell their products and services. With an eye on *process improvements* that lower the cost of doing business, management can improve the quality of everything they do—which, in turn, culminates in a better value proposition for customers. The successful Japanese penetration of the U.S. xerographic, photographic, automobile, motorcycle, lawnmower, video camera, television, video games, comic books, and personal computer markets testifies to this strategy. Only in service industries—such as investment banking and consulting—have the Japanese failed to date. The protracted slump in the Japanese domestic economy since 1990 was brought on, despite its revolutionary thinking about business processes, by its antiquated and inert banking and employment systems.

As consumers came to expect better quality in some products, they quickly came to expect it in *all* products and services. This has put business, industry, and professional service organizations in the United States under enormous strain to figure out how to improve their quality. This is quite obvious in the airline industry, for example. Airline companies (except, notably, Southwest Airlines) struggle to make a profit as higher levels of security as well as desperate measures to lower cost combine with a la carte revenue enhancers to frustrate customers.

The advent of internet-based consumer feedback tools that give customers ways to rapidly register their delight and displeasure with companies' products and services has produced a generation of consumers (and industrial wholesalers) who expect quality to be implicit, to be built in, to be there even when the price is lower. This has fundamentally changed the old business decision-making model that assumed an inverse relationship between price and quality. Consultants help their clients to achieve those "better" ends by redesigning and reengineering internal processes and recasting operating policies to improve, for example, the quality of people, standards of performance, and team building across the value chain, as well as the form and function of products and services.

Cheaper

If companies are to produce products of high quality at a lower price, then they must invest time and effort in finding ways to do business at a lower cost. Moreover, such efforts must reach well beyond reducing payroll expense and laying off employees. IT solutions, business process reengineering, revamping of organizational structures, and outsourcing strategies have enabled companies to dramatically improve their productivity rates (the ratio of unit input costs to output). Improvements in productivity have meant that, despite growing worldwide demand for products and services, companies have been able to keep their operating costs under control. Thus the *supply* of goods and services has risen, but at flat or lower prices. Price inflation remained at 2 percent—5 percent levels for the period 1980–2005. However, with global demand for oil increasing, prices in 2008 reaching $150 per barrel, credit problems in the banking system continuing into 2013, unprecedented U.S. government fiscal debt levels, and gold fluctuating between $1,500 and $2,000 an ounce, many signs indicate that inflation is threatening to increase. At the same time, even as prices rise customers will still be looking for the lowest price/highest value combination.

All industries must improve their quality and keep prices low if they are to compete successfully against Asian competitors that emulate the Japanese management, production, and process control systems. Countries like China and India have very low labor costs. Yet even in China, manufacturing is outsourced to Southeast Asian companies where the labor costs are even lower than in China.

Global pricing, merchandising, and global manufacturing have meant that not only can a consumer purchase the same article from a company anywhere in the world, but the consumer can also buy the same type of article from *many* companies anywhere in the world. Consultants help companies to understand and deal with those cost-value-productivity-market trends to retain fickle customers who can easily shift their purchases from one company to another with a simple click.

Management Conundrum

The biggest challenge is to help clients combine the four desired outcomes. It is relatively easy to explain how growth, lower costs, speed, and improved quality can each be accomplished separately, but to achieve them in combination requires both analytical and contextual thinking. Consider the challenge of doing the following:

- Speeding up decisions and improving their quality
- Investing in people and lowering cost with automation
- Raising overall quality and lowering costs
- Speeding up productivity with fewer people
- Increasing financial performance, investing, and lowering costs

But companies have no choice. They must take action—and they need their consultants to help sort out these problems.

Forces That Drive Business Consulting

In a global business environment, CEOs face many challenges: customers searching for the best possible price/value mix; rising raw material costs; pressure to keep prices low; profit margins shrinking in some parts of the world; consumer demand dropping from possible credit problems; and low-cost competition from Asian countries supplying U.S. consumers.

With so many complex, competing economic forces, executives and managers face quite a dilemma. This is grist for the mill for consultants.

Today's complexity can be simplified into a set of seven major forces that impact all organizations:

- Globalization of the economy
- Regionalization of the globe
- Changing regulations
- Privatization of public organizations
- Consolidation of industries
- Concerns about security
- Emergence of state capitalism

Globalization. The interdependence of financial markets, worldwide manufacturing processes, and use of the Internet to transact business have altered the opportunities for revenue, profits, and the nature of competition in all industries. The global economy has changed (and challenged) the basis of competition. All industries now contend with competitors from any part of the planet. Even dominant players in their domestic industry and markets must be concerned with competitors in other countries that now have the capacity and access to sell directly into the dominant players' home market. This means the number and range of competitors have increased dramatically. Company management must develop much more sophisticated and competitive strategies to compete in foreign markets, while defending their market share at home.

Regionalization. The global economy is in the process of reforming into a set of four or five large economic regions. Through formal treaties and agreements, informal processes, and trading infrastructure, because of globalization, nation states are integrating their political identities with their trading identities to create economic superstructures. This allows the European Union, for example, to maintain their cultural distinctiveness and various languages while creating larger geoeconomic entities to compete with the existing bigger players such as the United States or China, and emerging countries such as India and Brazil. The effect of this movement has been to fundamentally change the basis of competition and business trading, thereby creating untold opportunities and demands on company structures, strategies, systems and procedures, leadership capabilities, and infrastructure coordination.

Regulations. In every country, the government imposes rules and regulations on the ways in which companies can operate within its borders. Those regulations change in response to government parties, demographics, and societal preferences. At the same time that the globe regionalizes, global public institutions—such as the World Trade Organization and the United Nations—reinforce commonly shared policies in individual countries, thereby increasing the amount of regulations. Changes in regulations mean companies must also change how they manage their affairs, to ensure that their business strategies, internal systems, procedures, and policies are in compliance.

Privatization. With a few recent exceptions in South America, governments of many countries have chosen to turn their publicly run companies over to the private sector, in the belief that market economy promotes efficiency and provides more and better services at a lower cost to their consumers. Rather than control companies as government-run bureaucracies, legislatures have turned over their nationalized industries—such as transportation, energy, utility, and communications companies—to the free market system. We see this in similar industries—in China and India, for example, where in recent years the governments have moved toward privatizing some sectors of their economy. Because of privatization, with more competitors entering the market, business strategists must change the way their companies compete, and managers of newly privatized companies must learn new behaviors to operate successfully in a regulated yet open market system.

Consolidation. It is in the nature of a market-driven economy that industries move steadily from a state of open competition with many competitors to a condition in which a few major players dominate the market. Consolidation has occurred in industries such as oil, rail transportation, airlines, and electronics. Merger and acquisition strategies help companies to improve their revenue and help them to create a sustainable competitive advantage. As companies are acquired, integrated, and grow larger, they benefit from economies of scale and broader product scope. In this way companies can change and can grow their overall profits. To be successful, consultants help both acquired and acquiring companies take action to integrate a host of elements, such as their IT systems, organization structures, cultures, and policies, in anticipation of benefits gained through the consolidation.

Security. The terrorist attacks on September 11, 2001, have changed companies worldwide on many levels. All companies now realize they are at risk of a terrorist attack, and have taken measures to improve their security. Executives have always faced threats of kidnapping, property theft, and loss of propriety information. Companies now assess security risks more broadly and make contingency plans with preemptive measures to address terrorism, a worldwide force of unpredictable dimensions. Consultants help a company's management to assess, plan, train, and implement security measures.

State Capitalism. In contrast to the privatization movement discussed earlier, the emergence of state capitalism has also become a strong force in the global economy in recent years ("The Visible Hand," 2012). Western companies that have been managed with traditional principles of free market capitalism must now compete with companies that are controlled by state governments, especially in the energy, utilities, telecommunications, and financial sectors of the economy. Using principles of free market capitalism, these so-called "national champions" in China, Russia, and Brazil, for example, are some of the biggest companies in terms of revenue, buying resources around the world, and making huge profits. Government control is achieved through ownership of a significant percentage of shares. State companies get special privileges and access not available to private corporations, follow directives of government politicians, and are subject to the unpredictable attitudes and decisions of government officials about company strategies, management practices, and leadership. The "invisible hand" of trade and markets is giving way to the visible, authoritarian hand of the state. It seems likely these companies will need the help of consultants to facilitate their growth, while private corporations will call on the services of consultants to help them compete as the global economic playing field, players, and rules of the game change.

Influencing the Forces. Large multinational corporations (MNCs) have considerable financial power, with gross revenues in excess of many countries' gross domestic product. For example, in 2005 Wal-Mart, British Petroleum, General Motors, and General Electric had gross revenues greater than any one of the United Arab Emirates, Israel, Colombia, Chile, Malaysia, Hungary, Pakistan, New Zealand, or the Philippines (The Kassandra Project, 2005). Those MNCs are able to wield extraordinary power and influence in the countries where they are doing business. Many companies invest in political action consultants who may influence the direction of governmental laws and regulations. They develop relationships and make investments in ways that influence government policy and legislation. This is legal, but it means they can and do shape the very rules and regulations, policies, and practices by which they must abide. Compared to state capitalism, one might think of MNCs as the invisible hand controlling the state. Consultants help companies through political action committees and lobbyists to develop such influence; to a degree, consultants affect both the process of influence and the issues themselves.

The seven forces not only impact business strategies and operations; they also, of course, impact employees and consultants. Employees regularly deal with changes as a result of numerous management initiatives born of the seven forces. Employees may not fully understand the reason *why* changes are necessary, but they certainly are affected by them and therefore often react by complaining to anyone who will listen. Even if consultants are not helping management to launch change, they often find themselves in the middle of many change initiatives. Accordingly, management consultants must deal with a range of supportive and negative employee attitudes.

In summary, the forces are powerful agents of change. The impact of the forces varies depending on the local circumstances of companies and the nature of the industry within which they operate. But, it is the consultant's job to identify and explain the problems created by the forces and then to produce solutions that enable their clients to adapt—that is, to be faster, bigger, better, and/or cheaper. Consultants do this in many ways, providing analysis and recommendations that lead to, for example:

- Rationalizing headcount
- Restructuring the organization
- Reengineering processes
- Improving productivity
- Using information technology
- Moving production to less costly locations

Over the last thirty years, to remain competitive in the face of the external forces affecting their business, companies have taken many initiatives, such as the following:

- Rightsizing/downsizing
- Self-managed teams
- Telecommuting
- Decentralization
- Strategic alliances
- Flexible employment and career strategies
- Leadership and employee training
- Culture change: empowerment
- Quality circles and team building
- Total quality management
- Knowledge management
- Systems thinking/learning organization

- Feedback systems
- Business process reengineering
- Outsourcing

Many of the changes have been recommended by consultants. Despite the turmoil and disruption these changes have caused, management remains convinced that the benefits of those changes exceed the costs, confusion, and internal conflict they induce. Indeed, we are arguing here that companies *must* take such actions in order to survive in a global business environment. It is the consultant's role to help them do so.

Expectations of Consultant Services

Clients expect consultants to recommend changes that will give them a competitive advantage. In producing solutions to client problems, consultants are therefore change agents that drive and thrive on change (McKenna, 2006). The basic process they use to do this is shown in Figure 2.2, involving gathering data, presenting analysis, and recommending new policies and changes.

In the consulting fields of organization development, IT, and business strategy, for example, consultants conduct research, identify best practices, analyze alternatives, make recommendations, and in general help

FIGURE 2.2. CONSULTANT'S ROLE AS CHANGE AGENT CONCEPTUALIZES BUSINESS MODEL

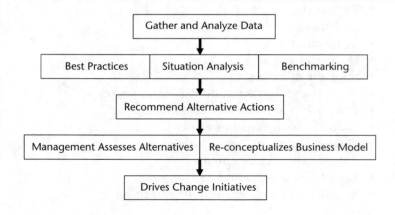

client management to reconceptualize their executive roles, business models, and business behavior. Clients, in turn, rely on the integrity of the analysis and recommendations and expect to be given the best advice. Following this work, clients then assume responsibility for deciding what changes to make and implementing them. Generally, clients do not expect their consultants to implement their recommendations. Exceptions to this would be where an actual product is produced, as in new IT software applications, tailoring of a process, system, or equipment to suit a client's needs, or benefits consulting and process reengineering. Those solutions must be tested and fully deployed. Clients then expect their consultant's service to include making sure the new product is fully operational before the consultant leaves.

Changes in Client's Business and Organization Needs

For most of the twentieth century, companies built their success on the principles of stability, order, and control. Stability was achieved by constraining investment, cost controls, formal structures, and conservative performance targets. Slow and steady growth was combined with tight controls and predictable managerial behavior. For a few companies that aspired to national or global success, *stability* was also achieved by dominating an industry and its markets to become as close to a monopoly as legally possible. In this environment, management's organizational model of running a business directed change at rational growth in size and increased order and control. Change was often limited to modifying and extending past practices into the future.

Order was accomplished with management practices reflecting a lack of trust in lower-level managers and employees. Because people could not be trusted to do the right thing with information, it was always on a "need to know" basis. Employees were not permitted to make decisions on their own unless it was within strict and limited boundaries of authority.

Thus businesses achieved stability and order by copying characteristics of the military and to some degree the church: top-down driven, command and control, high division of labor, role specialization, tight security on company information, strict adherence to the hierarchy, authoritarian management styles, and functions that were separated into silos. This form of control produced efficiency and dependency.

Control required strong central leadership with direction from the top and coordination systems such as performance appraisals and

FIGURE 2.3. COMPANY VALUE CHAIN

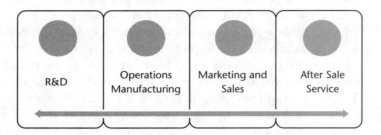

management by objectives to ensure alignment of business goals through-out the hierarchy to all employee roles and tasks. The values of conformity, analysis, logic, stability, and control prevailed. Therefore decision making tended to be slow, functions avoided cooperating with one another, and teamwork was resisted between levels and across the value chain (see Figure 2.3). Careers were a slow, grinding, politically intense struggle to rise up the functional ladder. This resulted in businesses that were inter-nally focused, complex, bureaucratic conglomerates run by rules and well-defined procedures.

The order and control model was not well suited to changing times. The models of the church and the military tend to work quite well once the institution has control over the environment. However, as the modern versions of those institutions have discovered, with globalization, keeping control of everything in their organization in such an the environment has become increasingly difficult. Now the very strategies and organiza-tional practices that enabled companies to grow and perhaps achieve dominance have become weaknesses, limiting their ability to adapt quickly enough to keep up with the changes in their environment.

Need to Change. By the late 1980s the major forces driving business, mentioned earlier in this chapter, intensified. Top executives began to hear from management and strategy consultants that the traditional busi-ness models, culture, structures, and management styles were no longer sufficient to ensure success. The amount of change going on was just too great. Companies could not adapt quickly enough, as the speed and direc-tion of change continued to accelerate and multiply. New strategies were needed to deal with global competition that was changing the rules of the competitive game. This was especially true as more and more companies found ways to create businesses using internet technology. Even though most of the dot-com companies failed to make money and survive, they surely set the direction for the twenty-first century.

It became clear that new uses of IT could turn time, productivity, quality, and efficiency into strategic weapons. Yet, to achieve those strategic advantages, a massive re-education program was needed to turn the burgeoning bureaucratic companies into nimble, innovative, and highly adaptive powerhouses of business profits. Companies had to change from slow bureaucracies to highly adaptive organizational "chameleons" that could quickly adapt to rapidly changing business conditions and customer demands, delivering goods and services on a global basis. Figure 2.4 depicts this shift, showing how companies have (internally) changed structurally and behaviorally in the last fifty years to successfully compete in the midst of powerful external forces—social, economic, political, and technological.

An important insight for leaders and consultants is that businesses need a more complex and sophisticated understanding of how to run their organizations. Good management is necessary but not sufficient for success in the twenty-first century. Kotter (1990) explains that managers produce stability, order, and control, whereas leaders produce change, adaptation, and growth. In the twenty-first century, organizations need both. And not just in their top-level leaders. Organizations need people who can lead *and* manage at every level in order to create businesses that

FIGURE 2.4. TEAM-BASED LEARNING ORGANIZATIONS CHANGE FORM WITH GLOBALIZATION

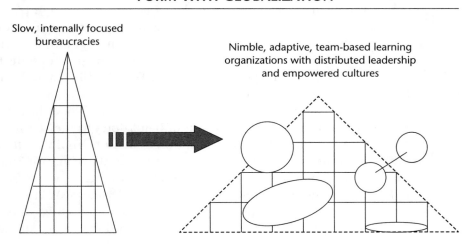

are FBBC, even though this appears to be a dilemma—and even contradictory. How can a company be stable and adaptive? Ordered and changing? Learning and controlled? Yet, that is the requirement in today's business. Companies need those outcomes—and consultants are expected to help resolve the dilemma for their clients.

Future Challenges

The business outcomes that management seek today are likely to be even more challenging to achieve in the future. The number and complexity of decision alternatives grow, because in today's business world everything is interrelated and possibilities seem infinite. For example, the demand for gasoline in China and India raises the price of gasoline in every small town in America; the quality of English language training in India affects the handling of service calls from American customers who need help with a credit card question; the price of vegetables depends on the availability of low-cost labor from Mexico. No element of commerce and consumption exists in isolation nowadays. Faced with this kind of interconnected complexity and the need to make smart decisions quickly, company management seeks the help and expertise of consultants who bring methods, resources, and relevant expertise to solving such management problems. Making ill-informed, bad, or wrong decisions has always been a threat; in this global market, it can be fatal. If one of the business variables is not satisfactorily met, the result of the FBBC effort will be reduced. If a dimension fails completely, then the enterprise as a whole will eventually fail. It is that simple and that brutal. Kodak is a good recent example; it failed to adapt its culture, technology, and management practices quickly enough to the consumer transition from film to digital photography and the market's demand for better quality digital technology—this despite having invented the world's first digital camera in 1975. The 131-year-old company filed for bankruptcy in 2012.

An excellent example of FBBC success is in the U.S. airline industry. We see airlines struggling to stay out of bankruptcy as they try to get the mix just right; some make progress, others do not. Ironically, they have the best practices and benchmarks right in front of them with Southwest Airlines. Yet none of the rest has been able to sustain success; not even JetBlue, the best recent competitor. Southwest Airlines (SWA) is an excellent example of a company that has gotten the four FBBC dimensions exactly right (see Table 2.1) and has replicated them in markets around

TABLE 2.1 SOUTHWEST AIRLINES FEATURES

Dimension	SWA Company Features
Faster	Fifteen-minute turnaround between flights
	Point-to-point travel between metropolitan cities
	No waiting for baggage check-in
	Employee rewards for consistent, excellent service
Bigger	Earnings per share
	Profits and cash flow
	Headcount
	Markets around the United States
Better	Reliable schedule and timetable
	Reliable airplane maintenance
	Relaxed culture on board the planes
	People-focused company culture
Cheaper	"Lowest cost for maximum volume" philosophy
	Competitive with ground transportation
	Lowest operating cost compared to major airlines
	Cheapest ticket prices for most routes

the United States for thirty years. During recession periods, including the "Great Recession" of 2008–2010, they have been the only airline to show a consistent profit. There is, of course, no guarantee of continued future success, and they may get into trouble should they try to penetrate international markets. Yet their remarkable achievement over the last thirty years cannot be denied.

One could argue that SWA did not need consultants to produce this highly successful business model. This is true mainly because they had the luxury of being a start-up company that understood the benefits of a different business model and had a completely new, integrated set of operational, strategic activities back in the 1970s. SWA *merely* ("merely" is my qualifier) had to replicate the model as it grew. Consultants are rarely needed for *inventing* a new business. However, they are needed for *innovation*. Airline companies have been trying to innovate their way to profits ever since SWA joined the industry. Any company wishing (and needing) to change in order to innovate on any one of the four FBBC dimensions will find it easier and more cost-effective to hire consultants—assuming the consultants have the right capability, expertise, and change management experience to help their clients innovate and compete.

It is generally acknowledged that consultants face a greater challenge at well-established, large, complex organizations—such as DuPont, American Express, or JPMorganChase—which have well-established cultures, systems, and habits, and well-established inertia. Yet it is precisely that greater challenge that makes the task more interesting for professional consultants. McKinsey is just one example of a successful consulting company that has helped many companies in all industries where the challenges and problems have been great. The size of the problem is not a deterrent to consultants with a "can do" attitude. Many new consulting methods and analytical techniques have emerged during such times.

The current market and economic dominance of a McDonald's or a Starbucks does not guarantee their future success. Such market leaders must be vigilant. Even the mighty Wal-Mart—with its global reach, $450 billion in sales, 4,300 facilities, and approximately two million employees worldwide (1.4 million employees in the United States) as of 2010—cannot rest on its laurels. As the company discovered with its recent failure to successfully penetrate the German market and with the Indian government's decision in December 2011 to stop Wal-Mart from entering India, it too must constantly seek to redefine its value proposition in the marketplace. It is this struggle to remain competitive and the need to constantly change that create the demand for consultants.

The powerful forces of globalization, innovation, and entrepreneurialism, combined with the human instinct for freedom to achieve and succeed, sustain the dimensions of that demand.

Conclusion

This chapter has attempted to answer the question: why are consultants needed? We have seen that in light of powerful external global forces, the "survival of the fittest" nature of free market capitalism requires the management of all business organizations to be adaptive; searching for ways to help them gain what Michael Porter terms "a sustainable competitive advantage." Porter (2009) sees strategic success as a company's ability to choose a unique *set of activities* that create value for customers and to deliver that value in ways that differentiate it from its competition.

Choosing the right set of activities is an area in which consultants play a big role. In a certain sense, the major strategy consulting firms—like Oliver Wyman, McKinsey, and Bain—are paid to help management understand and rethink strategic alternatives that help their clients choose where to place their bets. Change management consultants help managers to implement the changes needed to put the strategic activities in place and to optimize their delivery. Accenture, SAP, and IBM consult with companies to develop and deploy technology-based solutions that give management the information they need to make decisions about productivity levels, the status of operations, and how well the activities of the business strategy are performing. Individual academic consultants and firms—such as DDI, Forum, and PDI—are hired to build stronger teamwork, foster learning, and change values and attitudes.

Consultants help clients set the direction of strategic change and then work up, down, and across the organization's structure to ensure its implementation. As such, consultants help business organizations understand and deal with the intense, global, macro forces that impinge on daily operations. And they do so with the intention that their clients can achieve sustainable competitive advantage by being uniquely faster, bigger, better, and/or cheaper. This is why clients hire consultants.

In Chapter Three we provide a logical, sequential, and comprehensive model of a consulting process that can be used by consultants to build business cathedrals, address the problems discussed in this chapter, and deploy solutions that will exceed client expectations.

A MODEL FOR PROFESSIONAL CONSULTING

This chapter presents an overview of the model we will use throughout the remainder of this book. The model is an organizing framework that simplifies and depicts the process of consulting as a set of logical steps needed to find business, produce solutions that exceed client expectations, and, in the process, build a successful consulting business. This chapter describes how consulting is a logical process with a defined set of roles, tasks, and competencies that constitute a continuous cycle of activity. Examples of the application of the model are shown in summary form at the end of the chapter.

What Do We Mean by "Process"?

First, we need to define what we mean by "process," then apply it to consulting so we can understand how consultants do their work. *Webster's New University Dictionary* defines process as follows:

A succession of actions undertaken to bring about some desired result. A series of gradual changes moving toward some particular end; a forward movement; progression.

With this definition in mind, we can understand consulting as a series of actions and steps that progress from understanding a client's problem to producing a solution that solves the problem. This may be done by facilitating a process that enables the client to become "self-directed," as in organization development consulting, or by giving the client advice that effectively tells the client what to do, as in training or financial consulting. In either case, how we consult (that is, the process) must be logical and systematic, practical and flexible; consider the ends as well as the means; and reflect the scientific method. Yet, we must also acknowledge that it is a human endeavor subject to error and learning, requiring innovation and creativity along with efficiency and effectiveness. Our consulting model reflects those needs and describes a set of steps required to complete any kind of consulting. It also shows the roles and tasks that, at a minimum, a consultant needs to master to complete professional work. To consider oneself a professional consultant means that *one has mastered the roles and tasks with the acquisition of certain knowledge, skills, and abilities (reflecting one's values), so that one's actions ensure logical progress toward goals that ultimately solve the client's problem.*

The model has evolved over time and has been refined by years of consulting practice and experience, with the benefit of input from many practitioners. It is comprehensive in its stages, roles, and outcomes, and prescriptive in its key tasks and responsibilities. To that extent, it is a practical model of the process of consulting, not a general theory of consulting.

Subsequent chapters describe in detail and with great precision the steps, tasks, roles, and outcomes of the process. Appendix A provides a diagnostic instrument, the Consulting Role Preference Indicator (CRPI), which consultants and project teams can use to measure their role preferences across twelve competencies and forty-eight validated consulting practices.

A Framework for Consulting

Consulting needs a standardized model or framework that describes a process and practices that can be used in all forms of consulting. Organization development consulting uses "action research" (Lewin, 1946), and all consulting firms use their own proprietary models and analytical tools to complete their work. However, a general model of consulting has been illusive. The model must define methods and procedures, ways of diagnosing client problems and needs. It must incorporate a standardized series of steps, tasks, roles, and outcomes that are replicable in any consulting situation. In turn, each of these aspects must have a body of knowledge and skills that can be taught and learned so that practitioners can use the model to increase their professionalism.

For ease of discussion and to simplify complexity, the model presents consulting as a linear sequence of stages that one person would follow from start to end. In reality, consulting is a complex process of steps and cycles. Each logical step is followed by reflection and learning, which may take the consultant back to an earlier stage or forward to a new one. In large consulting firms, roles such as project management, client engagement, and analyst are filled by different people, not one. Often tasks are done concurrently, not in sequence. As the model shows, consulting has many moving parts. Describing how they all interact with one another is possible, but that is not the focus of this book. This book is trying to simplify and explain a phenomenon that is inherently complex. The model is one way to do that, its mechanistic depiction notwithstanding. That is the nature of explanatory models.

Figure 3.1 describes our framework for professional consulting. Over the past twenty-five years, the framework has been tested and validated

FIGURE 3.1. CONSULTING FRAMEWORK

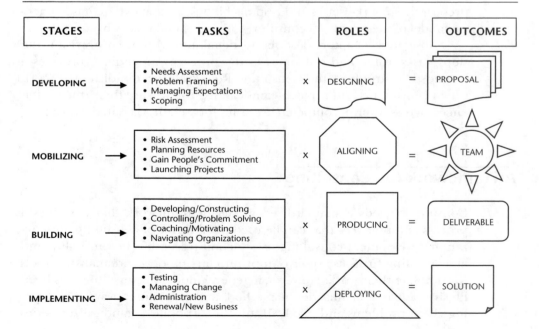

with a wide range of consultants. It has evolved and expanded to include new aspects of consulting. Important issues raised by the model include: (1) the cyclical nature of consulting; and (2) the central importance of the client.

Consulting as a Cycle. One of the obvious aspects of the framework is its cyclical nature. The model accounts for the fact that consulting is a continuous process, wherein consultants start their projects with step one, understanding client needs and problems, and end them with step four, deploying solutions, completing certain administrative tasks, and leading to new insights about consulting. In addition, as they complete each task, consultants are constantly alert to what they are learning that will enable them to build a solution that will solve the client's problem. Thus consulting follows a cycle: planning, action, learning, planning.

Importance of the Client. Where is the client in the model? In the framework the client is at the very center, and we should be asking ourselves vital questions such as these:

1. Who is the real client?
2. What are the client's real needs?
3. How does the client want us to work in the organization?
4. What are the client's vulnerabilities?
5. Will our proposed solution be the best for the client?
6. How do we build a long-term relationship with the client?
7. How can we become the client's trusted advisor?
8. What do we need to do to exceed client expectations?

Developing a client-focused mind-set is so important that we need to examine those client questions first, before discussing the specific elements of the consulting model.

1. *Who is the real client?* Sorting this out is often difficult and confusing. For example, the person who contacts the consultant enquiring about products and services may not be the person who makes the final decision or even controls the Consulting budget. In fact, these roles may be done by three different people. Or there may be a screening process for consultants to go through before the "short list" of prospective consultants is presented to the "hiring manager." For example, many consultants enter an organization through the human resources (HR) function where HR is a liaison with a line manager who has a problem that needs solving. Who is the client in this case? The line manager is the client (not HR). On the other hand, the line manager will have a supervisor who authorizes payment of invoices and has overall accountability to get the problem

solved. This person (the supervisor) may be the *real* client for the consultant. As challenging as it may be, it is very important that the consultant knows whom he or she is working for, that is, which person is the real decision maker and the most direct beneficiary of the consulting success (or failure). When this is unclear, many political mistakes can be made and long-term benefits lost.

2. *What are the client's real needs?* Discovering the client's real needs can be challenging as they may not be clear in the client's mind, may be deliberately hidden, or may require an in-depth study to define them. Furthermore, clients share their needs and problems in varying degrees of depth and detail, which may be mixed with personal biases. Therefore, early in the consulting process, consultants must be skillful at defining client needs by probing as deeply as possible the client's business context and business situation, by surfacing facts, and testing many assumptions. Embedded in the facts and issues are the real needs and wants, the real problem(s), and the real focus of the work. Because the results of this work end up in the proposal, this discovery process is critical and requires careful planning and questioning.

3. *How does the client want us to work in the organization?* All organizations have their own preferred ways of working, such as sharing information, reporting progress, demonstrating competence, showing commitment, making decisions, paying bills, and collecting revenues. An effective consultant learns as quickly as possible how the client works—its policies and procedures, protocols, and practices. Violation of any of these can be detrimental to the client-consultant relationship. The client may be forgiving, but others, well beyond the real client's jurisdiction, may not be. Although the maxim "It is better to ask for forgiveness than seek permission" has its place, effective consultants know that it can be risky to assume too much authority and risky to appear abusive of a company's standard ways of doing things. In other words, seek the client's advice about how to work inside the organization.

4. *What are the client's vulnerabilities?* A corollary to abiding by a company's protocols is understanding the client's personal organizational exposure. A client's *personal* vulnerabilities tend to center around the client's career—such as getting credit and promotions (or avoiding blame). Clients are concerned about how they are perceived in terms of power, authority, and influence, as well as their political exposure. It is imperative that consultants find ways to understand their client's vulnerabilities and to make sure they do not either negatively impact them or miss opportunities to reduce the client's organizational risks. Ironically, as a relationship

of trust grows, *clients* learn many things of great value about their *own* organization from their consultants. Consequently, effective consultants keep their clients informed as much as possible and try to reduce all negative surprises. Managers have a strong distaste for such surprises.

5. *Will our proposed solution be the best for the client?* Sometimes, a consultant is hired to evaluate the best solution for the client from a range of available solutions, including the consultant's own products and services. It is possible that the best FBBC solution is from another supplier. An effective and professional consultant uses a high level of objectivity to analyze and assess all solutions and recommends the one that is truly in the best interest of the client, even if it is not the consultant's *own* product or service. Candor and honesty in such matters always buys a tremendous amount of goodwill.

Another "best solution" concerns how to handle changes in scope that often occur when building and producing a solution for a client. In general, goodwill grows if the client is able to get more functionality and specifications in the solution without too much haggling over scope change and repricing. Always keep the client's best interest in mind (that is, think win-win, compromise, provide something for nothing). Such client focus may be a cost in the short run, but will pay off in the long run.

6. *How do we build a long-term relationship with the client?* Long-term relationships are built through professional behavior and producing results that exceed clients' expectations—results that the client (and sometimes the client's client) perceives as excellent. Honesty, integrity, credibility, responsibility, and accountability are the tried and tested qualities that build trust. Being trustworthy fosters trust building. Trust cannot be assumed; it must be earned.

7. *How can we become the client's trusted advisor?* Being a trusted advisor is the natural extension of having a long-term relationship built on achieving trustworthy results. As is discussed later in the book, becoming a trusted advisor takes time and effort and is a major professional milestone on the journey of becoming a highly effective consultant. Once a client trusts the consultant's advice, the client will seek advice on a growing number of areas—functional, organizational, strategic, and personal.

8. *What do we need to do to exceed client expectations?* It is not difficult to exceed client expectations. First, be exceptionally clear about the full range of the client's expectations; second, establish a metric for each expectation so you know whether it has been achieved; third, periodically recheck with the client to see whether the expectations have changed; fourth, seek feedback from the client during the consulting project to

assess progress against established and expected standards; and fifth, put in extra effort to give the client a little more than what was negotiated for and understood to be the finished product. The extras do not have to be expensive or highly visible to make a big difference. The key is to send the client the message that you are willing to make every effort to put the client first in the relationship.

With the client at the center of our thinking and work, and with the client's interests firmly in mind, we can undertake the journey of becoming a trusted consultant by following the stages and steps of the consulting framework. Our central purpose will be to pursue the stages and roles with a "can do" attitude that balances our own business needs with the goal of producing the very best solution for the client.

The Four Stages of Consulting

Figure 3.2 depicts four generic stages involved in undertaking any kind of consulting work. Every consultant must *develop business, mobilize people, build deliverables,* and *implement (present) solutions.*

Stage One: Developing. This stage addresses two basic needs of every consultant: (1) to find and develop consulting opportunities and (2) to develop a rapport with clients so a needs analysis and proposal can be completed. Whether working alone as an independent consultant or as a member of a consulting firm, *every* consultant must assume some level of responsibility for finding and *developing* business. In a consulting firm, a junior consultant who spots a business opportunity in a client's organization should then pass it on to his or her supervisor for consideration by the firm's practice leaders or new business committee. More experienced senior consultants will devote a significant portion of their time to business development. Owners and partner-level consultants may devote the

FIGURE 3.2. FOUR STAGES OF THE CYCLE OF CONSULTING

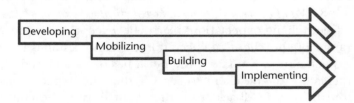

Developing

Mobilizing

Building

Implementing

majority of their time to such endeavors. Needs analysis requires balancing advocacy for using a particular existing solution (that is, a process, product, technology, or tool) with the advantages of inventing a unique solution governed by the client's unique situation. Both require excellent interpersonal skills.

Stage Two: Mobilizing. This is the stage when consultants must convert their proposal into a project plan, gather together other expert consultants to work with, and forge a team that is aligned around the individual and collective goals, roles, and responsibilities. Consultants rarely work alone. Even sole proprietor consultants acting alone as freelancers must work with client personnel to get work accomplished and therefore must learn how to team up with client workers.

Finding the right people for the right roles can be difficult if the people needed are not available or are not interested in a particular engagement. Consequently, two critical aspects of this stage are building people's interest in the project and mobilizing them to contribute their expertise. This can be difficult in a busy consulting firm with lots of concurrent engagements and consultants busy working on several projects at the same time.

Stage Three: Building Deliverables. In addition to any technical issues associated with producing a particular solution, stage three is when all the milestones in the project plan must be accomplished. Milestones are often interim deliverables concerning the design and development of some technical part of the solution, reports of findings from data analysis, presentations on progress, reviews with client management, and key meetings of the project team.

Stage three is a challenging and stressful time for most consultants, as many issues can arise. Challenges are likely to include varying from the project plan, negotiating changes in scope, navigating the politics in the client's organization, dealing with mistakes, and managing the performance of individual consultants and the team. Also, circumstances in the client organization can occur that may dramatically impact the consultant's work. These can include the loss of the project sponsor, changes in staff, a merger or acquisition, a dramatic reduction in profits, or a new government regulation.

Stage Four: Implementing. At this point, often clients have spent a lot of money and are anxious to see the final deliverable that will solve their problem. Whether that be a business strategy analysis, a new benefit program, an off-site team-building retreat, a fully integrated technology application, a training program, or the installation of lean manufacturing, everyone feels vulnerable. In stage four, training programs are *piloted* and tested, strategy documents and recommendations are *presented,* software solutions are *beta tested,* organization development initiatives are *phased in,* and process improvements are *subject to metrics.* At this final stage, getting the solution right (and within budget), along with helping the client with any change management consequences of implementing the solution, pays enormous dividends. By including an end-of-project feedback session with the client to understand the client's perception of our work, consultants can continue their journey of becoming a trusted advisor, which in turn may lead to more consulting opportunities and a long-term relationship.

The Four Roles of Consulting

Each stage of the consulting cycle requires a different role. Each role represents a set of behaviors required to perform a set of tasks that collectively are intended to achieve specific outcomes. By assuming the mindset of each role and learning how to perform the requisite tasks of each role, consultants will be able to produce the outcomes needed at each stage of the consulting cycle. Figure 3.3 shows the four roles.

Role One: Designing. The *science* of this role requires carefully gathering facts, analyzing the client's situation, and crafting a theory of the problem. The *art* of this role is a creative one; it requires well-thought-out questions, careful listening, and high emotional intelligence to arrest our own predisposition to provide immediate solutions, and to demonstrate very good

FIGURE 3.3. FOUR ROLES OF CONSULTING

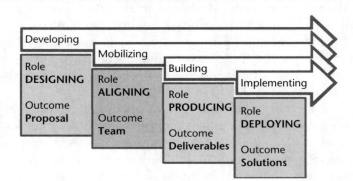

social skills and empathy. In this role we are trying to establish rapport and a relationship at a time when we are being tested and judged by the (prospective) client. The key tasks to perform in this role are:

- Assessing the client's needs
- Framing the client's problem
- Managing expectations
- Defining the scope of the work

Role 2: Aligning. The art of this role is getting people on board with the consulting project. This requires applying the people skills of stage one to the egos and needs of the additional consultants needed for the project, and combining those same human relations capabilities with leadership skills, to turn the new group into a team. The science of the aligning role is (1) using the proposal and project plan to make sure the right resources are identified for the scope of the work and (2) using the plan to communicate to the team the standards, specifications, and performance required to produce an excellent solution. The key tasks of the aligning role are:

- Planning and recruiting consultants for the work
- Conducting a risk assessment
- Enrolling and inspiring the team members
- Launching the project with the client

Role 3: Producing. The science of this role involves using the existing methods and procedures developed to produce the deliverables and, ultimately, the solution. Every consultant and firm has these, as they bring efficiency and effectiveness to the work. This role also requires using established formal management practices to set goals, track progress, solve problems, improve the performance of consultants as needed, and meet with the client to make decisions and keep them informed. The art of this role arises from the fact that sometimes established methods do not work and new ways must be invented. It also requires being sensitive to the client's organizational power structure, carefully handling changes requested by the client, and making adjustments when things do not go according to the plan. The key tasks of the producing role are:

- Using procedures to design and build deliverables
- Problem solving and decision making

- Managing the project according to the plan
- Navigating the client's organizational politics

Role 4: Deploying. Once solutions have been developed they must be deployed in the organization. The art of this role involves understanding and dealing with the dynamics of the client's organization. This stage is complicated and often politically charged for consultants, as a broader constituency of end users, beyond the client sponsor, are often involved. The consultant's handling of their perceptions and judgments is crucial for success. The role entails paying careful attention to any client resistance to ensure the adoption and use of the solution, and determining whether there are any new business opportunities. The science of the deploying role is using established procedures for presenting, testing, and rolling out the solution; managing change; fulfilling any final administrative requirements; and obtaining a client satisfaction metric. The key tasks of the deploying role are:

- Testing the quality of the solution
- Managing change and skills transfer
- Administration and documentation
- Assessing client satisfaction and renewal

The tasks of each role are explain in more detail in subsequent chapters, as each stage of the consulting model is discussed.

Consulting Competencies

So far, we have shown the tasks of each stage and role of consulting in order to translate the model's broad concepts into concrete actions needed to produce the outcomes. But what does a consultant need to know and be able to do, to perform those tasks? The final development of the model is to describe each role as a set of consulting competencies, which in turn can be described as a set of behavioral practices. Table 3.1 shows the competencies and practices; each is examined more closely in subsequent chapters.

With the model defined as a set of specific behavioral practices, training programs and diagnostic instruments can be created to develop those abilities in new consultants. The Consulting Role Preference Indicator in Appendix A is a self-scoring diagnostic instrument, which the reader can take to identify areas of strength and areas for development. The

TABLE 3.1 CONSULTING ROLES AND COMPETENCIES

Design (Approach)	Align (Team)	Produce (Deliverables)	Deploy (Solutions)
Needs Analysis/Problem Framing	**Project Resource Planning**	**Producing Deliverables**	**Testing and Refining**
• Rapidly identifies the major forces driving the client's business.	• Translates broad proposals into specific work plans, schedules, and task flow charts.	• Ensures that orderly progress is made on the assembly and development of deliverables.	• Ensures that solutions are tested before final delivery.
• Grasps the client's present business and how the client makes money.	• Uses planning documents to communicate people's roles and responsibilities.	• Makes decisions in the face of ambiguity and time constraints.	• Gives information so project teams can refine deliverables.
• Gathers, organizes, and systematically analyzes data about client needs.	• Assembles a consulting team for the work, when needed.	• Holds individual consultants accountable for agreed-upon goals.	• Actively seeks feedback about the client's satisfaction with the consulting solution.
• Asks questions to reframe and clarify issues that identify the real problems and needs.	• Ensures that team members have clearly delegated goals, roles, and responsibilities.	• Seeks constructive feedback about the effectiveness of deliverables as they are developed.	• Encourages people to try to exceed the client's expectations.
Managing Expectations	**Enrolling Others**	**Team Performance**	**Managing Change**
• Distinguishes the stated major issues and concerns of the client from the *real* ones.	• Communicates the project vision, plan, and strategy with enthusiasm and passion.	• Sets challenging but realistic team goals.	• Encourages continuous improvement in consulting work methods and processes.
• Works with the client to develop a strategy for producing a solution to the client's problem.	• Generates excitement about a shared vision and common goals among consultants.	• Builds people's confidence in themselves and their work with useful feedback and help.	• Explains any changes needed in the client's business and why the changes are necessary.
• Manages the client's expectations about the scope of the work.	• Listens carefully to the point of view and needs of the client and other consultants.	• Encourages team-based decision making when solving problems.	• Helps clients to manage the change process needed by the new solution.
• Tests the client's and one's own assumptions to ensure they are valid.	• Encourages the examination of differing views to build a consensus.	• Asks team members for their self-assessment of progress toward goals.	• Ensures that people are trained in the knowledge and skills needed to use the solution.

(Continued)

TABLE 3.1 (CONTINUED)

Design (Approach)	Align (Team)	Produce (Deliverables)	Deploy (Solutions)
Developing Proposals	**Launching Work**	**Navigating Politics**	**Closure and Renewal**
• Understands the client's strategy, plans, and goals. • Draws conclusions and makes recommendations from analysis of client data and information. • Prepares comprehensive proposals that summarize how the solution will be produced. • Identifies actions that reduce risks to project success.	• Demonstrates a command of the overall project requirements. • Conducts effective meetings with all relevant parties to launch consulting projects. • Uses influence in a way that builds trust to gain the support of others. • Ensures that everyone is heard, respected, and valued.	• Balances advocacy and diplomacy with clients to win support. • Understands how stakeholders in the client's organization use their power and influence. • Draws on informal contacts and networks of people to get things done. • Avoids taking credit for successful initiatives begun by others.	• Develops appropriate materials that document the solution. • Ensures that any project administrative problems with the client are resolved. • Conducts client meetings with diplomacy and tact in a way that grows the consulting relationship. • Helps clients to understand other business problems in their organization.

instrument can also be used for a 360 review to get the views and perceptions of other people, including consulting team members.

In the early stages of a consulting career it is important to know your strengths and weaknesses. Some consultants have preferences for certain stages of consulting work and may therefore be able to do a much better job at that stage than at other stages. For example:

- Technical consultants who prefer the producing role are very good at building and implementing solutions but dislike the political and project leadership aspects of the work.
- Some OD consultants may be very good at assessing a client's needs and defining the problem but avoid the "selling the firm" and winning business aspects of the designing role.
- A consultant may be excellent at energizing people and mobilizing a team but not so good at keeping things on track and delivering solutions on time.

Over time, with experience, training, and coaching, the goal is to be highly competent in all of the roles, competencies, and practices. Although more experienced readers of this book will almost certainly be at a very high level of ability, new consultants suddenly thrust into a project leadership role must make sure team members complement each other and one's own role preferences.

Conclusion

Clients spend a great deal of time developing vision and mission statements to provide overall guidance for their companies and employees. The practice of consulting needs the same effort. The profession needs a vision of an overarching framework that clarifies how consulting proceeds and ties together into an integrated whole. Consulting proposals serve this purpose, in part, by describing the phases of work, key tasks, deliverables, and a recommended process, and so on. But that is not enough. The consulting profession needs its own comprehensive, conceptual framework that guides how consultants work with clients. The purpose of this chapter has been to offer such a model.

For the sake of clarity and comprehension, the model presents a view of consulting that is linear and cyclical in nature, comprising a unifying set of stages, roles, and outcomes found in all consulting assignments. As defined at the beginning of the chapter, the framework is a process showing *a succession of actions undertaken to bring about some desired result moving toward a particular end state or goal.*

However, taken as a whole, a "process model" of consulting may appear deceptively simple. Consulting is messy, confusing, and ambiguous because it involves people—the client and the consulting team—even as the work is being done in a logical, sequential manner against plans and budgets. People often play multiple roles. In many firms roles and tasks are done by different people. Actions are taken not in a neat, linear fashion, but in parallel. Decisions are not always made rationally.

Despite the ambiguity of the real world, we hope the model provides an architectural foundation of the art and science of professional consulting practice. We hope it provides enough clarity to point the way for the kind of knowledge, skills, abilities, attitudes, values, and operating principles that (added to experience and examinations taken for professional education and certification) help practitioners achieve the status of a true *professional* consultant.

Appendix D provides case examples of the use and application of the model by showing each stage of the cycle for different consulting applications. We look at the process as if starting from the beginning; as if we have just received an opportunity to visit a prospective client to win the client's business. Then, assuming we have won the business, we show examples of the steps, behaviors, attitudes, and techniques that highly effective consultants use:

1. Putting together a consulting team
2. Beginning the business of building deliverables
3. Working in the client's organization
4. Producing solutions
5. Testing the deliverables
6. Implementing the solution
7. Helping the client with change management

At the end of the process, we return to the beginning. We recycle our efforts by asking the client to consider using us again in a new arena for consulting that the client has surfaced or we have identified along the way.

In Part Two, Chapter Four, we start to apply the model and provide details about what for many consultants is the hardest part of consulting, finding and winning new business.

PART TWO

APPLYING THE MODEL

STAGE ONE: THE DEVELOPING AND DESIGNING PROCESS

Consulting and consultants have become ubiquitous over the last twenty-five years. With the growth has come a wide range of opinions about their efficacy, value, definition, professionalism, and status. We stated earlier that a working definition of a consultant is:

A professional who can be trusted to use standard consulting methods and procedures, who gives advice and produces solutions to problems on behalf of clients.

The rest of this book shows how we can alleviate some of the concerns that clients have about consultants, if we follow certain procedures and use tested tools and techniques, with processes governed by strong professional values.

Stage one, the developing stage and design role, is explained in two parts, in this chapter and Chapter Five. These chapters show how this generic definition is turned into action that achieves the very important first step in any consulting assignment—winning business—using the competencies described in the model. In this first of the two chapters, we present broad components of stage one and discuss the preliminary actions needed to perform well in the design role, focusing on:

- Stage one competencies: winning business
- Understanding the client's business
- Aspects of making a good first impression when meeting with a new prospect for the first time

In Chapter Five we explain in detail the tasks of the first stage of consulting: conducting a needs analysis, managing expectations, and developing a proposal.

Stage One Competencies: Winning the Business

The purpose of stage one in the consulting cycle is to win business. This is a challenging mission made easier by understanding the client's business, conducting a needs analysis, framing the client's problem, making a very good first impression, managing expectations, and presenting a compelling proposal. Table 4.1 shows the three consulting competencies and twelve behavioral practices associated with this stage in the consulting model.

Winning business is essentially a *design problem*; that is, designing the best way to work with a client—involving both a human and a technical relationship—to solve the client's problem. The word "design" is used to mean plan, craft, create, and invent. The design role is a creative one that requires combining existing consulting procedures and perhaps known solutions, with imagination, innovative thinking, and tailored work. The essential role and function of the consultant at the beginning is to invent and articulate a plan to solve the client's problem by discovering the facts, making sure the problem is understood, and formulating an action plan. The extremely important first set of meetings with a prospective client focus on developing this understanding, and the resulting action plan ends up in the proposal. Once the business is earned, this plan then guides subsequent tasks during the stages of building a team, producing deliverables, and implementing a solution.

Winning business requires defining the client's problem through a *needs analysis*. It is not an easy task, as the client may mask the problem in many ways. When conducting a needs analysis, factors described by the client as problems are often just indicators of the problem and tend to be symptoms rather than the real problem. The consultant must peel away the layers to see what lies beneath what the client is saying. Additionally, the consultant is often working with so little information at this point that unless the consultant has experienced *exactly* the same situation before,

TABLE 4.1 DEVELOPING COMPETENCIES AND BEHAVIORAL PRACTICES

Purpose	Stage	Tasks	Role	Outcome
Winning Business	**Developing**	• Needs Analysis • Problem Framing • Managing Expectations • Scoping	**X Design**	**=Proposal**

Competency	Practices
Needs Analysis and Problem Framing	• Rapidly identifies the major forces driving the client's business. • Grasps the client's present business and how the client makes money. • Gathers, organizes, and systematically analyzes data about client needs. • Asks questions to reframe and clarify issues that identify the real problems and needs.
Managing Expectations	• Distinguishes the stated major issues and concerns of the client from the *real* ones. • Works with the client to develop a strategy for producing a solution to the client's problem. • Manages the client's expectations about the scope of the work. • Tests the client's and the consultant's own assumptions to ensure that they are valid.
Developing Proposals	• Understands the client's strategy, plans, and goals. • Draws conclusions and makes recommendations from analysis of client data and information. • Prepares comprehensive proposals that summarize how the solution will be produced. • Identifies actions that reduce risks to project success.

the consultant is using mostly guesswork, assumptions, and theories to define the problem. Therefore, for the consultant to gain insight into the client's situation and problems, it is crucial to ask many questions, test assumptions, keep an open mind, and help the client to open up.

Winning business involves *clarifying mutual expectations* and is often a complex and difficult task for consultants. Many prefer to leave this responsibility in the hands of a sales force. But smaller consulting firms often do not have a staff dedicated to sales, so individual consultants must find clients, clarify expectations, and win business themselves. When a firm does have a sales force, other problems occur, including salespeople overselling or overpromising their firm's consulting services. When this happens, the consultants who subsequently meet with the client (perhaps for the first time) must then realign expectations to ensure that they are practical and realistic. This conversation must be done very carefully and diplomatically so the client remains interested in buying the firm's consulting services, even with revised expectations.

When the consultant believes the client's business challenges are clarified, specific needs and problems sufficiently framed and understood, and expectations elucidated, then a plan can be designed and presented in the form of a *proposal,* which is the outcome or deliverable from the first stage of the consulting cycle.

During stage one, the client will begin to see how the consultant works, interacts, and communicates, which will tell the client a great deal about the consultant's style, values, skills, knowledge, and capabilities. Thus the consultant is already shaping the expectations of the client. It behooves the consultant to be very conscious of what is being shaped and to avoid language or ideas that may be biased, rude, prejudiced, premature, or presumptuous, given the consultant's limited knowledge of the client's situation at this point. The proposal itself—its accuracy, robustness, reasonableness, validity, clarity, and comprehensiveness—also sets and shapes expectations.

In the designing role, the consultant must be keenly aware of many things that shape a client's perceptions. Because the consultant wants to always be perceived positively, it is important to pay attention to the quality of questions asked, the astuteness of any insights presented, the style and language used, the appropriate use of humor, and the seriousness with which the issues are discussed. This stage of consulting calls for heightened awareness, as it is fraught with pitfalls and missteps. The relationship is very young. The parties do not know each other well, and both are trying to see whether the fit is right—whether the chemistry will produce a good working relationship.

To reduce the potential for mistakes, the consultant's mind-set needs to be one of frankness and candor, humility, and interest. Be frank about not knowing everything regarding the problem as it has been stated so far, and state how much more there is to learn about the client's organization, issues, and problems. It can be fatal to act with hubris by indicating that you have seen the problem before or suggesting it is an easy one to solve—if that were so, the client would do it without the consultant. Clients appreciate candor and honesty. If you do not know something, say so. In addition, the consultant must have enough humility to work collaboratively with the client. Urge the client to think about how to work as a team. Most clients want teamwork, and it can be a relief to the client to know the consultant feels the same way. Some clients simply demand this. At this stage of the consulting process, it is better if the consultant takes the initiative to acknowledge the working relationship as team-based and highly collaborative. Do not get upset if the client wishes to change many things in the proposal. Keep in mind the big picture: to *win* the business.

Winning business requires thinking beyond the initial contact person(s). An important best practice in stage one is to think about how to help the client deal with the client's internal constituency, which must also be convinced of the proposed approach, timing, staffing, and costs. The person at the first meeting may or may not be the decision maker. Even if the person is the decision maker, the client must still justify the use of consultants and their cost to other people in the organization, such as the client's immediate manager, the finance and accounting director, or perhaps a task force set up to monitor the problem. During the initial meetings find out whether anyone else is involved in the client's decision. Learn as much about this as possible, and think about how to help the client sell the proposal internally.

Because clients know their own organizations and preferences of internal players well, ask the client for advice on the best way to present the proposal in terms of appropriate language, style, content, length, format, and focus. If you think you have a good rapport with the prospective client, discuss how you can help with the person's internal selling process. All of those actions make a good first impression and reflect the style, values, and professionalism of the consultant. This signals to the potential client whether or not the consultant would be a good fit to do the work. The client is always privately asking questions such as "Is this the right person (or firm) for us?" "Will I feel comfortable working with this person?" "Has this person done a good job of really trying to understand my situation?" "Does the person have empathy for my vulnerability?" To the extent that the consultant is aware of those types of client concerns and fears and does a good job trying to allay them with emotional intelligence, honesty, and openness, the consultant will significantly increase the likelihood of winning the business and, perhaps more important, lay the groundwork for a long-term relationship in which the consultant ultimately becomes a trusted advisor.

Understanding the Client's Business and Industry

It is important to realize that clients do not expect you to know as much about their business as they do. Nor do clients expect you to know that much about how their organization works, let alone the client's specific problems. However, clients do expect you to have done your homework by studying certain key information sources (shown in Table 4.2). By studying as many of these as possible, the consultant will find it easier to develop a strategy and structure for the prospective client meeting and a set of questions that must be asked in order to understand the client's problem.

TABLE 4.2 SOURCES OF INFORMATION FOR PREPARING A CLIENT MEETING

Item	What to Look For
The organization's annual report	Business sectors, products, and services Change in financial condition by sector Chairman's introduction—key issues Board members' affiliations Names of key executives by function
10K reports (publicly available SEC filings)	Names of company officers Changes in structure affecting products Financial condition and concerns
Analysts' reports from services such as Value Line	Industry dynamics and key trends Business sectors, products, and services Performance of sectors Rationale for any forecasts
Newspaper and reputable magazine articles	Industry dynamics and key trends Business sectors, products, and services Performance of sectors Rationale for forecasts and conclusions Indications of culture (values, beliefs)
The organization's website	Business sectors, products, and services Chairman's introduction—key issues Names of key executives by function News items on the organization Indications of culture (values, beliefs)
Promotional literature the organization makes available	Business sectors, products and services Any commentaries—key issues Names of key executives by function News items on the organization Indications of culture (values, beliefs, stories)
The organization's service and product offering	Range and scope New products and services Markets and customer use Inventions and copyrights
Any existing information about the organization in your firm's files	Details of previous consulting assignments Reasons for success, failure Indications of culture Anyone you know who knows the organization

All of this preliminary work helps consultants to get organized, to be prepared and ready to meet with the prospective client. However, right at the beginning of stage one, before consultants even start their needs analysis and problem framing, they need to understand and constructively confront certain powerful, rational, and emotional dynamics that shape the quality of their relationship with the client. This stage often begins with the pressure of meeting the prospective client for the first time, and that starts with making a good first impression.

Making a Good First Impression

To help us understand the basic difficulties and challenges of stage one and how it works in context, in the real world, for the rest of this chapter let us *assume that we are starting right at the beginning of the consulting process.* We have an opportunity to develop new business with a prospective client, and we are meeting with a client representative(s) for the first time.

As a result of a concerted marketing effort, sales work, and reaching out to our personal network, at some point we get a call to meet with a prospective client to discuss their problems and to see whether we might be able to help. At this point we clap our hands and beam with excitement—we have been given a chance to talk about what we like to do; to talk about ourselves; to solve a problem; to enter a new client organization; to turn work into profits. We now have the great challenge of winning the business.

In meeting with a prospect for the first time, we must assume that the client is talking to other consultants and consulting organizations. This assumption should automatically trigger the desire to be as prepared as possible. We should ask ourselves:

- What is my goal for this meeting?
- What can I do to differentiate myself and my firm?
- How can I learn as much as possible about the client?
- What are the right questions to ask the client?
- How can I demonstrate an understanding of the problem?
- How can I make a good first impression?

It has been said: *Success is where opportunity meets preparation.* Preparing and asking oneself such questions is crucial, as that can help to make the first meeting discussion focused and clear—that, in itself, serving to create a positive impression. It also requires knowing exactly what to say about yourself and your firm. McKinsey uses the "elevator test" to make a good first impression (Raisel, 1999). This is the challenge of determining precisely what to say about ourselves, our work, and our firm, when asked by a client (that is, in the time it takes to travel down a few floors in an elevator with a client).

An important issue of fit and chemistry is the consultant's ability to explain exactly and clearly the mission and services of the consulting firm and his or her personal role in it. It is a good idea to write out a paragraph that succinctly describes exactly what you and the firm do. Then memorize it. At some point in the first meeting it is likely that the client will ask you to describe what you do, personally, and what the firm does. Even if the client does not ask, it is a good idea to be ready to provide a quick overview. It should be short enough to say in about one minute and in a language understandable by nonspecialists. For example:

> I am a senior information technology consultant with eight years of experience in designing, building, and implementing systems that integrate a company's different computer systems. I work with companies of your size and complexity and lead a group of technology specialists in my firm. My company has been in business for twelve years and has three locations in the United States. We have developed our own consulting methods for large-scale integration projects and use the latest project management techniques. The firm has experience in your industry and is a preferred supplier to Cisco and SAP. We have comprehensive skills in all the major technology systems and platforms.

Be prepared to back up everything you say, as the client may test you at this point. Depending on that person's role in the company (or who else is in the room), you will need to adjust the language to suit the technical expertise of the audience, using their own functional language. For example, in the finance department, speak in terms of numbers, analysis, and balance sheets. If the audience is general management, speak in terms of strategy, operational performance, and results. In the marketing department, speak in terms of sales, customer service, and products. In the legal function, speak in terms of compliance, regulations, and standards.

When discussing your firm and what you do as a consultant, a best practice is to find the right balance between using credible technical jargon suitable for the functional specialist sitting in the room (such as IT, marketing, or finance) and using the ideas, practices, and technical jargon of your consulting specialty. Always practice what you will say before meeting with the client. Always ask whether they have any questions about you or the firm.

Have references ready to offer to the client so you can give names and contact numbers on the spot. This creates a positive and credible impression and immediately increases trust and confidence in the mind of the prospective client.

First Meeting Dynamics

It is always a special time when consultants meet with a prospective client for the first time. It is fraught with subtle dynamics, multiple levels of communication, and important first impressions.

First Impressions

We understand that it takes only a few moments for us to know whether or not we like someone or feel comfortable around them. We pick up and tune in to positive or negative energy; we sense whether we are accepted or rejected, being judged or being dealt with fairly and openly, and with interest. It is important to tune into our feelings and be aware of how we are emotionally responding to the situation. As discussed in Chapter Seven, this is an important aspect of emotional intelligence (Goleman, 2006a).

According to Goleman, if we sense a negative, tough, judgmental atmosphere in the room, we have the potential, by tuning into ourselves and being conscious of our emotional response, to make the most of the situation by controlling that emotional response and directing our energy toward constructive, useful outcomes. The fact is, some prospects may use a difficult, aggressive style to test us; to see how well we deal with toughness, negative statements, criticism, or a deep inquiry into our qualifications. The prospect may be testing how well the consultant can deal with the challenges of the client organization; seeing whether the consultant can "take the heat" or function well under pressure. So if this happens, do not be discouraged by a cold atmosphere. Think of it as a test of your fortitude and mental toughness under pressure. See it as a challenge to demonstrate just how good you are!

Rapport

Experienced consultants look for ways to quickly establish rapport in the first meeting. Using good manners, being polite, and showing courtesy and respect are very important and obvious ways to make a good first impression. The following are additional practices that help to put people at ease and get things started:

- Be well-groomed and wear conservative dress that is neutral and does not draw attention. Clean nails, shiny shoes, and combed hair say a lot about who you are. If you are recovering from a cold or the flu and feel you might still be contagious, let the client know and keep your distance accordingly, declining a handshake if necessary. If you are ill, consider rescheduling; better to be clear-headed and not contagious.
- To show respect, reconfirm how much time the client has allotted for the meeting right at the beginning. Be led by the client's agenda and weave your own into it.
- Never violate the client's space by standing too close, prolonging a handshake, setting items on the client's furniture, asking to use the client's equipment, or commenting on the room temperature. Make comfortable eye contact, but avoid prolonged staring.
- Allow the client to indicate which chair to sit in and wait for the client to ask you to sit. Breathe deeply and relax.
- Always accept a client's offer for a beverage, even if you do not want one or cannot finish it. Accepting hospitality is a way of showing respect and being polite.
- Look around the client's office for signs of a common interest, such as sports trophies, family pictures, holiday pictures, degrees, awards, community recognition, collected artifacts, hobbies. Use these in the conversation to break the ice, show empathy, and be relaxed (but not too informal).
- Break the ice at the beginning with small talk about the weather, the view from the office, the commute, traffic conditions, positive statements about office architecture, something big in the news, or general business conditions.
- Use humor that is appropriate. Never make jokes that are vulgar or lewd, or personal about the client. Use self-deprecating humor. Smile a lot. Laugh at the client's jokes, but never compete with a better one.

All of these rational and emotional practices are part of forging first impressions; this is something that both parties are doing. Table 4.3 shows

TABLE 4.3 TACIT QUESTIONS ASKED DURING THE FIRST MEETING

Prospective Client	Consultant
How good are these consultants?	Can I communicate with this person?
Will this person be able to work with my people?	What does this person want?
Can I trust this person?	Can I have influence here?
How professional is this person's appearance and behavior?	Does this person like me? Like consultants in general?
How intelligent is this person?	Can I convince this person to buy our service?

the kinds of questions that the parties may be tacitly asking themselves in order to "size up" each other. Each is trying to assess whether or not the two of you will be able to get along and work with one another; at what cost in time and treasure; and whether it will be an enjoyable, productive experience. In short, is there chemistry or not?

Questions and Worries

One important aspect of the first meeting is that each may be experiencing a level of discomfort and anxiety about the whole situation. Table 4.4 shows the kinds of worries and concerns that both consultants and prospects can have at this stage.

Because there is a lot at stake in most consulting engagements, both sides worry about such things as political agenda, personal vulnerability, and the cost, timeliness, and quality of solutions. Previous consulting experiences can make the worries greater or lesser.

The key concern for consultants with the kinds of questions, worries, and fears outlined in Table 4.4 is that during the first meeting: (1) the client will hold back key information or will not be completely honest with the consultant; (2) how the client describes the problem will be impacted; and (3) because there may be just one meeting before a proposal is submitted, the consultant may fear that not enough of the right kind of information has been shared to enable the consultant to develop an accurate proposal.

Because the quality of the proposal is at stake, it is better to promptly take the risk of exploring any worries or concerns the client may have about working together, rather than ignore them. This may have the added benefit of revealing important aspects of client expectations, which we will discuss in Chapter Five.

TABLE 4.4 TYPICAL WORRIES AND CONCERNS OF PROSPECTS AND CONSULTANTS

Concerns of Both Prospective Client and Consultant

Organizational politics
I'll look unintelligent
The solution may not work
Lots of "people" problems
Problems outside my area of expertise
We won't like each other
Not getting what I want
Risk of failure
I won't be able to say "no" to something
Loss of control
Project will be late
Unrealistic deadlines
Project will go over budget

Client Concerns (about the consultant)	Consultant Concerns (about the client)
Isn't experienced enough	Is looking for someone to blame
Will not deliver on time	Has hidden agenda
Doesn't know my business	Will not negotiate
Does not have technical expertise	Doesn't know what is needed
Is not flexible enough	Is not fully committed
Has only "off the shelf" solutions	Behavior is part of the problem
Recommends more expensive solution than the problem requires	Is not the decision maker
Will discuss problems with my competitors	May be very slow in paying invoices
Will get transferred before the end of the project	Won't give enough time to the problem
Does not understand my constraints, such as budget	Has a one-track mind around a certain solution
Firm not able to handle the size of my organization	Wants a solution to symptoms rather than causes
May not fit my organizational culture	Has a reputation for being hard to work with
Will lack integrity	Wants something outside my firm's priorities or guidelines

Having All the Answers

Some consultants believe they must appear to be smart and have all the answers. Many clients dislike this attitude, because at this stage of the consulting process no consultant knows very much about the client's real problems. In fact, early in the relationship the client may just want to see how you think, test your integrity, and see whether you are capable of making a good effort. The client expects well-thought-out points of view that are backed up with experience, facts, research, and analysis, rather than quick, "off the shelf" answers or competitive arrogance. The client's style and demeanor can be deceptive. What seems like competitive—even defensive—behavior may just be testing to see whether the consultant is capable of understanding the challenges, drivers, and barriers to success, and the demands of the client's organization culture. So do not be baited into an argument.

Is the consultant mature and seasoned, able to handle the difficult questions and challenges that will inevitably arise? Consultants dramatically increase the possibility of winning the business if they take these first meeting impressions seriously, study the dynamics, consciously strive to increase the client's comfort and confidence level, and balance advocacy with inquiry and humility.

Communication of the Client's Problem

If the client is unduly anxious about the consultant or perhaps is worried about even entering into a consulting relationship in the first place, the client may deliberately or unconsciously misstate the problem. In general, the client may describe the problem too narrowly, too broadly, too ambiguously, or with too much complexity. The motivations behind such a description may come from the client's

- Ignorance of the true problem and hope that the consultant will find and define it
- Cautiousness about revealing too much at this stage of the relationship
- Reluctance to say too much, in an effort to keep the cost down
- Attempts to sound important and well informed
- Testing of the consultant to see what he or she will do with the problem description and information
- Confusion about the problem and inability to state it clearly

Regardless of the client's motivation, the job of the consultant is to keep *restating* the problem to verify whether it is accurate, *reframing* the problem to clarify and sharpen its definition, and *refining* the problem to define its scope. We can see here the importance of the interpersonal skill of active listening, as well as a questioning strategy to yield an accurate definition of the problem. To achieve this may require the consultant to be persistent and politely push the prospect to say more and to reveal underlying issues and broader implications. Consultants may be anxious about being persistent, assertive, or even confrontational, but that is part of the interpersonal skills requirement to be an effective consultant (Block, 1981).

At this stage in development, clients are looking for clues that will raise their confidence in the decision they are about to make. Remember, if the consultant is able to help the prospective client think through the problem aloud in a positive and constructive manner, then the client will be more likely to have a positive impression of the consultant's ability. Successful reframing of the problem by the consultant tells the client a lot about the consultant's professionalism, experience, seriousness, thinking skills, interpersonal strengths, and tenacity in accurately defining the problem to be solved. During this first meeting, in which the total time available may be less than one hour, creating such an experience for the client makes a positive impression, raises confidence levels, and improves the likelihood of winning the business.

Finally, consultants must not underestimate or ignore the existence of *their own fears*, many of which are listed in Table 4.4. As much as possible, use the presence of such fears and worries as messages and topics for discussion. They are real and should not be allowed to cloud your thinking or reduce your own confidence level. As difficult as it may be to give them voice, consultants must learn to recognize and face the fears and push through them; to speak up despite the fears. This is one aspect of having emotional intelligence (see Chapter Seven). These kinds of worries and concerns exist throughout a consulting engagement, so it is a best practice to periodically check with the client and discuss any fears and what can be done about them. If this is handled well, with diplomacy and advocacy, it will help to forge trust and a stronger relationship.

Conclusion

Stage one of the consulting process has three important ingredients. First, the consultant must do homework and prepare in anticipation of meeting the prospective client. Second, the consultant must be mindful of the behavior needed to make a very good first impression in the first meeting, and third, the consultant must have a strategy for conducting the meeting in order to do a good needs analysis.

This chapter has discussed the first two ingredients—preparation and the first meeting. Preparation requires researching the client organization to gain an understanding of its history, strategy, products and services, markets, management, organization structure, financial structure, growth prospects, and if possible, its business model. Current business issues and performance results can be discerned from articles and analysts' reports. Information about the person being met is also desirable, but harder to get unless the consultant knows someone who knows the person.

Because first impressions are critical and long-lasting, careful thought should be given to the consultant's dress, language, attitude, behavior, and message before the meeting to ensure that during the meeting mistakes are not made that would lower the prospect's confidence in the consultant.

Fully prepared with client information, meeting goals, an agenda, and support materials, and having prepared to make the first meeting a positive one, the consultant can then use the time available with the prospective client to conduct a needs analysis sufficient to write a proposal. Three basic skills are needed to do this: (1) asking the right questions, (2) listening effectively, and (3) structuring a question strategy. Those skill sets seem deceptively easy and obvious, but turn out to be difficult and crucial to winning business. We will examine each of these in detail in the next chapter, as core skills needed to frame the problem, raise confidence in the consultant's ability, manage expectations, and produce a proposal.

CHAPTER FIVE

STAGE ONE, CONTINUED: ASSESSING CLIENT NEEDS AND MANAGING EXPECTATIONS

In the previous chapter we introduced the three competencies required at stage one of the consulting cycle when we need to win business, and we discussed the importance of making a good, professional impression with prospective clients. In this chapter, we continue with stage one, covering the competencies in more depth by examining the issues and challenges of needs assessment, problem framing, proposals development, and managing expectations. We focus on:

- The purpose of the needs assessment and analysis
- Types of questions
- How to conduct a needs assessment—a question strategy
- Listening actively and effectively during needs assessment
- Proposal development and writing
- Managing expectations

The Purpose of Conducting a Needs Assessment

The purpose of conducting a needs assessment in stage one is to frame and define the client's problem(s). Both technical expertise and good human relations skills are required to conduct a successful needs

TABLE 5.1 NEEDS ASSESSMENT ANALYSIS

Current State	Future State
Finance focused	Customer focused
Confusing, old strategy	Focused, clear strategy
Independent databases	Integrated databases
Using manual procedures	Fully automated
Weak employee results	Consistent high performance
High-cost processes	Cost-effective processes
Costly employee turnover rate	Stable employee retention
Slow decision making	Fast decision making
Low return on capital	High return on capital
Average-quality metrics	High-quality metrics
High-cost operation	Low-cost operation
Centralized leadership	Distributed leadership
Strong competitive culture	Adaptive culture
Defined benefits plan	Defined contribution plan

assessment. After all, clients may hesitate to be open and honest in sharing their problems so early in the relationship, in part because of conscious and unconscious fears and natural caution. Nevertheless, consultants must do their best to frame the problem because it is the basis for crafting a proposal.

As a practical matter, needs assessment is an analysis of the gap between the client's current state (as is) and a desired future state (should be) (see Table 5.1). Solutions are then designed and built to close the gap.

Questions asked during a needs assessment gap analysis address the following (generic) issues:

- *Background:* History behind the current state
- *Dynamics:* Dimensions and dynamics of the current state
- *Rationale:* Reasons why the future state is needed
- *Vision:* Practical features or specifications of the future state
- *Causes:* Internal and external factors causing the gap
- *Context:* How one causal factor may affect another
- *Force field:* Factors driving and hindering closing the gap
- *Expectations:* Project management expectations (more on this shortly)

Getting answers to these questions requires asking "good" questions and very carefully listening. As easy as these actions sound, consultants may not have the necessary skills to do them well. The next three sections provide useful communication techniques to use at this point, to ensure that the client's problem is well framed and the consultant-client relationship is off to a good start.

Types of Questions: The Fundamentals

Effective questioning and listening demonstrate the art of tuning into the client's verbal and nonverbal communications and responding with questions that uncover deeper issues and insights that eventually reveal the client's problem. Effective consultants ask questions all the time, of many people and about many different things. However, to be *really* effective, consultants need to be thoughtful and strategic about the questions.

To be strategic, consultants must consider the form of the questions, their content, and the sequence in which they are asked. In this manner they can develop a *question strategy* in advance of the client meeting and so be much better prepared. As a result, the needs assessment conversation will go from general knowledge and issues to specific facts and productive insights about the client's current and future states and the gap in between.

First we will examine form and then address the sequence and content of questions before discussing how to listen effectively to the answers.

Questions come in a number of generic forms—closed, open, leading, or loaded questions—each yielding very different results. We will now cover each form in detail.

Closed Questions

Closed questions lead to "yes" or "no" answers or a choice among alternatives. Therefore closed questions tend to be quick and enable the consultant to get specific details. The client is "pinned down" and when answering such questions must share a mental decision made about the item under discussion. Such items include preferences and specific requirements regarding factors such as the scale, scope, or magnitude of the problem, or causes, effects, implications, and dynamics of the situation.

A good model for seeing the value of closed questions is provided by television interviewers who have a limited amount of time to get a guest to open up and share something interesting—without taking too much time to say it. The interviewer usually begins by asking the guest many closed questions to establish a context or certain facts. The strategic reason for using closed questions is to control the time the guest has to speak and to get certain information. This is also true for the consultant, who usually has limited time with the client during the first meeting but must elicit a lot of facts and insights very quickly. Closed questions are designed for those purposes.

Open Questions

On television, interviewers shift from closed to open questions. The intention is to get the guest to open up, to explain and describe, to elaborate and expand, and to provide a lot of information. Consultants must do the same thing. Open questions usually include phrases such as "Please explain," or "describe," or "expand." Such questions may take a long time to answer, so they must be asked sparingly and carefully. Long answers may require the consultant to interrupt with closed questions that guide and clarify the client's responses or help the client to explain more accurately. Open questions are key to gaining breadth and depth of understanding about the situation and the nature of the client's needs, but they carry the risk of the client going off on tangents and wasting time.

Leading Questions

Leading questions do just that—they lead to an answer the consultant wants, by suggesting the answer in the question. For example:

"Don't you think it is about time to stop others from having access to that information?"

"Wouldn't it be wise to choose a strategy of efficiency *and* quality rather than just one or the other?"

"If you wish to improve your leadership, will this decision be communicated sooner rather than later?"

Leading questions can be useful to clarify things, elicit action, or motivate a decision, but they must be used with caution. They may be perceived as premature or pushy—even inappropriate or arrogant at such an early stage of the relationship, when the level of trust is low and there are so many unknowns in the relationship. When they are used, they should be used wisely, thoughtfully, and politely. They can be softened with a preamble such as "Forgive me for saying this, but . . ." or "If you don't mind my saying . . . perhaps . . ." or "I know I don't know very much about the situation yet; however, could you . . . ?"

Loaded Questions

Inexperienced consultants or experienced consultants with low emotional intelligence who lack empathy may ask loaded questions. Loaded questions are similar to leading questions but usually convey a negative judgment and are often compounded by being asked at the wrong time and in the wrong way. For example:

"Do you think you will ever get it right?"

"How long do you think you will be in this job?"

"Wouldn't it be smarter to read the manual first?"

In general, loaded questions should be avoided, as they tend to make the client feel uncomfortable; the client may experience such questions as rude, controlling, or an attempt to get a preconceived answer.

Consultants must also be aware that questions can be asked in many ways: simple, clear, confusing, serious, humorous, and so on. Experienced consultants know how easily a poorly framed question, asked with the wrong tone, can reflect a personal bias, leading to misunderstanding, inaccuracy, and a distortion of the truth. The key is being intentional with our questions, such that we choose the questions we believe will enable us to achieve the needs assessment goals. The keys to asking good, mature questions are preparation, careful listening, avoiding confusion, using emotional intelligence, and knowing when to be humorous and when to be serious.

In summary, loaded, closed, open, and leading questions are options consultants can choose to use in any conversation during the consulting cycle, but during needs assessment meetings consultants must be particularly conscious of what they are asking, their tone, and whether the type of question used will yield the information they seek and contribute positively to building the relationship.

Obviously, effective questioning is a skill, and it must be practiced. One strategy that can help improve our needs assessment is bringing along to the client meeting a colleague who has the discipline and skill to ask the right questions in the right way. This enables one consultant to ask questions while the other listens and takes notes. However, listening itself is an art and requires attention, and is discussed in more detail later in this chapter.

Conducting a Needs Assessment: A Question Strategy

Armed with questions and listening skills, we can now develop more deeply the idea of creating a *question strategy*. A question strategy simply means that you have (1) thought through the questions you wish to ask and (2) decided on the sequence in which to ask those questions before meeting with the client. Both elements are very important. Asking a random set of questions that seem to have no logical starting point and then do not take the conversation to a practical end is useless and may confuse both the consultant and the client. Worse, the client may conclude that the consultant is not well prepared, or think she or he is "just fishing" and lacks the kind of mental discipline needed to solve the problem. Once such perceptions arise in the client's mind, the consultant has lost the business before even getting started.

One of the best ways to think about a question strategy is to use the ideas and excellent work of Neil Rackham (1988). In his book *SPIN Selling*, he discusses his research into the factors that differentiate highly successful salespeople from those who are not. He concludes unequivocally that salespeople who use a process of *inquiry* and *investigation* to "earn the right" to offer a product or service stand a much higher chance of success than those who do not. Earning that right is directly related to (1) the questions the salesperson asks (open, closed, leading), (2) the questions' content, and (3) the sequence in which the questions are asked. Customers and clients are much more likely to buy if the salesperson asks questions in a sequence that forms the acronym SPIN; that is, to first ask *situation* questions, then *problem-*oriented questions, then *implication* questions, and finally *need-payoff* questions. Thus a question strategy is a planned, logical sequence of questions that give the consultant the breadth and depth of information needed to draw conclusions about the nature of the client's problem and to yield insights into ways in which the problem may be approached and solved.

Situation Questions

These questions enable the consultant to add to the arsenal of information gathered during his or her preparation, and to gauge the size, scale, and scope of the *situation* to be dealt with. For example, if the consultant is being asked to design, develop, and deliver a training program in response to a performance problem such as workplace harassment or a drop in productivity, here are some likely situation questions:

- How many harassment accusations and cases have you had over the last year?
- Have you had workplace harassment training before?
- How many people need to be trained?

- Do you have internal training professionals who would need to be trained?
- How do you currently measure productivity?

Problem Questions

These questions focus on the precise nature of client problems, including breakage, loss, cost, quality, or timing *problems*; for example:

- What types of harassment problems have occurred most frequently?
- What concerns do you have about how the last harassment case was handled?
- How serious would you say the harassment problem is?
- How effectively has the company's training addressed the problem?

Note that the word "problem" or "concern" is used.

Implication Questions

With implication questions, the consultant can demonstrate an ability to think laterally about the problem and to get the client to see other problems that perhaps the client had not seen before. This has the effect of increasing the client's perception of the seriousness of the immediate problem and shows the client that the consultant's experience and skill enables him or her to see connections between internal problems, such as those that affect economic, cultural, political, or organizational issues. Such questions might be:

- If you reduced the number of harassment cases, how would this impact your recruiting strategy?
- If productivity training in this department is successful, how would that impact the corporate training budget?
- Do you think that the union contract negotiations will go better if you demonstrate immediate action in this area?

Implication questions enable the consultant to keep framing and re-framing the problem as it is being described, so that the actual problem is revealed as clearer, smaller, larger, or even more complex than previously believed.

Need-Payoff Questions

Need-payoff questions are used toward the end of questioning, so that the client can put the consultant's recommended approach or solution in context: the client realizes that any suggestions about products, services, or approaches to solving the problem are made with an informed opinion by the consultant. Because every organization thinks its situation is unique, clients generally are not receptive to hearing that a solution that worked for Company X will work for them. Although it may be true that the same solution could work, clients need to be reassured that the consultant's prior experience is merely the basis for addressing the unique aspects of the client's problem. Need-payoff questions examine potential solutions, how the client likes to work with consultants, and what the benefits would be by taking the approach being discussed to solve the problem.

In short, if the client believes the consultant has truly listened, understands the issues and the problem, and has asked relevant and helpful questions of the sort shown in Table 5.2, the client will be much more receptive to hearing the suggestions made by the consultant. The consultant now has earned the right to make such suggestions by using the SPIN questioning strategy.

We cannot overstress the importance of doing one's homework and being prepared before meeting with the prospective client. Developing a good SPIN questioning strategy and using active listening skills and emotional intelligence enables the consultant to be in the best possible position to win the business—at least on a straightforward and objective basis.

Problem Reframing

An effective questioning strategy, in combination with good active listening skills, enables the consultant to perform a critical task during the business development stage: reframing the client's problem. For many reasons (see "first meeting dynamics" in Chapter Four), clients may not tell you exactly what their needs are or the precise nature of the problem(s) to be solved.

Problem reframing is a process of asking questions, testing assumptions, and suggesting different ways to describe the problem in order to get closer to the true problem. For example, in an executive coaching session a client kept referring to his problem as the way his boss managed the senior team. After exploring many facets of the situation and thinking out loud with the client about other aspects that might be causing his difficulty in his role, it

TABLE 5.2 USING SPIN QUESTIONS TO WIN BUSINESS

Question Type	Characteristics	Examples
Situation	Questions are neutral and factual; gathers data about the client's organization and situation.	How many people work in the department? When did this start? What is this costing you? How many desktops do you have now? Do you have resources that could be used in this project? How many people could we interview? Is it possible to identify the problem right now?
Problem	Usually contains the word "problem" or "concern"; asks the client to state or describe the problem.	What are your immediate concerns about cost reduction? How would you describe the problem? What are your immediate needs? Is the problem high turnover or lack of training? What problems are you having with your current strategy?
Implication	Asks the client to connect the current problem with other problems that have occurred or may occur if the problem persists.	If you reduce the headcount this year, how will that affect morale? By replacing the system, how will you lower turnover or increase productivity? By how much will the restructuring lower costs and improve earnings per share? Will a new inventory management system change people's roles, and how will that impact the union contract?
Need-Payoff	Asks the client whether a specific feature, product, service, or approach would be helpful in solving the problem.	What would be the benefit of taking this approach? Do you think you would need to add your own people to our team? If you call up a screen with this feature, how would it help you? If we could start this month, would that help you with your budget?

Source: N., Rackham, *SPIN Selling*, 1988, McGraw-Hill, reproduced with permission of The McGraw-Hill Companies.

became clear that the problem was not his boss but the coachee-client, who was not taking enough initiative to craft and communicate clear direction for his own immediate team. By testing facts and assumptions; asking lots of situation, problem, and (especially) implication questions; and searching for alternative cause-effect relationships, the client reframed his own versions of the problem and recognized his personal communications style as a major problem. Subsequently he admitted that the *real* problem was his inability to decide on his own strategic direction for his area of responsibility. So rather than trying to help him develop more effective working relationships up the organizational hierarchy, the coaching focused on the reframed problem of working *down* in his organization.

Problem reframing is essential to distinguishing the real problem from assumed problems and hence to deciding what the proposal should focus on.

Needs Assessment: Listening Actively

Equally as important as asking the right question is having the right listening mind-set—to being fully attentive to the answers. Everyone hears, but do we listen? Listening has many problematic variants, such as listening superficially, intermittently, and judgmentally. People tend to either listen with "filtered" ears—filtering what they hear through their own biases—or be distracted by something happening in the environment. Generally, men seem to have a more difficult time with this than women, as women tend to be more relationship-oriented and more interested in people; men tend to be more interested in "things" or objects (Gilligan, 1993; Gray, 1993; Tannen, 1996). Luckily, listening is a skill that can be improved with practice.

To address the problem, we can use the most common listening skill taught in human relations, negotiating, influence, and management training programs: *active listening*. This is a skill that requires a conscious effort to use the enormous excess mental processing capacity we have in our brains. When we listen to someone speaking, we rapidly go through several stages of action and reaction. First we hear the words, and then we make connections in our brain to make sense of what we have heard. This is usually accompanied by some emotion. Then we think about a response and may even silently rehearse what we are going to say to the other person before responding. All of this happens in a brief moment and may be going on as we form a question we wish to ask, craft a counterargument, or prepare to relate a similar experience or tell our story. The problem is, while we are concentrating on our internal responses and rehearsals, we have stopped listening with our full attention; we are not *fully present*. This starts a downward spiral. The longer we rehearse and play our internal mental "movie scripts," the worse our listening becomes, until we completely lose touch with what the speaker is saying and thereby miss the person's points and ideas. When we suddenly realize we have not been listening or have missed something, we often feel too embarrassed to ask what the person just said, so we let it pass—perhaps missing some additional vital information as we become focused on our own feelings and then listen even less!

Again, we engage in internal conversations because we have excess processing capacity in our brain, and the brain is always processing information and "looking for something to say and do." The voice in our head wants us to focus on what *it* is saying, not the other person. Consequently, it can be even more of a struggle to concentrate on the other person if:

- The language is hard to understand.
- The concepts are too vague.
- The environment is noisy.
- The person speaks softly.
- The person has a difficult accent.
- The person has a unique accent.
- The person speaks too fast or too slowly.

With all those barriers to communications, it is necessary that consultants develop listening skills to put their brain's excess processing capacity to good use. Table 5.3 shows the questions to pose in order to actively

TABLE 5.3 ACTIVE LISTENING TECHNIQUES: ACRES

Active Listening Technique	Questions for Oneself
Attending	Am I *paying attention* and concentrating on the speaker's words and emotions?
Clarifying	Do I *understand* what the person is saying and does it need clarifying?
Restating	How would I paraphrase or mirror what the person has just said?
Empathizing	How does the person *feel* about what he or she is saying?
Summarizing	What are the *key points or messages* the person has just made?

listen. Active listening is a verbal, behavioral skill we consciously apply as we are listening to the words, ideas, logic, and expressiveness of a speaker. I call this having ACRES of listening—a handy acronym for Attending, Clarifying, Restating, Empathizing, and Summarizing.

ACRES can and should be used to improve mutual understanding during any conversation throughout the consulting cycle. When using SPIN during a needs assessment conversation, for example, we can use ACRES to make sure we understand the client's answers and to probe them more deeply, to uncover more of what the client is thinking. We can ask ourselves the five questions in Table 5.3.

Although the intent of active listening is very positive and does help to build rapport, as a *proactive skill* the consultant *must* from time to time interrupt the client by using any one of the five ACRES techniques. Interrupting can feel a little uncomfortable for some, even rude. This is an aspect of active listening that needs to be worked through. It becomes less uncomfortable with practice as consultants learn how to do it smoothly and naturally in a conversation.

Active listening assumes that the client will not be offended by the interruption, but in fact will become motivated to share more as it becomes obvious the consultant is really interested in what is being said. This is a very positive message that reinforces further communication. The client realizes (consciously or unconsciously) that the consultant *must* be listening, to be able to restate or clarify what the client has said. Even if the message was misheard, a good clarifying question shows interest and enables the client to correct the perception.

Be careful, however, to not interrupt too frequently and to summarize only at the end or halfway through a very complex presentation of data or ideas. One key to effective active listening is to ask oneself, "Am I conducting an interrogation here?" No one likes to feel interrogated. But people like to hear their own name mentioned frequently and to know that others are genuinely interested in what they have to say. Active listening does feel awkward at first, as if we are using a "technique." But if practiced and done with respect, it will become natural and will enable the client to continue with his or her line of thought, feeling good that the consultant is in fact, really listening.

To summarize, the habit of good listening has many benefits, including:

- Learning how to concentrate better
- Being fully present (not distracted or disengaged)

- Building stronger relationships
- Learning a great deal more from others
- Generating creative ideas
- Seeing patterns in information
- Being seen as courteous and curious
- Having others listen in return
- Increasing personal motivation to solve client problems

Effective consultants know that the skills of asking good questions and listening actively are extremely important not only for conducting needs assessment during the development stage, but in every role of the four steps of consulting. Both skills should be practiced and used frequently. By using SPIN and ACRES to gain a deeper, more accurate understanding of what the client is saying, consultants will be well on their way to becoming consummate professionals in this important area.

The Proposal Development Process

The first meeting or series of meetings during the business development stage should be used to gather the following information:

- The client's problem
- Technical requirements
- Organizational needs
- Procedures to be followed
- Timing
- Staffing
- Roles and methods to be used
- Limits, boundaries, and any other constraints
- If possible, some idea of the budget

Armed with as much accurate information as possible, yet acknowledging that much remains unknown until the work gets under way, it is now time to write the proposal. Table 5.4 shows the nine stages of the proposal process. Completing a proposal may take anywhere from a day to several weeks, depending on the size and complexity of the consulting work. Proposals for governmental agencies and many large companies that do a lot of work for the government usually have stringent requirements and demand a lot of backup documentation, details about the consulting firm,

TABLE 5.4 NINE STEPS OF THE PROPOSAL PROCESS

Proposal Stage	Key Actions and Issues
1. Identify proposal resources	Identify who will be involved in preparing, writing, and presenting the proposal.
2. Outline the content	This may vary, depending on the type of consulting being performed. Most established consulting firms have templates and standard formats.
3. Assess risks	For major consulting assignments, identify areas of potential risk in performing the consulting ahead of time and think through actions to mitigate the risk. Build time into the project plan as needed, to account for actions that may need to be taken.
4. Describe scope and deliverables	Describe the scope of the work, needs, problems to be solved, constraints, phases of the work, any interim deliverables, and final deliverables.
5. Identify the project team	Identify who may be available to perform the work; offer biographies and/or resumes in the proposal for individuals from whom the team may be selected.
6. Prepare a project plan	Develop a time-sequenced plan for each major task of the project, showing responsibilities, deliverables, interconnected deliverables, and completion dates.
7. Decide on pricing	Based on the project plan, develop a work plan based on assumptions about tasks, resources needed, time, and the client's contributions; calculate the cost by phase of work and overall investment by the client. Ensure that the project is profitable.
8. Present or submit the proposal	Send to the client and be prepared to meet with the client to discuss each aspect of the proposal. Revise as needed.
9. Ask for the business	When the client has had all questions answered and expresses any kind of interest (that is, "buy signals"), state that you want the business and ask the client what the next steps will be.

legal forms, specific descriptions of past consulting projects, competitive bidding procedures, details about staff resources to be used for the engagement, and a breakdown of costs. Putting all of this together can take a great deal of time.

Consulting firms often do a cost-benefit analysis on their proposal development process to assess the time and money required to complete a proposal versus the likelihood of winning the business once it is submitted. Such analysis is needed because some organizations, especially governmental agencies (which by law must receive a number of proposals and give each one a careful evaluation), announce a Request for Proposal (RFP) and then use their preferred supplier anyway. Another problem is that clients may use the RFP process to learn how to solve the problem, then ignore the proposals and (now that they know how to do it) solve the problem themselves.

Consulting firms' management know these tricks and may decide that if the complexity of an RFP is too great and the probability of winning the business too low, it may not be worth going to all of the time and effort to prepare a proposal, even if the contract is a large one.

Proposal Development

If a client requests a proposal, there are a number of logical and practical steps required to produce one. The nine steps of the proposal development process were summarized in Table 5.4; a sample proposal format appears in Table 5.5, followed by a brief overview of each of the steps.

1. Identify Proposal Resources In general, this means getting people to write (or at least contribute to) the proposal who will actually work on the project. The reasons to do this are simple: the more the consulting team knows about the project and the work, the more likely they will hit the ground running with detailed knowledge of the project, be more motivated, demonstrate the characteristics of an effective team early on, and be able to communicate effectively with the client. Several minds working on the proposal can make it a much better document in its coverage of the issues, client problem, the business case, and clarity in the writing. A best practice is to start the team-building process with the people who write the proposal.

2. Outline the Content Although the content can range quite widely, the proposal format in Table 5.5 depicts a proposal agenda used in actual consulting practice. In general, all proposals contain the following elements:

- An opening statement (or Executive Summary) that covers the content of the proposal document
- Details about the content areas relevant to the type of consulting being undertaken
- A section on professional fees, expenses, and billing
- A description of the scope of work, assumptions, risks, and any constraints such as intellectual property rights
- A closing statement, including next steps
- Qualifications of the consulting team members

TABLE 5.5 EXAMPLE OF A PROPOSAL FORMAT

Content Area	Explanation
Introductory Paragraph	This refers to the last meeting with the client and includes a thank-you to the prospective client for the time spent discussing the RFP. It outlines the proposal content.
Understanding of Need	Several paragraphs summarizing the history or background and facts learned during the first meeting(s), the stated problem and needs, and any client requirements.
Approach to the Work	This lists the discrete and logical phases of work that must be done to complete the work. It often includes data gathering and recommendations, design work, development of materials and deliverables, delivery of finished work, testing of solutions, and the rollout or implementation of the solution.
Professional Fees	Fees are best offered as an estimate and as a range of dollars rather than a specific number. Estimates are preferable because: (1) the extent of use of client resources may not be fully known; (2) the scope of work may incur more meetings than originally planned; and (3) if negotiations occur, profitability can be maintained within the range. A statement about agreed-upon expense reimbursement and the invoicing schedule is also included.
Schedule and Staffing	This is a simple statement of the estimated completion dates for each phase of the work and an indication of who will be project leader and the consulting team members. It is best to state that the team will be selected from among the biographies provided in the proposal, in case a specific consultant is not available.
Qualifications	This describes the firm's experience and relevant consulting and presents the consultants suggested for the team.
Closing Paragraph	This is a general statement of enthusiasm about working in collaboration with the client on an important and challenging assignment, with thanks for the opportunity to submit the proposal and an inquiry as to what the next steps will be (often a meeting to discuss the proposal or a Letter of Intent to commit both parties to doing the work).
Signature Line	Many consultants use the proposal as their contract; in this case, a signature line at the bottom of the proposal allows the client to sign and then return a copy for contractual purposes. However, many consulting firms have a separate contract, based on the proposal. An interim Letter of Intent may serve as a preliminary contract so the work can commence.

The proposal may be in a letter format to make it easier and more interesting to read. Proposals in information technology (IT) consulting are more cut-and-dried, stating just the facts and using a combination of IT language and legalese. Management consultants use a combination of letter formats and pithy, technical language. It is a good idea to make proposals user friendly, easy to read, and clear. To look professional, they must also be well formatted and have no grammatical errors. Many prospective clients use the proposal to judge the quality of the work they can expect from the consultant. Sloppy proposals lose business. To avoid errors, *always* have a second pair of eyes review the document before sending it to the client.

3. Assess Risks Risk assessment is the process of examining each aspect of the project to determine what could go wrong and planning actions to either: reduce conceivable risks or solve the problem if something does indeed go wrong. A good way to do this is to consider the *probability of occurrence* and *seriousness* of potential problems, suggest actions that could be taken to reduce the risk, and include them in the project proposal. Actions might include special meetings, training, or the use of more experienced consultants. Risk assessment methods are discussed in more detail in Chapter Six.

4. Describe Scope and Deliverables This description covers what is (and is not) included in the design, development, delivery, and implementation of a solution. Scope describes the boundaries of the engagement, which may include time, volume, specifications, functionality, locations, depth, speed, intensity, documentation, and people; for example, whether or not a leader's guide is included in a training program, or overseas locations are included in the deployment of a new information systems, or all competitors in the industry will be analyzed.

Deliverables are often described in terms of "interim deliverables," such as status reports, periodic analyses of data, studies, outlines, renderings, test pieces, presentations, and mock-ups or models. In the proposal, interim deliverables are used as milestones to indicate progress and show when certain pieces of work will be completed before a solution is finally delivered. This also serves to set expectations and increase client confidence that the consulting project is well organized. Another major benefit of stating interim deliverables is that it signals the client will (or may, depending on what is negotiated) be invoiced for them. Finally, because all deliverables and solutions must be aligned with the client's business strategy, a brief description of how solutions fulfill aspects of the business goals and strategy can be included in the proposal at this point, in an appropriate way, suitable to the nature, level, and scope of the work.

5. Identify the Project Team The proposal should indicate the likely team members from the consulting firm who will be assigned to the project. The qualifications section of the proposal describes the education, background, and consulting experience of each member of the potential team. Because people are not always available when the consulting work actually starts, it is important to maintain flexibility with resources by stating, for example, that team members will be selected from *among* the resumes enclosed, subject to availability when the project starts.

6. *Prepare a Project Plan* The project plan is a detailed description of the major tasks, timetable, and responsibilities of the project. It is a detailed analysis of who is responsible and accountable for the completion of each task. The plan shows, in chronological sequence, the start and the end of each task, milestones for interim deliverables, and the overall completion time for the engagement. The consultant needs to make sure everything is in sequence and is consistent with the client's expectations. Because the proposal is the main document that everyone uses to understand the totality of the engagement—the vision, mission and strategy, the timetable, performance expectations, and billing—the project plan represents a summary "template" of the whole project.

7. *Decide on Pricing* The *project plan* is a summary of the detailed *work plan*. The *work* (pricing) *plan* is a careful and accurate analysis of exactly what it will take to perform the consulting in terms of phases of work, resources, time, and cost (investment). The work plan is *not* shared with the client, for it explains the pricing strategy for the engagement. Table 5.6 depicts an example of pricing from a highly simplified work plan, showing resources and calculations. The work plan is a reflection of who is working on the project, how much time each consultant is contributing, the cost of that contribution, the administrative overhead used, and the target profit needed by the firm. Pricing of consultants includes each consultant's hourly or daily rates (per diem fees), which include the person's salary plus administrative overhead and profit margin. Differences in the daily rates of consultants are related to their level in a firm (from junior to senior to managing consultants), which usually correlates with their role (analyst to project leader). Engagement managers overseeing several single-client projects are usually senior/managing consultants or even partners in mid-sized firms, with correspondingly higher billable rates (see Chapter Six for how level and role tie to billable time and application rates).

Calculated for each task, the total price to the client is the aggregate of each consultant's chargeability or application, for all phases of work. Although not shown in Table 5.6, a range of professional fees is recommended to reflect an estimate of how long it will take each person to

TABLE 5.6 PROJECT PRICING FROM THE WORK PLAN

Phase	Task	Consultant Resource	Days	Per Diem Fee ($)	Task Total ($)	Phase Total	Project Total
I	A	Bill	3	2,500	7,500	20,500	
	B	Bill	4	2,500	10,000		
		Rakesh	1.5	2,000	3,000		
II	A	Susan	2	2,000	4,000	4,000	
III	A	Rakesh	3	2,000	6,000	43,500	
	B	Jay	5	1,500	7,500		
	C	Paul	10	3,000	30,000		
IV	A	Bill	3	2,500	7,500	28,500	96,500
	A	Hilary	3	4,000	12,000		
	A	Tony	3	3,000	9,000		
Extra	10%						9,650
Grand Total:							106,150

Note: The number of days may be stated as High, Medium, and Low to create a range of time; the "extra" is to ensure that any extra time the client demands is covered; the per diem fee includes salary, overhead, and profit margin.

perform the work or, subject to negotiation and as discussed during the needs analysis/SPIN meetings, whether the client will supply consultants to perform some of the work. Time to complete the work and use of client resources mean that a high, medium, and low (or maximum/minimum) calculation can be made and shown in the proposal as an estimated range of professional fees.

The keys to building a profitable consulting firm are *application* and *realization*. Application is the amount of time any consultant spends that is billable to a client (called "utilization" in Europe). Realization is the firm's ability to collect its income from clients once implementation has begun. Because cash flow is often a struggle for most consulting businesses, getting clients to pay in a thirty-day cycle is an important part of setting expectations. If the client has a policy to pay based on a ninety-day cycle, it may seriously hurt the consulting firm's cash flow and constrain its operational ability. Therefore, it may be important to design the approach to work in the proposal in such a way as to ensure that billing helps the consulting firm's monthly cash flow.

8. Presenting the Proposal Clients usually ask consultants to submit the proposal by mail or as an e-mail attachment; with this method, there is no chance to present the proposal in person and answer client questions. (Tip: If e-mailed, send the proposal as a password-protected file and make sure an original file is retained.) However, from time to time a client may expect a proposal presentation; if so, make sure the *best* presenter on the team delivers it. This may not always be the lead consultant. Make the presentation short and use a standard presentation tool such as Power-Point to support the presentation. Deliver the presentation in a way that allows the maximum time for the client to probe and ask questions. Any team member can answer questions.

When possible, ask the client for feedback on draft proposals before the final proposal is submitted. This is often achievable with work that is repeat business and where a long-term relationship has been established. Always remember that as consultants we are trying to help our clients be successful. Sometimes that means helping the client to sell the proposal to his or her *internal* organization, requiring the proposal have the right language, ideas, key phrases, and look and feel for a range of managers from different functions inside the client's organziation. In established, trusted relationships, clients often help their consultants with draft proposals to ensure that the best proposal is produced—one that helps both parties.

9. Ask for the Business As a general rule, consultants need to find language that enables them to communicate with enthusiasm about working with the client on the "important and challenging" assignment at hand. Remember, clients often need to have their confidence raised. So raise it—by demonstrating confidence in your own proposal.

Keep an eye out for buy signals. These may be questions about the benefits and improvements in performance the client will accrue by using your consulting services. They may be questions about client references, your availability, or attending a meeting with other client staff. For a full treatment of how to influence different buyers (user, coaches, economic, and technical buyers), see Miller and Heiman (1988) and Heiman and Sanchez (1998).

In general, at this point the consultant should convey gratitude for the opportunity, energy and passion for the work, and enthusiasm. Tell the client you *want* the business (not that you *need* the business) and indicate that you are able to get started right away. End the presentation or conversation with a question about next steps.

To make the proposal writing process easier, consultants normally use templates, prior proposals, or standard formats. Even though each proposal is unique in its content, the categories of information and the formatting are often standard. Templates keep the writing process as efficient as possible without sacrificing quality. But even with templates it is better to take extra time to reread the proposal before submission, rather than rushing, which may result in missed information or grammatical errors.

Finally, this entire proposal development discussion assumes that the consultant is writing the proposal and may periodically seek input from the client. It should be said that because of the particular focus and nature of organization development consulting, it is a common practice for the proposal to be cowritten by the two parties. This is part of the contracting process, essential for success in that kind of consulting (Block, 2000).

In summary, the proposal process can be time consuming and burdensome, but the final proposal is an important document that must be completed to the best of our ability. Unless built into the project plan, proposal development is done free of charge as part of the sales process and as the outcome of the business development stage. The proposal is the first document that brings the whole consulting engagement together in one place; it is a fundamental bridge between our firm and the client's firm. It is the basis for establishing a contractual and legally binding agreement.

Changes in Price

Once the proposal has been submitted, there can still be changes in price. Prospective clients will probably want to negotiate the price. And once the work actually begins, there may be many new discoveries about the client's operations, resulting in new and modified needs.

In general, once the contract has been signed, clients tend to view it as a *fixed price contract*. Consultants, on the other hand, want all contracts to be a *time and materials contract*, giving them the freedom to expand their scope of work to do a better-quality job—and getting paid accordingly. The tension between these two pricing models always exists and puts a premium on the quality of both sides' negotiating postures and skills. Changes in the scope of work and emergent needs require consultants to engage in negotiation meetings when they would prefer to be working on solving the client's problems. Clients, on the other hand, want value for their money and usually think in terms of getting their consultants to do extra work gratis.

In large firms the roles of engagement manager and hands-on consultant are filled by different people. This means that more experienced senior consultants, responsible for multiple projects with a given client, are responsible for negotiating changes in the original contract. Medium-size firms may use outside legal counsel to perform this task, as lawyers are usually trained to negotiate, but in small firms the consultant must do it all. Any consultants not trained to negotiate may make mistakes and give away far more than they should, either because they fear losing the work or upsetting the client, or out of ignorance. Clients who are already senior managers usually understand the strategies and subtle tactics of negotiating to get their needs met and find it easy to intimidate less experienced, junior consultants. A thorough discussion of negotiation is obviously outside the scope of this book; the reader would do well to read Fisher, Ury, and Patton (1991), among others, to understand modern negotiating ideas and skills and before negotiating with a client.

Managing Expectations

One of the critical tasks of winning business and successful consulting is to get the expectations right. The ability to manage expectations is part of a consultant's core competency and involves both external and internal people on an engagement. Basically, there are three sets of expectations to be managed: those of the client, those of the project team, and those of the consulting firm's senior management.

Clients' Expectations

It is crucial for consultants to openly discuss, test, and validate assumptions about the client's expectations for each of the following elements:

- Quality standards and how they will be measured
- Use of client facilities and equipment
- Access to needed information
- Client participation in project roles
- Number of updates and status reports
- Consultant's team members and their roles
- Completion dates of phases of work
- Billing schedule
- Handling of project expenses
- Impact of scope changes on fees
- Changes in solution specifications
- Client versus consultant responsibilities

Managing expectations means discussing them openly and honestly, being prepared to negotiate specific terms and arrangements, and trying to anticipate future circumstances in the life of the project that may affect results and the efficacy of the client-consultant relationship. Try to clear up any misunderstandings *before* completing the initial needs analysis discussions and before proceeding to write the proposal. Table 5.7 lists some of the questions consultants might ask to clarify expectations concerning roles, fees, accounting, deliverables, procedures, schedule, and tasks.

Needless to say, once business is won and the engagement is underway, expectations must be revisited and clarified throughout the next three stages of the consulting process. As the real circumstances of the client's situation, needs, and problems come to light, our initial agreement about expectations will inevitably change. Clients understand this phenomenon and may themselves introduce new requirements and changes in project scope. Such changes are common, and clients understand that although expectations are set at the beginning, they are subject to change and renegotiations at any time in the consulting cycle.

Project Team

Clarification of team expectations is typically led by the project leader. Chapters Six and Seven discuss in detail specific expectations involved in getting team members aligned and committed to a consulting project. These include:

- Internal norms that engender trust and productivity
- Internal communications among team members
- Use of standard procedures and processes
- Assessment of standards of work
- Communications with the client's firm
- Behavior in front of the client

Consulting Firm's Management

In large consulting firms, practice leaders and senior firm management watch their consulting projects closely, as each consultant can have a positive or negative impact on the firm's brand and reputation. Consequently, in such an environment it behooves each consultant and project leader to know their management's expectations concerning these elements:

TABLE 5.7 MANAGING CLIENT-CONSULTANT EXPECTATIONS

Issues	Questions
Project and Management Roles	• What roles do you anticipate you or we will play on this project? • What process should we follow to get access within your organization? • What are your project management requirements on this project? • Who is responsible for managing change during and after the project?
Fees and Accounting	• What, if any, budget parameters do you have? • What will be the invoicing schedule for this engagement? • What expenses are (or are not) paid?
Solutions and Deliverables	• How would you define the solution expected from the project? • Who will receive a transfer of knowledge and skills as a result of this engagement? • Do you expect us to do training and skills transfer? • What type of documentation will you need? • What criteria will be used to measure our success in providing deliverables?
Procedures and Processes	• How can we most effectively interact with your project manager and your team? • What are your expectations about how we will interact with other consultants in your organization? • How would you prefer us to communicate with you? With others in your organization? • What process do you feel needs to be put in place to ensure that the change is sustained? • How can we best involve you throughout the engagement?
Schedule	• When would you like to kick off this engagement? • When do you wish to complete this engagement? • When can a decision be made to proceed in order to deliver in this time frame? • Does your organization have other business dependencies that may affect our ability to deliver a solution? • What variables, if any, might affect our ability to meet this time target? • Are there resources available to support us if we determine that a lack of resources may prevent completion?
Work Rules and Tasks	• What procedures and protocols should we abide by in your management structure? • What is the best way to ensure that our two organizations cooperate? • How do you prefer we provide status reports as the project unfolds? • Do you know of third-party partners or other consultants who can work with us to complete the tasks?

- What constitutes quality work
- Professionalism
- Key success factors
- Best practices
- Productivity

To avoid misunderstandings and future problems, it is a good practice to examine as many specific expectations as possible with these three constituencies—the client, the project team, and one's own firm. Each can believe in the certainty of their own understanding about expectations. But such beliefs may be wrong. If left unexamined, beliefs about expectations (and assumptions about those beliefs) can dramatically affect results, change positive perceptions to negative ones, and in turn affect future business.

Conclusion

The preceding chapter examined how to make a good first impression to start the process of building a relationship; this chapter has focused on the steps and techniques for conducting a needs assessment, writing a proposal based on those needs, and the importance of managing expectations.

We discussed gap analysis and how to frame problems by preparing and using a SPIN question strategy. The SPIN technique is an effective way to conduct needs assessment, during which we can use active listening techniques (ACRES). If used faithfully, active listening will improve our comprehension and understanding of the client's problems and our relationship with the client, not only in stage one to write a proposal, but also throughout the consulting cycle.

The developing stage and the designing role demand many skills that reach well beyond a consultant's technical expertise. Consultants should always keep in mind that clients make buying decisions based as much on the fit and chemistry of the person as on the consultant's reputation and expertise. Thus, during the initial meetings of stage one, consultants must pay close attention to important human factors such as the rhythm of communications, pacing of speech, active listening, emotional intelligence, vocal tone, attitude, questions, humor, sharing of air time during conversations, team orientation, and managing of assumptions about expectations. All of those elements contribute to either winning or losing business.

In the next chapter, we will see how those human relations factors are put to use in the second stage of consulting—mobilizing and aligning—in which consultants need to build people's commitment to the engagement and forge a project team. We will also examine other important consulting competencies related to resource planning, project planning, and risk assessment, and, in the subsequent chapters, the dynamics of turning groups into high-performing teams.

CHAPTER SIX

STAGE TWO: THE MOBILIZING AND ALIGNING PROCESS

This chapter and the next discuss the second stage in the consulting cycle, as we must convert the proposal into tangible plans that can be successfully implemented by a group of consultants. At the heart of success at this stage is the need to launch the project effectively, with everyone in agreement (aligned) about the purpose, goals, and strategy of the project and their respective consulting roles and responsibility. This alignment is done first within the consulting firm and then with the client. In this chapter, we focus on

1. The competencies in stage two of the consulting process
2. Work and project plan reviews
3. Risk assessment
4. Launching a project successfully

In Chapter Seven we focus on understanding group dynamics and the challenges of building a consulting team that can create deliverables effectively and deploy solutions in the client's organization. These two chapters need to be taken together to really understand the mobilizing and aligning process.

Stage Two Competencies: Mobilizing and Aligning

Table 6.1 shows the three competencies and twelve behavioral practices associated with the mobilizing stage and the aligning role in the consulting

TABLE 6.1 MOBILIZING COMPETENCIES AND BEHAVIORAL PRACTICES

Purpose	Stage	Tasks	Role	Outcome
Launching a Project Team	Mobilizing	• Risk Assessment • Planning Resources • Gaining People's Commitment • Launching	× Aligning	= Team

Competency	Practices
Project Resource Planning	• Converts broad proposals into specific work plans, schedules, and task flow charts • Uses planning documents to communicate people's roles and responsibilities • Assembles a consulting team for the work, when needed • Ensures that team members have clearly delegated goals, roles, and responsibilities
Enrolling Others	• Communicates the project vision, plan, and strategy with enthusiasm and passion • Generates excitement about a shared vision and common goals among consultants • Listens carefully to the point of view and needs of the client and other consultants • Encourages the examination of differing views in order to build a consensus
Launching Work	• Demonstrates a command of the overall project requirements • Conducts effective meetings with all relevant parties to launch consulting projects • Uses influence in a way that builds trust to gain the support of others • Ensures that everyone is heard, respected, and valued

cycle. This stage begins with the client accepting our proposal and ends with the formal launch of the project at a so-called kick-off meeting. In between there are a myriad of human relations issues and challenges, from getting people to join the project, understanding roles, and group formation, to technical matters concerning project planning and delegation, risk assessment, and setting up a successful project launch meeting.

Work and Project Plan Reviews

A best practice in consulting is to use templates for work and project planning to make the process more efficient. Although each consulting engagement is in some sense unique, the planning elements are essentially the same. Applying standard planning templates, consultants can then devote time to carefully discussing and scrutinizing the logical sequence of what needs to done, by what time, and by whom, within the consulting firm and with members of the consulting team. As such, these plans serve as excellent tools to help build a team's understanding and commitment to the consulting engagement before discussing (and negotiating) the work with the client.

Basis of the Proposal

A proposal is constructed, in part, by conducting a careful analysis of the projected time and resources needed to solve the client's problem. The work plan and the project plan are the key financial and logical underpinnings for that analysis. Those documents are the governance structure for the conduct or implementation of the consulting, the technical requirements, timing of key events, the overall schedule, and at stage two, most importantly, team members' roles and responsibilities for the project. Those plans are used by the lead consultant (that is, project leader) to effectively communicate the details of the design of the work flow and project process.

Work Plan

In Chapter Five we referred briefly to the pricing plan that must be developed in order to accurately price a piece of business for the proposal; it includes details of the relationship of the work phases, tasks, people, and costs. Utilizing the assumptions in the pricing plan, the project work plan as shown in Table 6.2 depicts the phases of work in a time-phased plan.

Project Plan

The project plan describes the chronological implementation of the consulting process. It provides a map of who will be doing what (responsibilities) and start and stop times for phases of work (tasks). Usually phases end with a tangible deliverable. The project plan is a visual depiction of how pieces of the consulting process fit together. The project plan may also include key linkages of tasks, the critical path of key events, the precise moment when deliverables are delivered, and who is responsible and accountable for delivering results over the course of a project.

TABLE 6.2 TIME-PHASED PROJECT WORK PLAN

Phase	Owner	Jan	Feb	Mar	April	May	June	July
I	Rakesh	→						
II	Susan	→						
III	Rakesh			→				
IV	Tom		→			→		
V	Tom					→		
VI	Rakesh							→

Table 6.3 shows a sample project plan used in training and development consulting. In this case the plan is for the design, development, and delivery of an executive-level conference.

Application Rates

One of the keys to managing one's career in a consulting firm is managing one's own application rate. Every consultant has an application goal. It is also an important metric for managing a consulting firm. When constructing a project plan, the project leader must consider who has the right technical experience as well as who is available. The availability of people resources to do the work is directly related to a consultant's application rate.

What is an "application rate"? The term simply refers to the amount of consultant's time that can be billed to a client. As shown in Table 6.4, each consultant has about two hundred and twenty days each year to devote to work (three hundred and sixty five, minus weekends, holidays, vacation time, sick time, and floating days).

TABLE 6.3 PROJECT PLAN—EXECUTIVE, BUSINESS ALIGNMENT CONFERENCE

Key Tasks	Responsibility	February	March	April	May	June	July
Phase I, 2/6–3/28	Project Manager (PM)	↑					
1. Develop interview guide	Sue	↑					
2. Interviewing	Team		↑				
3. Data synthesis	Mike		↑				
4. Report development	Mike/Al		↑				
5. Editing	Joan		↑				
Phase II, 3/5–5/8	Project Manager		↑				
1. Conference design	Mike/PM		↑				
2. Design review, internal	Team		↑				
3. Design review, client	PM			↑			
4. Complete design	Team			↑			
Phase III, 4/23–6/15	Project Manager			↑			
1. Materials development	Mike				↑		
2. Client approval	Mike				↑		
3. Reproduction	Al					↑	
4. Shipping	Tom				↑		
Phase IV, 7/7–7/15	Project Manager				↑		
1. Conference delivery	PM						↑
2. Summarize data	Mike						↑
3. Report action plan	PM						↑

TABLE 6.4 APPLICATION RATE CALCULATION

365	Days in the Year
104	Weekends
13	Holidays
20	Vacation
05	Sick time
03	Floating days
(145)	
220	Consulting days available
70%	Target rate percentage
154	**Application Days (Goal)**

Of the two hundred and twenty consulting days a consultant is available for doing client work, how many days can be billed to a client? The rate varies by organizational level, consulting role, and responsibility, but in general the rate is between 60 and 80 percent (132–176 days). Although it is common practice in management consulting firms to account for time in days or per diem rates, accounting and law firms often calculate their billable time in terms of hours, not days, because they break client time into quarter-hour units of billable time and charge their clients accordingly.

Usually, more senior consultants have responsibility for managing the firm's operations and infrastructure. This is called "nonbillable time" and is used for business development, practice improvement, and management of the firm. Sometimes that means that senior consultants' application rates may be lower than 50 percent. Top management may not have *any* billable time, effectively putting their application rate at zero. Although this is a practical way to manage a consulting firm's use of time, profits, and growth, it also creates problems. For example, political problems arise and morale can decline among lower-level consultants when they start to believe they are carrying the burden of more senior, "overpaid" management. Consequently, the usual practice is that every professional in the firm, regardless of level, has some client responsibility and is therefore contributing to billable time, covering expenses, and producing revenue.

It is common practice for nonmanagerial consultants to use available non-billable days for some mix of the following:

• Contributions to improving consulting practice
• Contributions to improving the firm's systems and procedures
• Business development, marketing, and sales

- Personal professional development and training
- Supervising junior consultants
- Company meetings
- Special projects
- Attending professional meetings and conventions

Resource Challenges

After the thrill and excitement of landing a nice piece of business, a major challenge is getting the right professional resources to do the work. In most firms, and during normal economic conditions, consultants are usually very busy. They may be completely applied at their target level; they may be heavily involved in firm projects; they may be spending time on the weekends doing project work or even working on a graduate degree. It is usually the case that the best consultants are in demand and are the busiest building their "book of business." So when staffing a project, it can be hard to get the best people.

Even though it can be challenging to attract the best consultants on a project, there are a few incentives that can improve your chances: (1) presenting project attractiveness, (2) influencing firm management, and (3) timing the project.

Presenting Project Attractiveness

The first way to attract terrific people to your project is the direct approach and is similar to the one we recommend using with senior management. The more benefit the person can see from working with you, the more likely it is that he or she will join the team. It may take several tries. If the person is that good, it will be worth the effort.

Attractive projects have certain characteristics in common:

- They are professionally interesting and challenging.
- They offer new knowledge and experiences.
- They are big money earners (rainmakers).
- They provide high visibility with very important clients.
- They are career makers or builders.
- They offer a chance to work with other well respected consultants.

If any of these characteristics fits your project (or if it will eventually develop those characteristics), you should describe and use them in an influence strategy to make the consulting work attractive. Communicate those characteristics with conviction and passion, with enthusiasm and energy. How the message is conveyed can be as important as the content.

By extension, another way to make a project attractive is to consider the rule of thumb in business that employees usually start with the (albeit selfish) question: "What's in it for me?" Consultants ask the same question. Therefore it behooves team leaders and managing consultants to think through how to answer that question when trying to influence a top-notch consultant to join the team. Project leaders need to be able to state specifically how joining a consulting team will benefit each team member, so that a top consultant can see "what's in it for me."

Finally, experienced consultants know that over the intermediate to long term, a consulting career is either feast or famine. Even the busiest consultant today can find work disappearing during the downside of an economic cycle. For many businesses, the corporation's consulting expense is a variable and often a discretionary cost. When the economy declines, companies cut first advertising and consulting, then capital investments and payroll. Consultants are often the first to go. It never hurts to remind busy consultants of that fact. Most consultants know that although during the great IT boom of the 1990s virtually every IT consultant was fully applied (meeting or exceeding application goals and thinking they would never run out of work), when the bubble burst they suddenly found themselves "on the beach" waiting for work. Even in the big management consulting firms, many big egos had to eat humble pie. This has also been true more recently during the Great Recession of 2008–2009, which sent consultants from the beach to the unemployment line.

Influencing Firm Management

Another helpful way to resource a project is by going to senior level managers in your firm and persuading them that people need to be reassigned and made available to your project. Influence skills will be needed for this practice. One of the keys to accomplishing this is to communicate the following:

- Importance of the client to the firm
- Amount of revenue involved
- Sales development potential for the consulting practice area
- Long-term benefits that this immediate project will produce
- Benefits to application rates over the term of the project

- Anticipated project challenges that will need the best people to be successfully met
- How the success of the project will affect the firm's reputation

It is difficult to manage resources across many demanding clients, multiple projects, challenging firm goals, fussy account managers, vocal consultants, and disparate geographical locations. Executives of consulting firms must consider many factors in managing the human resources of their firm. They have an interest in developing their people to be the best, they want to distribute consultants across projects and engagements in relation to the areas where those consultants need professional growth, and they want to balance employee development with the growth of the firm.

A good influence tactic with top management is to use one or more of those managerial factors when making the case to get a particular resource. Explain how assigning a particular consultant to your project will provide the necessary balance among competing factors, economic interests, and resource issues of the firm.

A best practice is to consider resourcing your project as an (internal) consulting problem whereby your firm's management is the client. Do your homework and present a sound, thoughtful solution—not just the problem. A fact-based, reasoned argument will help to make it easy for senior management to make a decision. Lay the groundwork with other consultants, managers, or project leaders to support your request for resources. Get a full and accurate picture of the current and future workload of the person you want, and use a style that demonstrates an ability to give and take, compromise, and suggest attractive alternatives. Always walk into an influence situation with a positive mental attitude, consider the other person's needs, and leave the other person feeling good about the outcome. Do not burn bridges just because you did not get what you wanted. Always think long term and be politically savvy by being emotionally intelligent, just as you would with any client.

Timing the Project

Timing the project means working out with the client a project starting time that is mutually agreeable and that offers a good chance of getting the right resources for the engagement. This has the added benefit of adjusting the client's expectations. As already discussed, an ability to manage expectations is a key success factor of highly effective consultants.

When juggling time and resources, for example, it would be the kiss of death to promise one starting date, then start late, or to make a lot of excuses for delays just because it is hard to get the right resources for the engagement. The client does not want to hear excuses. If needed, project leaders can use the availability of special resources (such as third-party subcontractors) to negotiate the best starting date with a client. In a relationship built on trust, it is not unreasonable to ask the client to accommodate a later starting date.

Chances are that the client has chosen to do the business for a host of reasons (not just timing) and will be willing to wait for a short while until a key person is ready and available. Clients recognize that a busy consulting firm is so busy because it offers outstanding service and that busy firms are working with many other clients; in fact, that reputation could be one of the reasons the client went to the firm in the first place. The client may publicly complain and try to win a negotiation point (a lower price, usually) but privately feel reassured that the consultants are the right choice, as evidenced by their level of business activity.

When establishing a new starting time, do not fixate on one date; present options and alternatives to the client. Help the client to feel in control of the project and raise their confidence in how they can work with you on such matters. To achieve successful outcomes when renegotiating terms and conditions on such items, effective consultants are usually firm but flexible, serious and relaxed, grateful without being obsequious, and helpful without making concessions for free. Most deadlines are adjustable, and, with the right mental attitude and approach, clients will be willing to get the right consulting resource for the job by changing the starting time.

To summarize, at this stage of the consulting process we are trying to mobilize people to join *our* consulting project. One key strategy is to call a meeting of the relevant parties and use the proposal and project plan to describe the project. The goal is to encourage the right people to join the project and to motivate those that have been assigned by management to be on the project. Conducting an effective meeting to review the proposal and work plan is critical to getting everyone enrolled and *aligned*. You will achieve alignment when everyone's questions have been answered and all parties are clear (at least at this stage) about their roles, responsibilities, and expectations. Using strong influence skills, describing the attractive features of the client needs, and having an accurate understanding of each consultant's other work will help to get the right people on board.

Risk Assessment Factors

Clients as well as consultants face many risks when they engage each other. Risk can arise unexpectedly and have dire consequences. In one example, where risks were not adequately considered, a client hired a major IT consulting firm to produce a system that would centralize the company's international insurance broking. The consultants buried themselves so deeply in the client's technology department that it became in the consulting company's best interest to slow things down, keep information to themselves, and maintain their handsome cash flow. After years of not seeing the final deliverable, the client became so frustrated with the consultants that they decided to get rid of them. In the end, the client ended up having to pry the IT firm out like a parasite in order to take back control of the project. Unfortunately, after many years, millions of dollars, and changes in IT management, the system was never actually delivered in an acceptable form to the end users. This example highlights a common client fear—the risk of losing control of a project's deliverables, deadlines, and cost.

Dealing with Unknowns

In general, risk is about future unknowns and control. Risk increases as future events are hard to predict and, should they occur, hard to control. However, because many organizations have experience with disasters, mistakes, and failures, it is possible to identify the likelihood of the occurrence of a risk event and the seriousness of the impact if it does occur. Once these risks have been identified, we then can think of actions we need to take (insurance) to lower the risks. Insurance underwriters and actuaries spend their lives evaluating statistics to determine what could go wrong, the probability of an occurrence, and the associated financial loss. Based on this they offer insurance to cover the loss and charge premiums in relation to the calculated risk. Managers of insurance companies hope the premiums paid by clients will (in the aggregate) exceed the payout claims made each year. The underwriter's approach to risk suggests that risk management requires that decisions be made based on a judgment of existing conditions, the costs of failure, expected future scenarios, and actions needed now to offset future losses. In consulting, there are four factors used to analyze and mitigate risk:

- The size of the project
- The change in client's environment

- The use of various methods and technologies
- The structure of the project

Project Size

The size of the project is directly related to the number of people involved, including those in the client's organization. It is also related to the number of "moving parts"—such elements as legacy systems involved, locations affected, departments impacted, management oversight, committees, and management mechanisms that can influence the quality of the work. Project size also includes such factors as the visibility level, dollar value, scope, organizational-wide impact, and costs. Because every one of those factors can be very important to success, consultants must be skillful in handling how each affects the many stakeholders and vested interests in a project. In general, very visible, high-dollar-cost projects with many moving parts and great complexity are risky. They require careful coordination, highly effective communication, and careful problem solving and decision making by seasoned consultants.

Changes in Client Environment

This factor refers to risks in the client's business and organization that will be affected by executing the consulting project and implementing the solution. The bigger the scale and scope of the consulting, the bigger the potential risks. Risks include such possibilities as disturbances to suppliers and customers, disruptions to the client's organizational culture, changes in policies and procedures, interdependencies between the solution and existing systems, the lack of control over potential impacts caused by the dependence of the client on other projects, whether or not existing organizational systems will need to be replaced, how strategic the work is, and the client's level of commitment to the project. In general, the greater the amount of change in the client's organization as a result of the consulting, the complexity of the changes, and the extent to which they can or cannot be controlled during the four stages of consulting, the greater the risk.

Methods and Technologies

There are risks associated with the project team's knowledge and expertise in using their methods and technologies, such as analytical methods, software, systems, case formats, change management procedures, implementation techniques, and total quality management in the design, development, testing, and completion of the solution. There are also risks associated with the quality of information available to do the work and how accessible it is, as well as its value. Each team member needs to be well versed in the consulting firm's own standard tools and techniques, created to make work efficient and to reduce error and variances. In general, the greater the team's experience with the methods and technologies used and the more reliable those methods and technologies are, the lower the risk. If the team's experience is low, finding stronger team members, as well as training and coaching, can lower the risks in this area.

Project Structure

The structure of the project refers to both technical systems and team relationships. It includes such elements as the scope agreed to, the clarity of the client's requirements, the closeness or remoteness of team members' locations in relation to the client's locations, the quality of existing documentation about legacy systems, the amount of time team members and management can devote to the project, the clarity of team members' roles and responsibilities, the team's prior experience with each other, and the understanding of procedures for handling mistakes, making decisions, and handling client protocols. In general, the clearer the structure and the more experience people have working together, the lower the risks.

Table 6.5 describes some of the actions that IT consultants, for example, can take to lower their risks in each of the four factors. These are illustrative and highlight only some of the possible actions, and are not meant to be comprehensive in the treatment of this important topic.

A thorough risk assessment is especially important in large consulting projects. Such an assessment is conducted several times throughout a consulting project, first by the project team while developing the proposal, again during the project kick-off meeting (with the client present), and periodically as the project moves through the consulting cycle.

Project Launch Meetings

At some point in the mobilizing stage, when the consulting team has been assembled, the first important event is the "kick-off" meeting that officially

TABLE 6.5 RISK MITIGATION ACTIONS IN CONSULTING

Risk Factor	Mitigation Actions
Size of Project	1. Use experienced consultants. 2. Create a steering committee to oversee the entire project. 3. Increase the number of project reviews. 4. Communicate project issues regularly and broadly. 5. Keep project documents and databases up to date.
Client Change	1. Ensure that client management provides regular updates on changes affecting the project. 2. Establish a change management process. 3. Procure and use existing client documents. 4. Provide ample training on the transition to new systems and procedures. 5. Include the highest possible level of client management in the consulting team.
Methods and Technologies	1. Require team members to be trained in the methods and technologies used in the project. 2. Develop systems to keep everyone current with the latest developments, versions, and performance metrics. 3. Identify alternatives as fallback positions or actions in the event of a failure. 4. Use recommended client methods and technologies, if relevant and efficacious. 5. Use consultants with significant experience in the methods and technologies used.
Structure of the Project Team	1. Use team members who have worked together before. 2. Clarify roles and responsibilities with charts and project plan documents. 3. Communicate frequently, using all available methods. 4. Ensure backup and overlap of skills and capabilities in the team. 5. Use a client senior manager or steering committee to provide overall guidance and assistance.

launches the project. We will examine the structure and agenda of the meeting in this chapter, then in the next chapter discuss other related and important issues, such as meeting dynamics and meeting management.

Exhibit 6.1 provides an outline of the structure and discussion items that can be used for a project launch meeting. Broadly speaking, the launch meeting has four basic parts: premeeting, opening, discussion, and close. When leading this meeting, it is useful to think about breaking the content into these four components so that each phase is given the attention it deserves.

Exhibit 6.1 Structuring a Consulting Kick-off Meeting

Circulate agenda (discussion items below) in advance, if possible.
  Lead consultant (project manager) runs the meeting.
  Someone takes meeting notes to be followed up after the meeting.

Opening:
  Welcome
  Introductions
  Review of agenda
  Ask for additions or changes to agenda
Discussion:
  Purpose of project (business and technical)
  Deliverables (in general terms)
  Project plan—tasks, milestones, dates
  Review procedures, due dates, risks, and expectations
  Team members' roles and responsibilities
  Guidelines for working together
  Action items for each member
  Schedule upcoming project meetings
  Set up next meeting date—ask for agenda items
Closing:
  Revisit purpose and importance of the project
  Enthusiasm for the project and this team
  Ask for final comments and issues
  Thanks again—"meeting closed"

Premeeting Phase

Most people complain about meetings because there are too many of them and they are often poorly handled. One way to manage meetings effectively is to circulate the agenda ahead of time and ask for comments or additions to the agenda discussion points. If some people need to make a presentation at the meeting or lead the discussion of an item on the agenda, circulating the agenda in advance will give them the opportunity to prepare. Assigning responsibility for agenda items, requesting people to prepare, and setting time limits for agenda topics all help to set and manage expectations for the project launch team—and to prevent long, boring, ineffective meetings.

Opening Phase

1. *Welcome.* It is usually the duty of the lead consultant or project leader to run the meeting, provide a warm welcome to everyone, and break the ice. This should be done before the meeting officially starts, in a relaxed way, with courtesy, humor, warmth, and a smile. Make sure all attendees have what they need, then call the meeting to order.

2. *Introductions.* When launching a consulting project, there are likely to be people present who do not know each other, including employees from the client's organization. Start by asking all to introduce themselves briefly by providing a little background; such things as work experience, consulting experience, special skills and talents, thoughts about the project, and, if known, role on the consulting team.

3. *Review of Agenda.* Because the agenda has been sent out ahead of time, people should know what is on it. At this point you need to clarify any areas of confusion; indicate who will handle which agenda topics; identify time frames and parameters for each topic; mention how discussion items, data, and decisions will be recorded; and identify any meeting rules that everyone ought to follow to make the meeting effective and efficient.

4. *Ask for Additions or Changes to Agenda.* Be prepared to add or change agenda items and to negotiate how they will be handled in the time frame set for the meeting. Flexibility at this point helps to set a positive tone and make people feel they can influence the course of the project.

Discussion Phase

The topics and amount of content of the discussion phase depend on whether or not team members have read any prework and prepared agenda items. The set of topics listed here are suggestive and comprehensive, and may be culled or shortened as time permits for the meeting.

1. *Purpose of the Project.* People may be confused or unsure at the beginning of the consulting process. Spend time going over the proposal, starting with the purpose of the work in both technical and business terms. Clarify technical issues as needed. Whether it is strategy, training, organizational change, systems development, or implementation consulting, each type has its own "technology"—the language, methods, protocols, and so on used to do the work. Also, because all consulting work affects a client's business in some way, review the purpose of the consulting in terms of the needs discussed in Chapter Two, to help the client's business

become fast, bigger, better, or cheaper (FBBC). Help the team see the bigger picture and larger context of the work they are about to undertake. Make sure everyone has read the proposal and is crystal clear about the purpose.

2. *Deliverables.* To the extent that deliverables are understood at this point, at least conceptually, describe them as the intended outcomes of the work so that the team can visualize the end result. Be clear that "deliverables" means what is delivered according to the project plan (subject to adjustments needed as things progress). Deliverables may be a strategic analysis report, a training conference, or a new set of computer screens used to run a help desk; these are measurable and explainable outcomes. Describe deliverables sufficiently to make sure team members can see how their roles, both individually and collectively, contribute to achieving them.

3. *Project Plan.* Review the plan, first from a broader perspective of timing and deliverables, then in detail in terms of tasks, milestones, and the interactions of each activity. If a "critical path analysis" (see a standard text in operations management for a detailed explanation of this tool) has been done, describe it and show how the activities on the critical path impact the progress, timing, and cost of the consulting and deliverables.

4. *Roles and Responsibilities.* Every member of the team should have a specific role—such as leader, manager, quality control, trainer, analyst, documenter, designer, or developer. Each team member should have a document that describes the various roles on the team, the owner of each role, and the broad responsibilities of each role. It is important to make sure that the client's roles and the consultants' roles are clear and differentiated. If they overlap, make sure the overlap is clear and explicit. Organizational charts and team structure diagrams will help clarify roles and responsibilities among team members. Avoid guessing games and creating speculation about who does what and who is responsible for what.

5. *Review Procedures.* This concerns the *formal* interactions of the consulting team with the client organization, including procedures for gaining access to the client organization, use of confidential information, protocols for meeting with senior management, expense management, and understanding and complying with relevant client policies.

6. *Guidelines for Working Together.* This refers to the formal and informal ways in which team members interact with one another. Formal guidelines include rules for team meetings, disseminating information, making decisions, documenting progress, confidentiality, and disclosing deliverables. Informal guidelines (or norms) include dress code, handling

disagreements, using appropriate language, the ethos of team building, and encouraging active collaboration.

7. *Action Items for Each Member.* It is important that every team member leaves the launch meeting with something to do. This helps to build motivation, momentum, and responsibility. People with something to do feel important and that "things are happening" already. There may be actions that need to be discussed at the next meeting. Make sure that people know they will be expected to report on their progress.

8. *Schedule of Project Meetings.* To avoid any misunderstandings, ask all attendees to note in their diaries the dates of all project meetings. These dates could change, but you should at least launch the consulting project with the expectation that these meetings will be held (according to the project plan) and that everyone will attend.

9. *Set Up the Next Meeting Date.* Review the next meeting date and identify any item from this kick-off meeting that needs to be added to the next meeting agenda.

Closing Phase

1. *Revisit.* Spend a minute reviewing the project vision, mission, scope, and purpose. Keep it general, and reinforce the key points discussed during this meeting. Summarize any new and important items that arose from the discussion, any decisions that were made, and all action items for the next meeting.

2. *Enthusiasm.* As the person leading the launch meeting, it is very important that you be energized and excited about the work and the people. Communicate with passion and enthusiasm. Articulate exciting possibilities that may result from this assignment, and state how important this is for the client's organization and business. Think positively, be positive, and demonstrate genuine pleasure at the prospect of working together as a team.

3. *Final Comments and Issues.* Take a moment to give anyone in the room an opportunity to make a comment or to raise an issue. Keep the momentum going, and if necessary, take the issues off line (that is, discuss them outside of the formal meeting time). Sometimes people want to talk and may take the meeting into overtime. Be polite, but take firm control and bring it to an end.

4. *Thanks and Adjournment.* Take a brief moment to say thank you again and state: "The meeting is adjourned."

This design for a project launch is comprehensive, and if this is a large project with a large team it will take some time to complete. Kick-off meetings can be short and concise—they do not have to take many hours—but the question of how long such a meeting should run is an important one. A best practice is that it should be long enough to answer all questions from all persons present. With questions answered, project goals and timing clarified, action items assigned, and sufficient energy and excitement about the work, two to three hours will be enough for a large project.

Finally, as mentioned earlier in the chapter, one of the key items addressed in the launch meeting is that of *managing expectations.* Just as we endeavor to effectively manage client expectations during the business development and proposal stage, we are now trying to set consultants' expectations for working as a team—aligned, committed, and motivated. People are all motivated, to some extent, by what they expect to happen in the future. The team will be mobilized to pursue its goals if it can reasonably assume that the immediate future holds the prospect of interesting and challenging work. The kick-off meeting is designed to create those expectations.

Conclusion

In this chapter we have explored a number of actions needed to mobilize the project team. We have examined aspects of a consultant's leadership, communications, work planning, risk assessment, and kick-off meetings to launch a consulting project. In Chapter Seven we turn to the task of building a consulting team.

We have seen that it is the responsibility of the consultant to be in the alignment role to find the most appropriate and best resources for the consulting work, shape how things will be managed, clarify roles and responsibilities, and help everyone to contribute to producing a smooth and successful work experience. As these factors are discussed and clarified with the team members, they affect expectations and work norms and, in turn, produce alignment with and commitment to the consulting vision and goals.

At the individual level, the project leader is helping each member to declare what that member is taking responsibility for in relation to project deliverables (along with expectations about such norms as timeliness, quality of work, collaboration, and being client focused). By declaring this responsibility at the kick-off meeting, each individual recognizes that a personal commitment has been set that must be fulfilled. This is the essence of professional integrity—keeping one's word. All of this helps to build a cohesive sense of joint and mutual accountability—of succeeding together and being mutually bound by the agreed-upon rules and procedures for the team's operations. In this way, a group of disparate and perhaps skeptical consulting specialists begin the process of being molded into a team.

This leads to the whole question of the team *process*. What is a team? What are the characteristics of high-performing consulting teams? How can consultants turn groups into a team? This is the subject of the second part of mobilizing and aligning the project team, and the subject of the next chapter.

CHAPTER SEVEN

STAGE TWO, CONTINUED: TURNING A CONSULTING GROUP INTO A TEAM

A full treatment of the issue of teams and team building is beyond the scope of this book, but this chapter provides a basic set of models, steps, and skills needed to turn a group into a team. We examine:

- The definition of a team
- The stages of group development that end in a team
- Behavior that helps or hinders team development
- Diagnosing group and team problems
- Project leader style and actions that help group members become a team

Appendix E provides an overview of various diagnostic procedures and instruments that can be used in team development.

Defining a Team

Many consulting firms proudly advertise to clients that teamwork is one of their core values, but the same firms often drive internal performance with financial reward systems tied directly to individual application rates, revenue generation, and individual performance—not to teamwork. Also, by their very nature, consultants are knowledge-workers who like to work independently, may dislike group work, and are often (contrary to their self-perception) competitive rather than collaborative. Faced with this reality, project leaders may have to work that much harder to build a team. It helps if project leaders have a rudimentary knowledge of group psychology and strong skills in managing people. At the same time, consultants need to understand, respect, and trust the value of teamwork. This requires a sensitivity for the human relations issues applicable to projects in all types of consulting—not just organization development consulting—and a willingness to improve.

Building a team is very difficult work. A consultant who assumes the responsibility of leading other consultants on a project must grapple with a mix of client pressures, scope creep, shifting tasks, time constraints, various personalities, hidden agenda, emotional volatility, and the leader's own natural desire to perform well as a leader. As the project leader endeavors to turn a group of egos into a team, it helps to know what a team *is*. In its most simplified form, according to Katzenbach and Smith (2003), a team is defined as follows:

A team is a small number of people with complementary skills who are committed to a common purpose, performance goals, and approach for which they hold themselves mutually accountable.

1. A *small number* means between five and eight members. Of course, some teams are much larger, but if the size can be limited it makes the job of team building that much easier, as the complexity of the variables involved is reduced. As a practical matter, team size depends on the situation, the size of any given project, and the scope of the work to be done. The number of members is often determined by the number of *functional specialties* needed by the assignment as the project leader tries to match the project's needs with members' skills. In IT consulting, situations requiring the development of a complex system or applications using "agile" and "scrum" development methods increase the team size considerably, as both consultant and client developers work side-by-side in rapid interaction. It is common practice in IT consulting, for example, to have the following functional members:

- Engagement manager
- Project leader
- Architecture design
- Systems development

- Testing and quality assurance
- Training and skill transfer
- Documentation

Another example is a consulting team working on an executive leadership development conference that has the following members: project leader, 360-degree survey designer, project administrator, three conference design consultants, and a technology consultant (for an electronic voting system). In addition, the client may include their own consultants to work on the project. Although team size can vary quite a lot, it can be reduced when team members have multiple roles.

2. *Complementary Skills.* A group of consultants usually brings different technical, human relations, and process skills to the problem-solving and decision-making process. It is virtually impossible for just one or two people to have all of the necessary skills and capabilities needed to run a large and complex assignment. The team leader needs to assess the skills needed for the team while the project proposal is being developed. Identification and selection of people for the team is then done on the basis of who is available and who has the right skills, in order to fill out the team with sets of the skills, experience, and capabilities needed for the project.

3. *Common Goals.* The importance of the project launch meeting was discussed in Chapter Six. The objective of this meeting is to achieve team alignment and build members' commitment to the consulting project. At this meeting the team develops common purposes, goals, and processes. The launch meeting is so important to team building that without the requisite alignment, a group of people may never become a team; the dynamics and interplay of the members may never quite produce something greater than the sum of the individual members' contributions. Consultants who join a consulting project start as a loose group of people *without* a common approach to things, *without* goals, and with only a *vague* purpose. To turn such a group into a team, the project team leader uses common goals to (1) develop *shared values and beliefs* that enable individual members to overcome their natural resistance to teamwork, and (2) develop conditions that motivate people to collaborate with one other.

4. *Mutual Accountability.* Team members' motivation to collaborate comes, in part, from (1) understanding the larger purposes and goals of the team's existence (that is, solving a client problem in a particular way); and (2) understanding how they can contribute to success (exceeding client expectations). This includes team members' holding each other responsible for results. This is what Katzenbach and Smith (2003) mean

by "mutual accountability" in their definition. Ultimately, real collaboration comes from all members having a willingness and an ability to contribute. Achieving this with each team member is one of the central and often the most difficult tasks of team leadership.

Accordingly, Katzanbach and Smith provide us with the means to achieve teamwork. These four broad qualities and the properties of each are needed if a group is to be a team. But achieving the goal is challenging, as project leaders must be able to convert disparate attitudes, conflicting values, resistance, and varying personalities into a cohesive, collaborative, and efficient team of people. It is important to note that because consultants are knowledge workers and may have in mind an "ideal version" of how a high-performing team looks and behaves, they expect to be led by someone they respect; someone they view as a role model for teamwork, team attitudes, team skills, and team values. Accordingly, consultants who assume a team leadership role must be particularly sensitive to their colleagues' expectation of credibility and integrity, as they look to them to be experts in facilitating the process of developing a team.

Stages of Team Development

Team development is challenging work, but it can be made easier if project leaders develop their own skills in facilitating the process of team building. Here are the basic requirements for project leaders:

- Internalizing and believing in the definition of a team
- Acknowledging their personal role and impact on the group's work
- Diagnosing problems in group performance
- Giving group members ways to openly discuss the quality and effectiveness of their behavior—what helps and what hinders collaboration
- Using proficiencies in negotiating, influencing, and politics (discussed in Chapter Eleven)

Research on teams and team-building has found that groups go through stages of development on their way to becoming high-performing teams (see, for example, Lencioni, 2002; Moosbruker, 1995). One of the earliest models, developed by Tuckman (1965), demonstrated that groups go through four stages: forming, storming, norming, and performing (later a fifth stage, adjourning, was added). Table 7.1 summarizes Tuckman's model and provides a useful way to think about the general set of

TABLE 7.1 STAGES OF TEAM DEVELOPMENT

Stage Issues	Behavior	Leader's Actions
Forming: "Checking Things Out" • Where do I fit in? • Who are these people? • Why are we here? • Will I be accepted? • How do I find my place? • Will I perform successfully?	Excitement Nervousness Passivity Confusion Complaints Frustration	• Establish expectations. • Agree on goals. • Determine how work will be accomplished. • Identify and tackle key issues. • Test people's perceptions.
Storming: "Thrashing Things Out" • Do we really have to do this? • Who has the real power here? • How much influence do I have? • I don't think we can succeed. • How do I find my place here? • Can I get off this team?	Arguments Conflict Resistance Tension Grandstanding Frustration	• Review vision and purpose. • Seek common ground. • Assign responsibilities. • Agree on goals, process, and steps needed to accomplish the project. • Confront and discuss the tension. • Assert expectations of each other.
Norming: "Working Things Out" • What are the rules? • Who isn't following the rules? • How are we doing? • How do we overcome obstacles? • Who can I help? • How do we keep the momentum?	Establishment of rules Acceptance of rules Enthusiasm Friendliness Cohesion Conflict avoidance Cooperation	• Discuss team's vision, mission, strategy, and goals. • Revisit basic purpose of the team. • Meet deadlines. • Clarify and maintain ground rules. • Share successes and progress. • Learn from each other.
Performing: "Getting It Out" • How close are we to finishing? • How do we keep the momentum? • How do we overcome obstacles? • Who can I help? • What do we do when we're done?	Sharing Openness Enthusiasm Cohesive effort Ownership of results Conflict resolution Process focus	• Revisit vision and purpose. • Keep to milestones and deadlines. • Seek creativity and innovation. • Provide public recognition and thanks. • Celebrate progress and results.

dynamics, issues, and leadership challenges that accompany each stage, as well as actions that can be taken to turn a group into a team.

Diagnosing Project Team Performance

At a project team-building meeting, the four stages can be used as a model to discuss and diagnose the team's effectiveness. For example, members can discuss their current day-to-day behavior (observable and normal constructive and dysfunctional behavior) to see where they fit in the model at the moment, diagnose what is helping and hindering their ability to achieve results, and agree on actions needed to move to the next stage. Groups may find they break down and cannot get past the storming stage in the Tuckman model. This occurs when the exertion of power and control by members grows in intensity, leading to a general breakdown of group cohesiveness. If such problems become too big, project leaders may need the skills of an outside consultant to deal with the issues and make progress.

Recent work by Lencioni (2002) provides another simple and useful way to diagnose team effectiveness in terms of five levels of issues and problems: trust, conflict, commitment, accountability, and results. The model is hierarchical, with the most basic issue being trust. Consultants who do not trust each other will have problems with the other four issues and ultimately be unable to produce high-quality results. His book includes a simple diagnostic questionnaire that can be used to measure and discuss the presence or absence of problems in the areas described in Table 7.2.

Diagnosing group performance requires observation, data gathering, analysis against standards and goals, and a process that enables group members to diagnose themselves. Self-diagnosis is an important part of the process; it may be done by surveying and discussing the group's views, attitudes, and behaviors in these areas:

TABLE 7.2. COMMON PROBLEM AREAS FOR TEAMS

Problem Area	Evidence to Be Observed
Trust	People do not risk being vulnerable with one another.
Conflict	There is low engagement in debate, and artificial harmony prevails.
Commitment	There is much ambiguity about roles, goals, and responsibilities.
Accountability	Standards of performance are consistently low.
Results	Outcomes are attributed to only one person or to the leader alone.

Source: Adapted from P. Lencioni, *The Five Dysfunctions of a Team*, Jossey-Bass, 2002. Reproduced with permission.

- Clarity and agreement on team goals
- Clarity and understanding of roles
- Use of team's work processes
- Quality of member relationships
- Team synergy and output
- Clarity and agreement on priorities
- Quality of team spirit

The sample team diagnostic questionnaire in Appendix E can be used for gathering data about each of these factors. Once each team member has anonymously filled out the questionnaire, the data can be aggregated, analyzed, and presented to the team members as strengths and weakness of the team, trends and patterns, and key issues that need to be discussed and resolved.

How Team Building Is Conducted

Project Leader as Change Leader. The most difficult aspect of team building is getting team members to talk openly and constructively in an open forum about their own behavior and that of other team members, especially the behavior of team members that is preventing the team from achieving its goals. Because these conversations are difficult and make people feel uncomfortable, project leaders have a choice: to manage the conversations with the group personally or to hire an outside consultant that specializes in helping companies with team building. If the project leader decides to do the team building personally, it may be done off-site or in-house, but in either case requires the ten-step process outlined in this section. An outside team-building consultant would follow the same steps.

If done personally, the consulting project leader needs to create a "safe space" that allows members to level with each other, share authentic feelings, and speak openly about their perceptions of team effectiveness and people's behavior. Ground rules need to be set for sharing, giving, and receiving feedback, as such levels of candor can be emotionally difficult and politically risky. But avoiding such straight talk can only makes things worse and may either accelerate the storming stage of team development or cause the group to regress back to it. The principles and steps of POISE coaching (an acronym for *purpose, observation, impact, solution,* and *expectation,* covered in Chapter Eight) can be useful in setting the right tone and structuring the discussion, if needed, and the diagnostic questionnaire in

Appendix E can be used to develop the issues to be discussed. The discussion usually begins with relatively safe group-level issues and evolves to the more difficult issue of the behavior of individuals.

If the team is really in trouble, facing major hurdles in its performance, and the team leader feels ill-equipped to handle the group effectively, an organization development (OD) consultant may be used to conduct a team-building retreat. This person is an expert in group process and team facilitation and possesses the necessary people skills, political neutrality, and objectivity to help team members discuss their thoughts and feelings regardless of how difficult the issues may be. The consultant can get to the heart of a matter and, when necessary, protect members who may be vulnerable to attack or fearful of subsequent recriminations. Such consultants usually follow an *action research* process (Block, 2001), which includes the following ten steps in the design and delivery of their work:

1. Clarify retreat purpose and values.
2. Set ground rules.
3. Generate data.
4. Discuss group issues.
5. Address individual problems.
6. Support everyone.
7. Identify specific action steps.
8. Ensure that team members are accountable to one another.
9. Debrief the retreat.
10. Follow up on all action items

It is wise not to treat this work superficially. Whether using an external OD consultant or trying to do team building oneself, it is well worth reading Block's book *The Flawless Consulting Field Book & Companion* (2001) to understand the objectives, steps, values, subtleties, and key success factors in this specialized area of consulting.

Special Problems in Building Project Teams

Let us not lose sight of why we are discussing the dynamics of group behavior and team building. The purpose for doing all this work is to ensure we have consultants who are motivated to be on the engagement and aligned around the project goals, and who can work together as a team. Even though team member roles are often performed separately and individually, the members must collaborate to produce deliverables and, from the point of view of the consulting firm, be seen by clients as one, unified team. At the same time, clients expect teamwork among their own employees and therefore expect the same behavior from their consultants. With this in mind, project leaders need to be cognizant of some special problems, such as member resistance, that occur with teams.

Team Problem: Resistance

The heart of team building is the effective handling of change. Part of the content or substance of any team-building retreat is discussing the reasons for change and what new behavior looks like, helping people to behave more effectively, and overcoming people's natural resistance to something new.

For some members, the process of team building can be threatening and may cause them (and perhaps the whole team) to resist the changes needed to become more effective. According to Warner Burke (2008), there are at least four ways in which groups resist change:

1. *Turf Protection and Competition*—The group fights for its survival and "will muster every rationale, fact, and guilt-inducing behavior to justify its continuation."
2. *Closing Ranks*—By "circling the wagons," group members protect their identity.
3. *Changing Allegiances or Ownership*—Group members avoid the conflict of change by seeking ways to redefine its vision, mission, and stakeholders.
4. *Demanding new leadership*—Group members revolt against the legitimate team leader through an unconscious collusion to get rid of the leader by assuming the leader is incompetent.

The challenge of overcoming resistance to change has been the subject of much research (see Bridges, 1986; Block, 2000; and Hambrick & Cannella, 1989), which is recommended as a place to begin developing an understanding of this thorny issue. The project leader or OD consultant must be able to help team members recognize when they are resisting and help them both to understand the underlying human dynamics of the resistance and to discuss ways to overcome such resistance.

Team Problem: Dominant, Damaging Member

The level of performance can be lowered by a vocal team member who cannot or will not try to exceed previous performance levels because of the belief that: (1) the payoff does not warrant trying harder, (2) the "rules" prevent trying something new, (3) the client's or manager's expectations are unreasonable and never ending, (4) the team's process cannot be improved, or (5) current performance is satisfactory. The situation will be worsened if this vocal person is an opinion leader to whom people listen carefully, or a loud team member, or someone who threatens to quit the team. Project team leaders must take immediate action to coach such individuals, lest that "attitude virus" spread to other team members.

Team Problem: Loss of Members

The loss of team members obviously creates huge barriers to team performance. Team members may leave for a host of reasons, including apathy, frustration, anxiety about change, worries about not having sufficient skills and competencies, or feelings of being ignored, belittled, embarrassed, or confused. To prevent such losses, both informal leaders and the project team leader must be alert to signs of withdrawal, persistent errors or mistakes, or physical behavior that signals negative emotions, as well as comments about the team. If such signs are detected, the project leader must take coaching action immediately to uncover the causes and find solutions before the team member leaves.

Team Problem: Ongoing Maintenance

Even when a consulting group has become a high-performing team, it is not likely to stay that way permanently without proper maintenance. Over time, deterioration may occur, and the team will need frequent, regular maintenance to fine-tune its performance. Maintenance is needed because consulting work changes, old habits return, bad habits get formed, new members join, and old members leave. All of these can reduce the team's performance, so the team leader must be vigilant to spot any regression. The leader must then have the courage to address such issues in another team-building retreat.

Without the leader's vigilance and attention, a team will likely regress to an earlier stage and may well end up getting stuck in "storming" once again. If any of the team's regressive behavior negatively affects deliverables, it will result in very serious consequences with the client. However, as can be seen from this discussion, team members and team leaders can take action to prevent regressive behavior if they are attentive to group dynamics, diagnose themselves, and remain clear about what the team needs to do.

Characteristics of High-Performing Teams

When a team is at peak performance, it manifests a certain climate and behavioral characteristics. For example, when you observe a top basketball or volleyball team, certain behaviors are obviously present. Just as sports coaches can observe these characteristics in their teams, so, too, project leaders can determine whether or not such characteristics are present in their consulting teams and, if they are not, take action to create them. High-performing teams act in ways that "make the task the boss," and they work on continuous improvement in *what* they are doing and *how* they are achieving results. The following are some of the obvious behaviors of high-performing teams:

Obvious Behavioral Characteristics:

- Challenging but realistic goals
- Lots of communication
- Inclusion of every team member
- Climate of fun and excitement
- Practice and skill building
- Learning from mistakes
- Helping each other
- Brainstorming and ideation
- Listening to each other
- An ethic of "can do" and "let's try"

Interestingly, although some behaviors are obvious, others are subtle and even counterintuitive.

Counterintuitive Behavioral Characteristics:

- Leadership of team discussion floats to the person with the next best idea.
- Pressure to perform comes from external sources.

- Metrics are used that create higher expectations.
- Consistency of performance blends with rule bending.
- Competitiveness is used to generate energy.
- Routine behavior combines with a vigorous challenging of assumptions.

In summary, at its core, team building requires *dealing with reality*. Sometimes this reality can be difficult to surface and acknowledge, let alone discuss maturely, especially when the problems involve people's attitudes and emotions. However, with the identifiable stages, issues, and team-building processes described here, and with consultants willing to take on the challenge, the team can make considerable progress toward achieving high performance. We end this chapter with a description of the personal skills needed by project leaders to move a group though the stages and levels of team development.

The Project Leader Style Needed for Team Building

Research on team effectiveness shows clearly that the best leadership style to use in a business setting (especially with professional knowledge workers like consultants) is a democratic style—one that fosters full participation, involvement, open debate, and consensus decision making (Francis & Young, 1979; Knowles, 1972; Kouzes & Posner, 2012; Kreitner, 2009; Schermerhorn, Hunt, et al., 2010). Autocratic micro-managers may get a greater volume of work accomplished, but this is often at the expense of fulfilling people's need for strong socioemotional support and team cohesion. Autocratic, coercive leadership tends to make group members operate on the basis of fear and compliance rather than commitment. Fear in the work environment inevitably results in people feeling insecure and not giving their best performance. This can lead to group member turnover and higher costs (Deming, 1987).

Given the challenges of building a team in stage two of the consulting cycle, a democratic style of leadership is likely to produce faster, bigger, better, and perhaps cheaper results. The values, focus, and skills of a democratic style increase the probability of successful group development because project leaders with such an approach will be naturally interested in group dynamics and willing, if not better able, to frame issues, confront problems, listen carefully, resolve conflicts, coach people, communicate shared interests, reinforce common goals, and build consensus. Armed with such a style, project leaders will be able to overcome dysfunctional behavior among members and thereby build a stronger consulting (project) team.

Skills of a democratic style combine a strong focus on ensuring that team tasks and goals are accomplished with a strong focus on the human relations qualities needed to get the work done in the collaborative environment of a team. Emotional intelligence is needed when this combination raises tensions.

Emotional Intelligence

Daniel Goleman's (2006a,b) research has provided an understanding of the skills needed by project leaders to deal with consulting situations that are emotionally difficult, full of tension, and perhaps full of outright conflict. Goleman explains that we can learn to be more emotionally intelligent by paying attention to how we automatically *respond* in moments when our emotions are strongly aroused and we feel threatened. Such situations can easily occur in team building when strong positions are held by team members and the atmosphere is uncomfortably tense. At such moments the project leader needs to think through and rationally decide what to do with each of the five elements of emotional intelligence: *self awareness* (label the emotions aroused), *self control* (objectify feelings to control them), *internal motivation* (decide what outcome is really important), *empathy for others* (see the world from the other person's perspective), and *social skills* (adjust response to be kind, understanding, and diplomatic).

To Intervene or Not to Intervene?

On occasion, when the team-building problem is internal to the team members and not affecting the client directly, as project leader you may let the team members work out a solution for themselves. Let them coach each other as necessary. Let them learn for themselves how to work through the stages and be high-performing. Intervening may not always be necessary; in fact, it may build a dependence on the leader, inhibiting the group's maturity.

On the other hand, if the problem directly affects the client, then the team leader needs to intervene and exert greater influence and presence with the team to resolve the problem. Knowing that he or she must represent the team's work to the client, the project leader must have firsthand knowledge of any issues affecting performance and make sure they are resolved.

Finally, when working at the level of an individual team member's specific role and task, the project leader need not worry about being able to perform the task as well as the team member. The leader's role is to be a big-picture generalist with some specialized technical expertise, to ask the right questions that uncover root causes to problems and improve quality, and to provide guidance on creating solutions. This is the coaching role of project leadership.

Equally, when leading the team as a whole, the project leader need not worry about having to impress the consulting group with a lot of specialized technical knowledge. The leader's job is bigger and broader, focused on making sure team members' complementary skills produce the kind of synergy that enables the team to produce solutions in the next stage of the consulting process and throughout the engagement.

Conclusion

In this chapter we have looked at the key principles, factors, elements, and actions needed to get a group of technical specialists mobilized and turned into a consulting team that is energized and aligned around the engagement. This is not an easy task. For the new consultant charged with the responsibility of leading a large and visible consulting assignment, it can be a daunting task indeed. However, many consultants have done it before, and the keys to success are known. Once the consultant has the mental desire to lead the process, the tools and techniques discussed here will engender success.

As leaders, we are likely to encounter resistance and challenges, just as we did when we were trying to win business by convincing the client of the value of our specific approach to solving their problem. During stage two, mobilizing and aligning, consultants on the project team may resist many things: their roles, tasks, the plan, other team members, the timing of events, goals, the methods and techniques to be used, even the project leader. This is common. Strong-minded, expert consultants always want things done their way. At the same time, clients sometimes like to challenge who is really in charge of a project in order to get *their* way. Amid all of those challenges, someone has to lead. Ultimately, it is the responsibility of the lead consultant or the project team leader to face any fears and be that leader.

By studying and deploying the team leadership skills articulated in Chapters Six and Seven, consultants will find the tasks in this phase of the consulting cycle made easier and the challenges of the next phase in the process—building and producing deliverables—much less daunting.

CHAPTER EIGHT

STAGE THREE: THE BUILDING AND PRODUCING PROCESS

The purpose of the building and producing stage is to make sure that project teams complete agreed-upon interim deliverables and a solution to the client's problem. It is a crucial stage in the consulting cycle that should be studied carefully. This is the stage in which time and budgets become most sensitive to waste, pressures mount, consultants must be vigilant in managing expectations, and clients can be delighted with progress—or really disappointed.

This chapter examines the practical skills needed to deal with the challenges of stage three, the time when project leaders must produce results by integrating their technical expertise with skills in managing people, all within the political context of their client's organization and the demands of their consulting teams. We focus on:

- Competencies in building and producing
- Data gathering
- Performance management
- Coaching of consultants
- Motivating of consultants
- Progress review meetings
- Organization politics
- Project management issues

With the many risks and vulnerabilities inherent in any project, in order to delight clients, project leaders must be able to exercise exceptionally good management, and each consultant must work hard to ensure that this stage is extremely well executed.

Stage Three Competencies: Building and Producing

It is hard to make stage three run smoothly, because once the action starts, original project plans rarely reflect the reality of getting things done. Clients fear mismanaged project plans, delays in deliverables, cost overruns, mismanaged expectations, or results that lack value.

Table 8.1 shows the three competencies and twelve behavioral practices associated with the building stage and the producing role in the consulting cycle.

Successful development of these competencies and practices enables consultants to overcome the many challenges of this stage. Producing

TABLE 8.1 BUILDING COMPETENCIES AND BEHAVIORAL PRACTICES

Purpose	Stage	Tasks	Role	Outcome
Building Deliverables	Building	• Developing/Constructing • Controlling/Problem Solving • Coaching/Motivating • Navigating Organizations	× Producing	=Deliverables

Competency	Practice
Producing Deliverables	• Ensures orderly progress is made on data gathering, analysis, assembly, and development of deliverables • Makes decisions in the face of ambiguity and time constraints • Holds individual consultants accountable for agreed-upon goals • Seeks constructive feedback about the effectiveness of deliverables as they are developed
Team Performance	• Sets challenging but realistic team goals • Builds people's confidence in themselves and their work with useful feedback and help • Encourages team-based decision making when solving problems • Asks team members for their self-assessment of progress toward goals
Navigating Politics	• Balances advocacy and diplomacy with clients to win support • Understands how stakeholders in the client's organization use their power and influence • Draws on informal contacts and networks of people to get things done • Avoids taking credit for successful initiatives begun by others

deliverables requires political intelligence, teamwork, and applied technical expertise by all consultants on the project, and good management skills by consultants in a leadership role who are responsible for the implementation of everyone's work.

The consulting firm that manages the building stage and the producing role exceptionally well will earn a competitive advantage for itself and start to build the kind of trust that leads to long-term relationships and more business.

Data Gathering

To design and build a deliverable, consultants must gather a great deal of data and gain insight about their client's existing set of circumstances—for example, depending on the type of consulting, information is marshaled and synthesized about industry issues, legacy systems, existing performance standards, new performance requirements, general business conditions, the existing organizational structure, and the company's culture, procedures, and existing documentation. These disparate items of information form the starting point for the designing, building, and producing of deliverables. At McKinsey and IBM, for example, data gathering must be very systematic, fact-based, and focused on the right issues, and must validate hypotheses and use analytical and contextual thinking and a wide range of data-gathering methods. Consulting at such firms is very demanding; it requires that consultants refine their thinking and findings and be prepared to have their conclusions tested and validated.

Systematic Data Gathering

A data-gathering process (such as in action research) requires careful planning and implementation. It must have a clear scope, goals, and a strategy. It must be done in a disciplined way by people trained in various data-gathering methods who can ensure the highest level of objectivity. Procedures for the collection, collation, synthesis, and reporting of data must be rigorous and used uniformly by all consultants performing the data gathering. Many consulting projects broaden the data gathering to include new areas of research, or go to new levels of detail regarding the problems or hypothesis being investigated. As new insights are garnered from each iteration of data gathering, it may be necessary to change the research strategy to ensure that the scope of the problem is examined sufficiently and in sufficient depth to ensure that all facts and possible explanations for the problem are identified. The fact-based consulting performed at McKinsey, for example, involves ten steps:

1. Create a logical structure to organize the problem and needs analysis.
2. Based on what is known, develop causal hypotheses of the problem.
3. Validate all hypotheses by testing their underlying assumptions.
4. Create an issue tree for each hypothesis, describing areas for research.
5. Formulate questions for each area of research.
6. Develop a plan for the research intervention.
7. Select methods of research.
8. Research the facts to either support or reject hypotheses.
9. Based on validated hypotheses, develop recommendations for change.
10. Present the client with recommendations for solving the problem.

McKinsey's process is designed to ensure that their recommendations are grounded in analysis that is systematic, fact-based, logical, and complete and fulfills a standard they call being "mutually exclusive and collectively exhaustive" (MECE) (Rasiel & Friga, 2001).

Hypothesis Driven

A hypothesis is a tentative explanation of the cause-effect relationships in a problem, such as: "lowering taxes creates jobs." There may be several hypotheses believed to be causing the problem; each must be investigated and tested for accuracy and validity. Data gathering produces facts about a situation and provides the evidence that each hypothesis is either right or wrong. Once a hypothesis has been proved or disproved, we are in a position to develop solutions to the problem based on that cause-effect discovery. Of course, how we describe the problem shapes the very hypotheses we develop to explain it, and, accordingly, the strategy we use to test it through data gathering. Therefore, we must be very careful about how we frame the problem in the first place and give very careful thought to the various ways in which a problem can be viewed (see Chapter Five). Making this process even more complicated is the very way in which the human mind works—our "thinking styles"—that is, the ways in which we process information both analytically and contextually.

Analytical Thinking Style

The most natural and normal thought process we experience in everyday business and consulting life is *analytical* thinking. It is a way of thinking ingrained in us from years of training and education, a direct use of the western scientific tradition known as "empiricism," which uses the objective observation of reality and the testing of hypotheses to establish and assert truth about reality. Analytical thinking is data driven, reductionist, comparative, rational, and logical. It takes a problem and breaks it apart into its constituent elements in order to see granular cause-and-effect relationships. Causes of problems are determined from these relationships.

With analytical thinking, consultants ask questions such as: What is broken? What does not work? How does this compare? Contrast? Consultants look at results compared to standards and deviations from the norm. Analytical thinking uses tools and methods such as root cause analysis, the program evaluation and review technique (PERT), flow charting, experimentation, de-engineering, mathematics, scorecards, statistical sampling, controls, value chains, supply chains, planning, Gantt charts, variation analysis, and budgeting.

Contextual Thinking Style

Contextual thinking (also known as *systems thinking*) examines a problem as it exists in relationship to the larger space or environment of which the problem is a part. Contextual thinking requires seeing the whole as a collection of subsystems; for example, an organization's composition of layers of management, coordinating systems, and business functions. Each of those organizational subsystems has its own organizational purposes and functions, which can be understood (in part) by the way it *interacts* with other subsystems. Interestingly, a problem may reside in the interaction *between* subsystems as much as it may reside *within* any one of them (see Burke, 2008, pp. 49–64). This is a very useful perspective for consultants to consider in the building and producing stage of consulting to ensure that the right problem has been solved and, when solutions are implemented, the impact of the solutions on other organization or business systems.

Whereas *analytical* thinking focuses on the inner workings and logic of a subsystem, *contextual* thinking considers both the purpose of the subsystem and how it interacts with the other subsystems; for example, how one business function—say, manufacturing—is connected to other business functions, such as marketing and human resources, or how one department interacts with other departments. By thinking contextually, consultants may discover that the real problem lies in how subsystems (in an organization) *interact* with one another, rather than in any given functional subsystem.

Clearly, analytical and contextual thinking are both important methods and perspectives for solving problems during *all* stages of consulting. Consultants must keep both ways of thinking in mind as they decide on the data that must be gathered to understand the nature of the problems they have been hired to solve, and the focus of the questions that in turn influence which data-gathering methods will be used.

Methods of Data Gathering

The data-gathering process for consultants is similar to the "discovery" phase for lawyers. It is important that consultants do a thorough job of fact-finding. McKinsey, for example, prides itself on its fact-based analysis of business problems, and they assiduously use facts to support or deny the validity of their working hypotheses about the causes of a problem under investigation. Data gathering is critical for building and producing excellent deliverables. Solutions must be grounded in business and organizational realities, and analysis must be fact-based in order to create realistic and practical solutions. For useful distinctions between hypotheses and facts, see Dawkins, (2009).

The importance of fact-based data gathering requires consultants to be well-trained in the various tools and techniques used to complete this phase of the consulting process. Each consulting firm has its own preferred methods, tools, forms, systems, and procedures for data gathering. However, there are standard methods used by all consultants. The most common data-gathering methods used by consultants are:

- Interviewing
- Surveying
- Focus groups
- Documentation analysis
- Observation

To fully understand the pros and cons of each method, we recommend consulting a standard text on research methods (see, for example, Bryman & Bell, 2003; Lehmann, 1989; Sekaran, 2003).

There is no perfect method for gathering the facts. All data-gathering methods are subject to bias and data distortion. Consultants must be conscious of those sources of bias and try to eliminate them as much as possible. Because there are many subtleties to research and research methods and because bias is common, it is highly recommended that in addition to receiving formal education in research methods, junior consultants also receive coaching by experienced senior consultants before they perform any data gathering in a client's organization.

Obviously, the soundness of deliverables, solutions, and recommendations are directly related to the efficacy of the data gathered and the value of the insights found in the information. Consultants must be competent in statistical analysis, detecting themes and patterns in the data, as well as drawing conclusions and recommendations from their analysis. Consultants must be trained in understanding how to remain objective as they interview clients, how to ensure that random samples are taken of client populations, and how to conduct precise observations of client operations.

The Heisenberg Effect

Before a consultant enters a client organization to conduct what in the legal profession is called "discovery," formal training must be provided not only on data-gathering methods and objectivity but also on the impact of the data-gathering process itself on the perceptions and feelings of clients' employees. Data gathering is an intervention into a client's organization, and careful consideration of the impact of such an intervention on client responses is very important (Block, 2001). Because the data-gathering phase of any consulting engagement is a time when consultants work closely with individual employees, groups, departments, and the management of a client's organization, the very act of gathering information changes the client system (Burke, 2008). This phenomenon, whereby the presence of a consultant-researcher affects what it is being examined, is called the *Heisenberg effect*. In essence, the act of data gathering affects the data gathered.

Considering the problems of bias, effects on the client systems, and the specific skills needed for each type of research method, consultants must be well-trained to perform data gathering professionally. Before the process starts, it is wise to ask questions such as these:

- What data-gathering methods will be used?
- How will data be gathered, synthesized, and reported?
- Who will do the data gathering?
- Are the researchers trained and qualified?
- What impressions will researchers make and what effects will they have on the client system?

- What sources of bias are possible in gathering data and how do we guard against them?
- How will we test the validity of our hypotheses about what is causing the problem?

In the journey of becoming a trusted advisor, it is critical to perform data gathering in the most professional way possible, using the best interpersonal, diplomatic, and politically sensitive skills. Clients will judge the quality of both the individual consultant and the consultant's firm on how well this phase of work is accomplished. In short, consultants can generate enormous goodwill and cooperation if they conduct this work correctly, or client cynicism and resistance may result if they do not.

Performance Management and Coaching

By *performance management* we mean a process by which the results produced by each consultant and the entire consulting team are accomplished as set forth in the project plan, while allowing for creativity and unexpected events. The performance management process consists of (1) goal setting, (2) performance tracking, (3) coaching, and (4) appraisals. This process enables the project leader to be systematic and logical in managing people, holding consultants accountable for results, and, at the same time, allowing for initiative and creativity.

The term *performance management* is indicative of our assumption that performance *can* be managed. This requires that project leaders implement the four steps of the performance management process, beginning with goal setting.

Goals are important for at least three reasons. First, they are basic to human motivation. Each of us lives to achieve goals of one sort or another. In consulting projects goals provide a motivation to produce results. Second, with a set of project-related performance goals in place, project leaders can use them to assess each consultant's future performance against the accomplishment of those project goals. Third, nonproject goals ensure that broader professional development of employees and the firm are achieved. For a firm to grow, consultants' goals should include acquiring new skills, insights, and knowledge, and they must contribute to the firm's financial health.

Each consultant ought to have a small number (four to six) of manageable goals, and each goal should be detailed and specific as well as

TABLE 8.2 GOALS FOR CONSULTANTS

Goals	Focus
1. Project plan related	Roles, tasks, specific deliverables
2. Personal and professional training	Knowledge, skills, and abilities
3. Consulting practice development	New procedures or processes
4. Application rate	Billable or chargeable time
5. Sales and revenue	Money or percentages and market development
6. Client development	Adding clients and account penetration

practical and achievable. Consulting goals can vary, from sales revenues and account penetration to consultant professional development and office expansion, but usually cover the categories shown in Table 8.2.

A practical way for consultants to ensure that their goals are written clearly is by using the classic SMART method—a simple, well-known set of criteria that are used by business managers and easily adaptable to the consulting environment.

SMART Goals

The acronym SMART stands for *specific, measurable, achievable, realistic,* and *time-bound.* Each of these criteria has specific requirements, and collectively SMART goals serve to set very good performance standards against which results can be tracked, coached and appraised.

○ *Specific.* By specific, we mean the goal must be described as a concrete outcome or result. Consultants often make the mistake of describing a goal as a set of activities; these are *inputs* to producing an outcome, not the goal itself. For example, if an IT consultant had to produce a report that recommends the selection of certain application software, a *specific* goal would be stated as: "Deliver a software recommendation to 'X' client." In strategy consulting, it might be: "Recommend a marketing strategy for the sole proprietor insurance business."

○ *Measurable.* This means there is a metric attached to the goal that enables a consultant to know the level of accomplishment required. In our examples, it simply means that *one* report is to be delivered. Once the report is written and delivered, we know the goal has been accomplished. In the second example we might state it as *three* alternative strategies for the Chicago market.

○ *Achievable.* This means the goal can be accomplished given the skills, expertise, time frame, and logistics the consultants need to perform the work. It is usually a good practice to set a goal with some "stretch" in it (that is, an increase that exceeds the last goal) to ensure that consultants have the opportunity to grow their professional capabilities and improve their performance, whenever possible. In our example, that might mean adding that the work will be done across two departments in the firm— *applications development* and *sales*—or limiting the strategic alternatives to the top one hundred firms by sales revenue, in order to limit the scope of the study to an achievable amount.

○ *Realistic.* This means that the goal needs to be in the context of the consultant's work, the firm's mission and strategy, and the client's needs. It also means that the time frame and the scope (of the report) are both practical and achievable. All of this must add up to a conclusion that the goal is relevant and realistic, given the context, demands, and expectations of the consulting work.

○ *Time-Bound.* This means the goal must be accomplished within a specific time period. In our example, this could mean that the report is to be delivered to the client on *October 18, 2013.* The date must coordinate with existing project plans and the client's expectations.

By structuring our thinking with the aforementioned criteria, we have a complete "SMART" goal:

Deliver a sales applications software recommendation report to client (X) by 10/18/13.
or
Deliver three marketing strategies for the sole proprietor insurance product for the top one hundred firms in the Chicago market, by October 18, 2013.

It may seem a bit cumbersome making each consultant write a set of SMART goals. However, not only will the goals be sharper, but the thinking that goes into making them SMART compliant will improve. With practice it becomes easier to write goals in this fashion, and it makes the rest of the performance management process easier, not only for tracking performance, but also by simplifying the subsequent coaching process, as improvements can be tied to the goals.

Coaching Consultants

Coaching is the art of helping someone to learn a new skill, gain new knowledge, or acquire a new ability. Every professional can benefit from coaching. Coaches help professionals achieve their highest level of performance and then helps them *stay* there! Even the world's best tennis player or golfer requires coaching. Consultants need to be coached as well.

Coaching is a best practice for consultants (and client managers) and is a skill anyone can learn. In the consulting world, consultants who work with peer-level colleagues or manage others in some capacity can use coaching to improve people's performance in any role and tasks in the cycle; for example:

- Conducting a SPIN meeting with a client
- Moving a group through the stages of team building
- Improving the use of a research method
- Making a presentation
- Writing a report
- Handling a client political issue

In addition, coaching is a *consulting service* provided to business managers by external consultants who specialize in this form of consulting in order to improve an individual manager's personal performance. This so-called *executive coaching* helps managers to improve in areas such as these:

- Dealing with an employee's leadership (consulting) style
- Overcoming interpersonal problems
- Assisting in building specific skills
- Creating individual development plans
- Providing career transition help
- Supporting employees acquired through a merger

Figure 8.1 shows how coaching can be used with fellow consultants on a 360-degree relationship basis. Commonly, project leaders coach their team members, but team members can coach each other and coach their more senior colleagues; they can even coach the client. (The Consulting Role Preference Indicator in Appendix A can be used in the same way to coach employees on their strengths and weaknesses across the four roles of the consulting model.)

Positive Coaching

Positive coaching is a best practice and skill that can be used to enhance, improve, develop, and increase anyone's abilities. An important point is

FIGURE 8.1 360-DEGREE COACHING RELATIONSHIPS

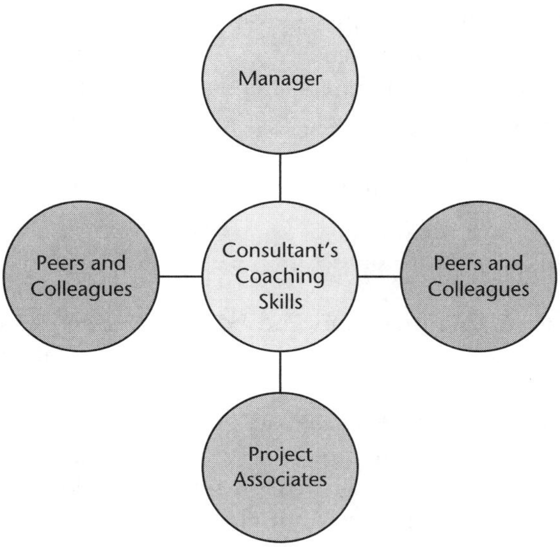

that coaching of subordinates is not used only when they have done something wrong or have made mistakes. When coaching a tennis player, the coach does not just point out what the player did wrong, but instead may place the focus on a change in tactics or physical movement, in order to help the player exceed current performance. In this sense, positive coaching simply raises the "skill and performance bar." In consulting, project leaders can coach in the same manner and with the same intent as sports coaches. Thus we have one consultant helping to redirect other consultants to achieve higher standards in the goals of their respective roles, or helping the team improve within the context of the project plan. This is positive coaching.

Corrective Coaching

Lead consultants can use coaching to correct a team member's performance. Corrective coaching is necessary when mistakes like the following are made:

- Not producing a deliverable on time and specification
- Violating a company policy
- Inappropriate language with a client

- Not respecting cultural norms in foreign countries
- Introducing bias when using a research method

Whether handling mistakes or pushing for higher standards of performance through positive coaching, consultants can use "coaching moments" to effectively make changes—that is, to help others avoid making the same error twice. Effective coaching is easier if there are a set of coaching competencies that can be learned, and if there is an organizing framework or a coaching model to follow. The next section explains how to coach.

Coaching Models

In most training programs and books on effective coaching, the practice of coaching is boiled down to a logical and rational decision-making process: identify the problem, generate alternative solutions, evaluate each solution, choose a solution, and implement the solution. This is what consultants and managing consultants do naturally to solve problems. However, to this scientific process must be added the art of coaching. The art of coaching involves human motivations, introspection, creativity, behavioral skills, dialogue, reflection, and contextual thinking. The coaching process requires skills such as:

- Enabling someone to acknowledge that a problem exists
- Putting the current performance in context
- Discussing the fact that performance could be better
- Searching for ways to improve the performance
- Providing and selecting a preferred approach
- Expecting and encouraging attempts at a new approach
- Learning from experience
- Being persistent in expectations and results

The characteristics, elements, and dynamics of coaching can be organized into a simple, logical framework with five steps called POISE: *purpose, observation, impact, solution,* and *expectations and encouragement.* Consultants can use this model, summarized in Table 8.3, to conduct face-to-face coaching.

POISE Coaching

First, the coach (that is, a senior consultant, team leader, or managing consultant) tells the person the *purpose* of the meeting: to give the person

TABLE 8.3 USING THE POISE METHOD TO COACH CONSULTANTS

Steps and Themes	Purpose	Examples
1. Purpose Rapport	Set a positive tone Get in step with each other Break the ice Create an open atmosphere	"Thanks for getting together. Let me review what we plan to cover today." "I look forward to spending some time to review how we're working together." "What questions do you have before we get started with today's session?" "I'd like to take a few minutes to talk about some things I've observed."
2. Observations Relate	State the issue or problem Provide examples State facts Talk directly about it	"Yesterday I heard you say . . ." "I have seen you . . ." "Over the last week, I have observed you . . . " "At the meeting you said . . ."
3. Impact and 4. Solutions Resolve	Discuss impact of the problem Define optional resolutions Choose a course of action Define new behavior	"Do you see the impact of what you are doing?" "What changes in [programming behavior] make sense?" "How will this new method or technique improve your results?" "How will we know that the situation or problem is solved? "When you do that, it affects me [this way] and others [that way]."
5. Expectations and Encouragement Reassure	Provide empathy Create a "safe" place Offer help Give encouragement	"I know it's difficult to change, but I know you can, and I appreciate the effort." "How else can I help you with this?" "We'll talk about this again to see how things are coming along." "Do you have any final questions about what we've discussed? Thanks!"

some feedback. Second, the coach provides specific *observations* made about the person's performance, including both positive and negative observations. Third, the coach describes the *impact* of the person's performance on the work environment. Fourth, after discussing what may be causing the current level of performance, identifies potential *solutions*. Once a solution has been found, discussed, evaluated, and agreed on, the coach ends by balancing expectations with encouragement and support. The coach acknowledges that it may be hard to change behavior and improve, but sets the expectation that it is necessary to try. The coach also explains that help is available by giving the coachee opportunities to practice, offering performance tips and suggestions, and sharing insight about any other future benefits accruing from change and improvement. The coaching session should end with a few simple words of thanks and support.

In summary, the steps of the POISE coaching model are:

P = Purpose of the session or meeting

O = Observations that are specific, both positive and negative

I = Impact on others, the work, and oneself

S = Solutions and support

E = Expectations and encouragement

The first three steps in the POISE model focus on telling, sharing, and explaining. The rest of POISE is a dialogue and discussion: asking questions, listening carefully, probing and testing assumptions, and examining conclusions to make sure they are valid. One good coaching practice involves the coach's taking a "partner posture" with the coachee; this means treating the person as an equal in searching for and solving a problem, using a friendly communications style and a positive tone. A simple but useful question for coaches to ask themselves is "How can I help this person learn?"

On the other hand, raising one's voice, rebuking, and treating people harshly (often seen in coaches handling sports teams) are not best practices and should be avoided in all professional consulting environments. Such behavior has a negative and often humiliating impact, making the recipient feel ashamed, embarrassed, or hurt. Obviously, this creates barriers to learning, change, and improvement. A good coach does not need to use such demeaning tactics. A good coach can be serious and demanding as well as friendly and respectful.

Coaching Tips

Coaching is a change management strategy. It is useful to remember that the goal of coaching is simply to *help the consultant learn* new ways of thinking and behaving that change the outcomes the consultant produces. Keep in mind the following:

- Learning is always enhanced if the consultant uses a coaching style that treats people with respect and dignity.
- People may have different learning styles from that of the coach and therefore may have different ways of understanding the problem and see different ways of solving it (see Skills Transfer in Chapter Nine).

- Age is a factor. Older adults often find it more difficult to learn something new. As people age, their thinking patterns become reified and their behavioral habits strengthen; mature adults tend to like routine.
- If possible, conduct the coaching in private; many people may be self-conscious and easily embarrassed trying to demonstrate a new skill in a public environment. Adults often find it hard to admit "I don't know how to do that." If pushed too hard, they will resist.
- Use POISE to plan and prepare the content of the coaching session and to develop the right focus, tone, and attitude toward the consultant being coached.

Inevitably, we will find ourselves working with other consultants of varying age, ethnicity, gender, race, and experience. Those factors must be taken into account as the team leader or managing consultant manages the performance of team members. And although POISE provides a standard process for planning and conducting coaching, the coach must be mindful of the complexities and subtleties presented by these factors. Human relations skills are extremely important when working with clients and fellow consultants around the world. In general, all of us will benefit from having a deeper understanding of the thinking, behavior, perceptions, and expectations of cultures other than our own.

Coaching Through Resistance

Resistance to personal improvement and change is natural and, to some extent, to be expected from knowledge workers and experts who may find it difficult to admit they do not know or cannot do something. The reason consultants resist being coached or resist the changes required from coaching is deeply psychological. A full treatment is beyond the scope of this book; however, anyone interested in coaching as a consulting practice ought to study this psychology more thoroughly. Block (1981), for example, explains that resistance may arise from fear, lack of control, or feelings of vulnerability. Hambrick and Cannella (1989) discuss three forms of resistance: blind, political, and ideological. Burke (2008), in discussing the context of individual, group, and organizational change, suggests that resistance is not as bad as apathy (apathetic people are indifferent to change or do not care whether they change or not). Burke goes on to explain that resistance is actually a normal human response; and that coaches need to respect people's defense mechanisms as they deal with shifting away from known to unknowns, from what is familiar and comfortable to situations that are not, and from certainty to uncertainty.

Clearly, when managing the performance of consultants through coaching, it is important to acknowledge and respect their resistance, but also to seek an understanding of what lies behind initial statements such as "I can't do that," "I don't think that is right," or "I don't want to do that." Is the person resisting because of a lack of understanding about *what* to do or *why* something needs to be done? Does the person not know *how* to do it? Is the person embarrassed to admit a lack of knowledge about something, afraid to admit openly that they are not sure what to do? Does the person fear repercussions from exposing a lack of expertise?

Rather than jumping to conclusions, the savvy coach knows people resist for a reason and so asks questions, and takes the time to discover the root causes. The coach listens with an open mind, creating a safe, open, positive, and supportive climate for the discussion. Coaching through resistance requires a combination of emotional intelligence, compassion, and a deep interest in developing consultants who, after all, have been trained to provide answers and solutions, not to share fears about their vulnerabilities.

Finally, when working with consultants—and, for that matter, with resistant clients—it can help to use language that helps to shift the consultant's psychological perspective. Table 8.4 provides examples of what to say in situations in which the coach encounters avoidance or opposition. A paradigm shift from "can't do" to "can do" can reorient thinking to what is possible rather than what is not, to benefits rather than costs, and to new behavior rather than rigid attitudes. In the broader context, throughout the consulting cycle, consultants must have the emotional resilience and vocabulary to challenge the status quo in order to counter the normal and natural tendency to resist change from clients and team members alike.

Motivating Consultants

What motivates consultants? The subject of motivation has been studied for many years, and many theories of motivation have been formulated. The following are the most prominent among the theories that relate to business and consulting (Kreitner, 2009; Burke, 2008):

- Behavior modification—B. F. Skinner
- Motivation-hygiene theory—F. Herzberg

TABLE 8.4 SHIFTING PERSPECTIVE TO OVERCOME RESISTANCE

Cannot Do	Can Do
We've never done it before.	We have the opportunity to be first.
We don't have the resources.	Necessity is the mother of invention.
It will never work.	We'll give it a try.
There's not enough time.	We'll reevaluate priorities.
It's a waste of time.	Think of the possibilities.
We'll cannibalize our sales.	We'll do it before they do.
We don't have the expertise.	Let's network with those who do.
We can't compete.	We'll get a jump on the competition.
Our vendors won't go for it.	Let's show them the opportunities.
It's good enough.	There is always room for improvement.
We don't have enough money.	Maybe there's something we can cut.
We're understaffed.	"We're a lean, mean machine."
We don't have enough room.	Temporary space may be an option.
It's not going to be any better.	We'll try it one more time.
It can't be done.	It'll be a challenge.
No one communicates.	Let's open the channels.
Isn't it time to go home?	We need to get going on this before time runs out!
I don't have any ideas.	I'll come up with some alternatives.
Let somebody else deal with it.	I'm ready to learn something new.
We're always changing direction.	We're in touch with our clients.
It takes too long for approval.	We'll walk it through the system.
Our clients won't buy it.	We'll do better at educating them.
It's contrary to policy.	Anything's possible.
It's not my job.	I'll be glad to take the responsibility.
I *can't*.	I *can*!

- Expectancy theory—V. Vroom
- Need for achievement—D. McClelland
- Hierarchy of needs—A. Maslow

These are all psychologically based theories about human nature, our needs and drives. Each has merit and helps to explain what drives people and why they have such tendencies. However, most consultants are not psychologists and find it difficult to apply these theories to the workplace. A more practical approach can be found by completing the short motivation exercise found in Exhibit 8.1.

Exhibit 8.1 Motivation Exercise

Read through the following eighteen types of rewards and recognition and consider which you find most meaningful and more likely to motivate you to maintain or improve your performance.

1. Getting a letter from my manager praising my performance
2. Doing consulting work that is challenging and interesting
3. Receiving a good performance review
4. Getting more vacation time for years of service
5. Working with people I enjoy working with
6. Being coached and getting special attention from my manager
7. Getting "perks" such as complimentary food and beverages, my own parking space
8. Being listened to when I give my opinion on an important issue
9. Seeing my views and ideas being put into action
10. Receiving verbal praise from my manager
11. Getting a special bonus because of my job level
12. Completing a project that makes a difference to the firm
13. Receiving a promotion based on my past performance
14. Learning new things
15. Getting a raise based on my performance
16. Getting a special reward for doing something
17. Being praised by other consultants for doing good work
18. Getting time off for having given extra effort

Circle the numbers for the nine rewards that you find most motivating. Then fill in the score sheet by placing a check next to your chosen item numbers in the three columns.

Are most of your "motivators" in column A, B, or C? Results show that of the hundreds of people who have taken this quiz, *100 percent* have the largest number of motivators in column C. These items are what motivates people most effectively at work—based on the results of all of the consultants who have taken the quiz.

Motivator Score Sheet

Group A		Group B		Group C	
Item 1	____	Item 4	____	Item 2	____
Item 3	____	Item 7	____	Item 5	____
Item 6	____	Item 11	____	Item 8	____
Item 10	____	Item 13	____	Item 9	____
Item 16	____	Item 15	____	Item 12	____
Item 18	____	Item 17	____	Item 14	____

Column A on the Exhibit 8.1 score sheet includes those items that *managers control*, which may or may not be done for employees, depending on particular circumstances and aspects of employees' employment situations. Column B lists items set by *policies* of a company, which therefore represent items subject to standardization; employees and their colleagues may or may not receive them. Although managers may do them, they are largely out of the control of individual managers, as they must abide by company-wide standards and rules. Column C items are the motivators. These have to do with working with interesting people, learning by doing interesting and challenging work, and being listened to and having an impact at work. Throughout all industries, companies, functions, organizational levels, and roles, these are the *predominant* motivators; these are the enduring characteristics of employment that motivate employees. They are the factors that people seek in searching for new jobs, making an internal job transition, or getting promoted.

This suggests that to increase motivation, project team leaders ought to emphasize column C items in their projects and try to align team members with their preferred roles and responsibilities. Make sure consultants have a voice and are heard; give people "stretch" assignments that enable them to learn and grow in their knowledge and skills; put together teams of consultants with high competence and complementary skills.

Even though it is impossible to get a perfect fit with every consultant's needs, project team leaders should look for aspects of the work that can be made more interesting and challenging. Recognize team members for having an impact on project performance; put together a team of people who have fun together and enjoy each other's contributions; build the project team to bring out the features of column C; challenge the team by setting higher standards; coach people to help them learn and grow, both professionally and personally. Listen—*really listen*—to people.

Items in columns A and B are also important and can provide short-term motivation, but they are not as significant and enduring as column C factors. For example, over time, we all need more money, and that drive seems never-ending. But it seems clear that honorable and noble work, that allows people to learn and work with great people, generally trumps money. That explains, in part, why people work in hospitals, museums, charities, and schools, where often their psychic income is far greater than their financial income.

The motivating power of Column C items is consistent with Herzberg's (1968) concept of job enrichment and Hackman and Oldham's (1980) diagnostic approach to job design, including such factors as skill variety, task identity, task significance, autonomy, and job feedback. These are core characteristics of work designed to motivate professional knowledge-worker consultants. By extension, Conger (1998) has found that these and other factors meet the needs of Generation X employees who were born after 1985. Schermerhorn, Hunt, and colleagues (2010) embrace them and offer project team leaders a practical and simple set of questions for consultants:

- Do they find the work intellectually interesting?
- Are they working with people who help them gain new insights into their work?
- Are they able to expand their knowledge?
- Do they have opportunities to work on new problems?
- Can they share their knowledge and skills?
- Can they apply newly gained insights and learning?
- Can they teach, coach, and mentor others with their knowledge and skills?
- Are they able to see the results of their work quickly?

Pondering the answers to such questions, team leaders should give serious thought to how they can rearrange work, organize assignments, create new working relationships, expose consultants to new and interesting things, and help consultants to pursue their personal areas of interest. This, of course, can be difficult, and it may not be possible with every consultant on every assignment. However, if project leaders communicate a desire to do so and periodically take such actions, team members will know that management cares about and understands their needs. Our experience indicates that, in return, consultants are more likely to be cooperative, work harder, enjoy their work, and contribute to a pleasant work climate for the team.

Motivated consultants are easier to manage. At performance review time it will be easier to focus on evaluating the work and results produced, instead of getting sidetracked by debating such things as effort, how things were done, emotional issues, or personality conflicts. But because consultants are not always motivated and progress review meetings can be difficult, in the next section we cover how to conduct one, with individuals and with the project team.

Progress Review Meetings

Progress reviews are important occasions in which the consulting team meets, either privately or with the client, to assess how well it is performing against expectations and the project plan. Such status meetings focus on a range of matters during the building and producing stage and examine issues such as lessons learned, successes, problems with individual behavior, technical issues, progress toward objectives, teamwork, or addressing client concerns.

Client Focus

Throughout this book, we have emphasized the need to be client-focused in our consulting work. Progress review meetings should be designed to ensure that such a focus is maintained and that client issues are the overriding focus in all assessments of the team and team members' performance. Whenever possible (and whenever politically practical), it is a good practice to include clients in such meetings, not only to keep them up to date, but also to include them in developing solutions to problems that may be occurring. Discussions should be accurate, reliable, and clear so everyone knows exactly where things stand. Such discussions should include both positive progress and problems.

Consultants cannot avoid problems. After all, consulting is fundamentally about change, and when a situation with many "moving parts" changes, there are bound to be mistakes, anxiety, and confusion. Clients understand that change is difficult, and they look to their consultants to help them with the change management process, including providing comprehensive and relevant communications. Maintaining a client focus means keeping clients informed, giving them information in advance, giving them time to digest the situation, including them in the search for solutions, and generally treating them as equal partners in the building and producing process.

Clients <u>must</u> be included on issues concerning the client's organization, such as discovery of a significant consulting error, changes in solution functionality or specifications, or plans for accessing the client's systems or databases and budgetary matters. These responsibilities are shared between the consultants and the client. The issues may have sensitive political dimensions. When such client matters are on the agenda, clients should be invited to attend the regularly scheduled progress review meetings.

Individual and Team Behavior

There may be problems that are strictly internal to the team that need not involve the client. These could be discussions about routine analyses, administrative matters, documentation, or clarifying procedures. Another reason to exclude the client would be if there were serious breakdowns or interpersonal conflict among the consulting team members which, if discussed in front of the client, may reduce the client's confidence in the consulting team. Less serious but important breakdowns might include:

- Personality clashes
- Debates about what is best for the client
- Disputes about scope and pricing changes
- Significant changes in deadlines or milestones
- Decisions about changing a team member

Consultants who are very technical may believe that nontechnical discussions are unimportant, so they avoid, ignore, or take a cynical view of those issues as a waste of time. This is a mistake. For example, if a consultant fails to show up for meetings, or treats meetings disrespectfully, or if a consultant makes inappropriate remarks in front of the client, then such incidents require examination and resolution. Unprofessional behaviors are risky and must be examined and addressed. If one or two consultants are at fault, strong off-line individual coaching is needed. However, behavior problems may also exist at the project team level (which suggests that the group is not an effective team!), indicating that in addition to the normal meeting agenda, team coaching may be in order.

Progress Review Meetings Agenda

Internal team problems and issues should be kept internal to members (and perhaps the consultant firm, if warranted). They should be resolved before meeting with the client and, if possible, without needing to ask the client to join the discussion. Review meetings of this sort are called "internal reviews" and are best conducted in the consultant offices.

Project plans usually include periodic meetings with the client to review progress made on deliverables. The agenda for such meetings can cover a large number of issues related to people, project plans, processes, and producing results. A standard agenda for a project status review meetings is shown in Exhibit 8.2.

Exhibit 8.2 Project Status Review Meeting Agenda

- Welcome (Project leader or meeting owner)
- Review Agenda
- Overall Project Status:
  - Degree completed
  - In process
  - Not yet started
  - Off schedule; why?
- Deliverable Owner(s)
  - Current status toward completion
  - Problems, opportunities, significant changes
  - Needs; resources requirement changes
  - Any changes to scope (deliverable or project)
- Organizational Intelligence
  - Client feedback (not team members, not affected by the projects)
  - Client feedback (from those directly impacted by the project)
  - Project team member's feedback
- Risk Management Assessment (people, financial, business, and so on)
- Action Items:
  - Summarize for deliverables
  - Summarize for overall project
  - Owners of each action item
  - Next steps
- Next Meeting Date (for project status review)

The agenda is generic and covers all items that *might* be included. Certain items may not be included in some meetings at the discretion of the project leader, who must decide the most productive use of the time available. In general, the agenda covers the following items.

1. *Welcome.* This self-evident item should open all meetings, using a positive tone to set the right climate for discussion and problem solving.
2. *Review Agenda.* Go over the items to be discussed and note who is responsible for each, with an indication of roughly how much time should be spent on each item.
3. *Overall Project Status.* Provide the big picture by showing where things stand in relationship to the overall project plan as well as progress since the last review meeting.
4. *Deliverable Owner(s).* Review each deliverable so that deliverable owners can share and discuss problems, get help, present progress, and show accountability for results. Some problem solving and action planning may be necessary.
5. *Organizational Intelligence.* This should give the team a chance to learn as much as possible about anything going on in the client's organization that affects their work. Some problem solving and action planning may be necessary.
6. *Risk Management Assessment.* Even though a risk assessment may have been done before the project commenced and at the project launch, it is always a good idea to check with the team to see whether anything has changed. Item 5 on the agenda, organizational intelligence, may help to assess old and new risks.
7. *Action Items.* Good meetings are ones in which people have a good discussion, resolve issues, and leave with a feeling of responsibility for the performance of the project team. Owning an action item helps to build people's commitment.
8. *Next Meeting Date.* Make sure everyone knows when this is and clarify any follow-up responsibilities to be reviewed at the next meeting.

Meeting Effectiveness

Because it can be difficult to get busy consultants to attend meetings, one of the outcomes team leaders do *not* want is the impression among their consultants that they are constantly attending poorly run meetings! Exhibit 8.3 shows twenty guidelines that can make meetings more effective. They are designed to help the project leader or "meeting owner" produce a positive, upbeat atmosphere, be well organized, and get things done.

Exhibit 8.3 Running an Effective Meeting

- Select a *time of day* best for meetings.
- Have a clear *purpose* to the meeting (sharing, decision making, getting input, brainstorming).
- Have a clear *objective* in mind.
- Issue a clear *agenda* and all information or materials in advance.
- Have a *seating arrangement* helpful to the group process and discussion.
- Start and finish *on time.*
- All attendees should arrive *prepared.*
- Ensure that there are *no interruptions.*
- Use meeting time *for the meeting.*
- *Stick to the agenda* (including time limits).
- Ensure that there is some means for keeping a *permanent record* (traditionally, meeting minutes).
- Create *a record*: use flip charts, whiteboards, overheads, laptops.
- Deal with *facts,* not guesswork.
- Seek *each person's opinions* and ideas.
- Treat others' opinions with *respect.*
- Seek *consensus,* not compromise.
- Speak up if the session is *unproductive* or seems to be getting nowhere.
- Recommendations made by the group should be *agreed to by the whole group.*
- Make any *assignments clear* during the meeting.
- Circulate any and all *follow-up materials* immediately following the meeting.

At project progress review meetings, the goal is usually to understand the current status of technical, people, political, process, or team issues. When problems inevitably occur, it is worth bearing in mind that the challenge of review meetings is *not* necessarily finding a solution in the shortest possible time. The goal is to remind the team of their job: to control the project in a manner that keeps the client's confidence level high at all times.

Navigating Organizational Politics

Organizational politics is more likely to come into play during the building and producing stage of consulting than at any other time. This stage is when consultants may be "swarming" around the client's organization, asking hard questions, poking around for issues and problems, challenging long-held employee assumptions, and testing management's thinking. It is likely that feathers will be ruffled, tense debates may ensue, and the client's natural instinct to protect and preserve the status quo may surface as win-lose power plays. If consultants are not careful, they may be seduced by the client's political games, co-opted on issues, driven to despair, or perhaps become cynically competitive. A few concepts about the nature of organizational politics and skills in dealing with it can be helpful at this stage.

Political Perception

The first thing that consultants must realize about organizational politics (OP) is that it can be a *good thing* as well as a bad thing. Most of us have positive and negative experiences with organizational politics, starting with our personal family, in which we learned about the use and abuse of power, authority, influence, and rewards and punishment. Many people carry the negative aspects of family politics into adulthood and thus into the workplace, where perceptions and feelings are often reinforced with additional bad politics. People associate organizational politics with hidden agendas—situations in which someone is taken advantage of, or someone gets hurt, or someone gets ahead without merit, or someone is overlooked who deserves recognition, or someone is deliberately set up to fail. All of those are real experiences from the past and can leave us with very bad beliefs about organizational politics, thus impairing our ability to deal with it realistically and effectively.

However, organizational politics can also be looked at in quite a different way. An organization is a group of people with common and personal political agendas who have come together to accomplish something they could not achieve on their own. This collective agenda is the primary reason for political collaboration, but it exists in tension with people's private agendas, as individuals seek to accomplish their private aims along with the common goals of the organization. This tension is a source of both internal competitiveness *and* accomplishment. It is natural and normal, and it is the reason organizational politics is often perceived as both a positive and a negative human phenomenon.

Politics Is a Conversation

Organizations are made up of people interacting with one another through ad hoc, coordinated, and orchestrated conversations. Therefore we can conceive of organizational politics as essentially a series of normal and natural political conversations designed to accomplish individual and collective goals. This view raises these important questions about such conversations:

- What is the focus, nature, and quality of the conversation?
- What is its content?
- Who is leading it?
- What issues are included or excluded?
- Who is in the conversation and who is not?
- Are the conversations credible and reliable?

The answers to these questions tell us about the nature of how they make decisions, get things done, and a client's organizational politics. It follows that consultants must be in on the political conversation of a client's organization to so they can learn what will help and hinder the success of a particular engagement.

How to Think About Politics

The central role of organizational politics is the exercise of power and influence to get things done. In fact, it is the primary way in which things are done—through the political conversations among people as they communicate, solve problems, and make decisions, day in and day out. This is a positive and constructive view of organizational politics, one that is both *natural* and *necessary* to moving an organization forward.

It does not mean that organizational politics cannot be negative. That depends on the *values* of the people exercising power and influence. Political conversations can be intended for personal gain at other's expense, solely for personal credit, or even to eliminate rivals. They can also be used for a good cause; that is, directed toward the common good. Effective consultants learn to be aware of the political conversations going on and decide *how to be a part of them*. To ignore organizational politics or view it with fear or disdain is to put oneself at a disadvantage and to be on the outside of the inner workings of the client organization. Therefore the political goal for consultants is to become part of the inner circles of power and influence in the client's organization. Being part of that inner circle is evidence of being a trusted consultant.

Developing Political Skills

The most effective consultants take organizational politics seriously and spend time developing their political competency. Figure 8.2 outlines the

FIGURE 8.2 STAGES OF POLITICAL SKILL DEVELOPMENT

Avoiding	Experimenting	Intentional
Fear	Help me	Natural
Victim	Help you	Normal way
Retreat	Trial/error	Alliances
Paralysis	Experiment	Coalitions
Toxic	Learn	Influence
Danger	Risk taking	Network
Cynical	Play the game	Perception

major attitudes and skills required to develop political capability over time: Defensive, Tactical and Strategic.

Many consultants find it hard to comprehend organizational politics and even harder to see it in a positive light. But trying to avoid it is both naive and a mistake. As organizational politics is both necessary to getting things done and a natural phenomenon among people in a social organization, consultants must start the journey of becoming politically savvy by developing a political strategy. (For a valuable perspective on the characteristics and tactics of mechanistic, mixed, and organic political strategies, see Tichy, 1983.) Developing political strategies requires four steps: (1) developing personal political awareness, (2) diagnosing the political landscape, (3) creating a political activity plan, and (4) shaping one's reputation (that is, impression management).

At the start of a consulting career, consultants often have strong negative feelings about organizational politics, seeing it as toxic, petty, dangerous, and to be avoided. This attitude can leave a consultant disenfranchised, disempowered, unable to exercise influence, and, worst of all, unable to add value because of the consultant's disengagement from the inner workings of the client organization. Developing political skills requires acknowledging that the game of politics is going on all the time and everywhere in the client organization.

Political Process

The first step to developing political skill is to "get in the game" and to learn as much as possible about the players, issues, and decisions driving power, the rules, timing, goals, winners, and losers in the game. Figure 8.3 shows the process of becoming politically savvy. At the earliest opportunity, effective consultants shift from avoidance to thinking tactically and acting strategically, by:

1. Assessing where the power lies
2. Identifying the powerful people who can impact the engagement
3. Developing a plan to build a network of relationships
4. Engaging the identified network to learn about their goals and needs
5. Sharing the consultant's own consulting work
6. Being alert to how power and influence are used by the client
7. Becoming aligned with the power network
8. Influencing the network to gain direct support and assistance

Consultants with a political strategy empower themselves with knowledge and relationships. They learn about organizational priorities, build a network of relationships, and gain access to people in the client organization who, for their own personal reasons (including their perception of the consultant's growing power) want to foster a relationship *with the consultants*. Over time, by testing, exploring and learning about the client's political climate, issues, and dynamics, consultants expand their political competencies and increase their understanding of what it takes to be politically successful. Courage replaces doubt; skills replace confusion. As a consultant's scope of projects expands, the political goodwill with one client can be brought to the next.

The professional consulting goal is to so internalize this process that organizational politics becomes a natural way of working in client organizations; organizations, by the way, of any size and complexity. Experienced consultants recognize the turning point in this development when, at the beginning of an engagement, they automatically think strategically about the political landscape affecting an engagement. They then engage their plan of building a network of alliances, seeking people's support, time, resources, commitment, and help.

FIGURE 8.3 DEVELOPING POLITICAL SKILLS (SAVVY)

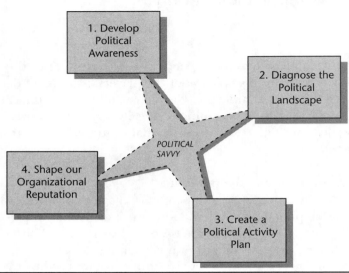

STEPS	ISSUES AND ACTIONS
1. Develop Political Awareness	• Personal experience with politics • Current level of political skills • Desire for growth and development • Emotional and political intelligence
2. Diagnose the Political Landscape	• Players' power distribution • Political intelligence data • Position on the issues • Political culture
3. Create a Political Activity Plan	• Networking plan • Engagement plan • Alignment plan • Negotiation plan
4. Shape our Organizational Reputation	• Consulting project goals • Career interests • Power enhancement • Issues analysis

A Final Note on the Game

Consultants will not always win the political game. As we discuss in Chapter Eleven, it is normal that in some client settings there will be managers and employees who simply do not like consultants. It is as if they want the consultants to fail and to disappear. This is a political issue involving the raw exercise of power and influence. Politically savvy consultants know this resentment may exist and may cause them to lose a political fight. However, they should not let it be a barrier to progress. Drawing on their power bases, politically savvy consultants can counter this pressure by developing and drawing on the widest possible coalition of support—one that is multifunctional *and* multilevel.

When client management believe that a consultant is powerfully connected, this serves as a natural antidote to political sabotage. Keeping their own futures in mind, savvy client managers will be cautious about what they say about their consultants. They will be more inclined to provide support than to withhold it. So long as consultants "live their values," do not break confidences, always put the client first, and find ways to help client management by supporting them in achieving their goals, the consultant stands a good chance of winning the political game. Not winning at the expense of the client, but winning through building long-term, trusted relationships.

Project Management Issues

The building and producing stage in the consulting cycle demands that consultants take care of a number of management tasks, using tried and tested methods to manage knowledge, project meetings, conflicts, and performance problems.

Building and Development Methods

Every consulting company has its own way of doing things, its own methods and protocols. Part of learning to be an effective professional consultant is learning those methods and processes. Certainly, clients expect their consultants to use tried and tested ways of working; they may also expect consultants to use the client's own internal systems and procedures. Table 8.5 shows typical (high-level) steps used by firms in each type of consulting.

TABLE 8.5 TYPICAL PROCEDURES ACROSS CONSULTING APPLICATIONS

Type of Consulting	Typical Procedures
Strategy Consulting	Fact-based data gathering, issue analysis, hypotheses testing, summary analysis, conclusion, presentation of recommendations
Organization Development Consulting	Needs analysis, contracting, intervention, commitment to action
Training and Development Consulting	Needs analysis, diagnosis, recommendations, design, development, program testing, rollout delivery, train-the-trainer, transfer
Technical Consulting (Tax, Accounting, Law, Medicine)	Checklists, discovery interviews, document analysis, examination of precedent, evidence analysis, case development and conclusion
Information Technology Consulting	Systems analysis, architecture development, application coding, prototype testing, skills transfer deployment, rollout, follow-up

Earlier in this chapter we touched briefly on standard research methods for data gathering but did not explain them in detail. Similarly, it is beyond the scope of this chapter and book to discuss the numerous methods, analytical models, and processes used across the many types of consulting conducted by the firms covered in Chapter One. There are many textbooks and company websites that explain those that have become industry standards, and the reader is encouraged to study them. In the field of professional consulting they form an underlying structure behind project plans and contribute to determining how clients and consultants work together to solve problems and achieve goals.

Documentation

Throughout the entire consulting engagement, consultants must keep records of meetings where decisions are made regarding such things as plans, budgets, delegated assignments, scope changes, constraints and risks, key issues, and insights. Documentation is a tedious task for consultants, who generally prefer to spend their time applying their knowledge and expertise to solving problems, not to keeping administrative records. Yet it is imperative to keep accurate and up-to-date records on file, for legal reasons as well as for the purpose of good project management.

Knowledge Management

One way in which consultants add value is by expertly managing the storage and dissemination of knowledge. Through the course of an engagement, data and huge amounts of information are generated and as a result important questions arise, such as:

- How can this information be captured, secured, and accessed?
- What needs to be reported and in what format?
- To whom should information be reported and for what purpose?

As solutions are developed, consultants see and hear about a broad range of managerial, operational, and strategic issues facing the client organization. Clients expect to be kept abreast of the consultant's insights and learning. Files and databases of information need to be kept orderly and up-to-date. Appropriate confidentiality protocols must be established and implemented. Every day, each consultant must update files, summarize data collected, report insights uncovered, and show progress made against the project plan. Project leaders and engagement managers must be able to access the files and know exactly where things stand on each issue under investigation and the status of each deliverable. On large engagements this is key to synthesizing findings and ultimately to making valid recommendations. Effective, professional consultants standardize their knowledge management practices and develop efficient processes for their implementation.

Administrative Systems

In addition to knowledge management, consultants are expected to use standard administrative systems in their work. Sometimes they are expected to use their clients' systems. Consultants must have their own systems for planning, budgeting, controlling, and reporting progress throughout an engagement. This is especially important during the stage of building deliverables, when important decisions are being made across a host of issues critical to the delivery of a solution.

Usually deliverables are built according to a plan of agreed-upon specifications and against deadlines. Consultants must demonstrate that they have detailed project plans and can deliver according to the plan. Client management will accept missed deadlines if they believe there are good reasons (especially those caused by the client). Consultants must be able to show the detail, data, and documentation, and explain deviations from the plan. They must be able to provide good reasons for their actions and, when necessary, be able to effectively negotiate new goals with client management.

Project Meetings

We have already looked at the basics of running a good meeting. Needless to say, clients expect consultants to be able to lead meetings effectively. Kick-off meetings, technical reviews, project status meetings, and review meetings with management and steering committee updates all must be handled professionally, following the guidelines outlined earlier in this chapter.

Conflict Resolution

From time to time consultants may face severe human relations problems with people on engagements and projects. There may be significant performance problems with team members, disputes with client management, disagreements about scope and specifications, or the need to deal with dramatic new expectations that arise on any long-term project. Consultants and the team leaders have an obligation to handle conflicts professionally. It is a good practice for consultants to assume responsibility for conflict resolution and to demonstrate how to resolve problems in a timely and professional manner. This is part of the added value that consultants bring to their work. A consultant can be more skillful at conflict management if the origins and sources of conflict are understood (Kilmann, 2004).

Generally, the origin of tension between people can be traced back to three factors: miscommunication, blocked intentions, or unfulfilled expectations. Tension turns into disputes when people disagree over four issues: goals, values, methods, and facts (Schmidt & Tannenbaum, 1960). Tension can occur if the one party suffers from *automatic negative thinking syndrome,* that is, having "ANTS" on the brain. Another possible cause of conflict is an inappropriate response stemming from low emotional intelligence. When we lack consciousness of the sources and consequences of our negativity, which in turn produces problems, we need POISE coaching. Conflict resolution requires clarifying what the disagreement is about (goals, values, and so on) and the source of the tension (communications, intentions, or expectations), understanding the impact of the conflict, patching up hurt feelings, searching for and reaching mutually agreeable solutions to the conflict, and confirming a commitment to implement the solutions.

Professional consultants know that conflict must never get in the way of building trust and long-term relationships. Sometimes, just keeping those two goals (trust and relationships) in mind can help the client, and especially the consultant, to overcome emotional barriers and frustrations. The key is to simply acknowledge that there are more important issues at stake than satisfying short-term, selfish motivations. In the midst of an intense emotional dispute, such "superordinate goals" can shift our way of thinking from always focusing on what is wrong to focusing on what is possible—from *cannot do* to *must do*; from thoughtlessly criticizing others with ANTS, to focusing on nurturing relationships.

Poor Performance

Generally speaking, clients care less about the process used by their consultants than they do about the results. To some extent, clients will even allow subpar performance for a while if they know performance problems are being resolved internally by the project team. However, clients do expect their consultants to resolve the performance problems, and, if it involves the client directly, to be a role model for the problem-resolution process. Team members make mistakes. Team members do not always do what they are supposed to do. Team members can and do perform poorly. As discussed earlier in this chapter, the answer to poor performance is coaching. Poor performance cannot be tolerated or allowed to worsen; it must be dealt with in a straightforward, adult manner. It is the obligation of all consultants on the team, as well as the team leader, to take the coaching responsibility seriously.

Celebration

Normally consultants celebrate twice: when they first win the business, and when they complete an engagement. Unfortunately, with all of the pressures and stresses that accompany many assignments, consultants do not celebrate enough and may celebrate only once—on winning a piece of business. Even that celebration may be truncated when someone faces reality and points out that *now they must deliver the business*!

Occasionally clients may be generous and ask their consultants to lunch or dinner to review and debrief the production of important deliverables; however, usually they do not. So it is up to the consultants to make sure some kind of celebration occurs. Celebrations are important moments to reinforce cultural values, boost morale, and build team cohesion. It can be an enjoyable experience to enjoy a few drinks and have a few laughs with colleagues while reviewing how deliverables were produced. It can be a great source of learning, insight, and even creativity that can be carried forward to the next deliverable, and ultimately the engagement overall.

Conclusion

This chapter has focused largely on important tasks in project management including the political aspects of getting project work accomplished. We have tied this discussion closely to stage three because very good project management skills are essential for building and producing deliverables, and it is the most complex part of consulting, fraught with potential tensions and barriers to success.

Now we are working inside the client's organization. That organization is *not* a consulting firm full of semi-independent entrepreneurial consultants with highly specialized analytical skills. More often than not, client organizations are very large, complex, politically intense bureaucracies full of employees trying to get ahead (or to simply hold onto their jobs). Competition among employees is high, pressure to produce results is constant, and most feel overwhelmed with the amount of work to be done. This puts a premium on consultants having very good people skills.

Building and producing deliverables requires being able to become a temporary "employee" of the client's organization while retaining professional distance. It requires being politically smart by advocating and advising while listening and being diplomatic. Producing deliverables demands the use of tested procedures and protocols that ensure steady progress toward milestones and expected outcomes. Building deliverables requires teamwork, a bias for action, collaborative behavior, building consensus, and an ability to handle complex problems amid confusion and inadequate information.

This stage of consulting is a logical extension of the roles, tasks, and competencies required in stages one and two of the consulting process and draws on the entire set of core interpersonal skills already mentioned in previous chapters.

Because consultants are commonly, to a degree, resented by clients, consultants must maintain a positive, can-do attitude. It is important that consultants resist cynicism about client attitudes and positively relate to the client's business, organizational culture, internal language, and ways of working.

Consultants need a full range of professional, technical, business, and interpersonal skills during this stage, as they are commonly applied among a diverse workforce and often across all business functions and levels of management.

Stage three, building and producing deliverables, is the time when clients scrutinize every aspect of consultants' roles and competencies—and when consultants demonstrate their true level of professionalism as they show the results of their work in the face of client resistance, criticism, skepticism, and caution.

If the work of this stage is done well, however, consultants can move smoothly into the final stage of work: implementing and deploying solutions—the last step to becoming a trusted consultant.

CHAPTER NINE

STAGE FOUR: THE IMPLEMENTING AND DEPLOYING PROCESS

Up to this point a lot has happened in the journey of a consulting engagement. Consultants will have completed the steps of producing a proposal, forming a team, and building interim deliverables. They will have faced the challenges of designing an approach to solving the client's problem, getting people and resources aligned and working, and producing results against budgets and plans. They will have used a range of expertise to understand the issues, gather extensive data, and frame the problem after careful analysis of the issues and facts. They will have developed and validated hypotheses; crafted, tested, and modified deliverables; and finally, presented recommended solutions. The next step is implementation.

Implementation entails taking actions with the client to ensure that they can use the solution to the benefit of their organization. Consultants can render three types of service at this point: (1) offering advice on how to manage the changes in the client's organization as a result of adopting the recommended solution; (2) designing and delivering training that transfers to the client the skills needed to use the developed solution; or (3) working in the client's organization to execute the changes required by the solution.

The extent of consultants' involvement in implementation and deployment varies considerably from firm to firm. Management consultants such as Monitor, Booz, and McKinsey rarely go beyond making recommendations, whereas the business models of Bain and Capgemini emphasize making revenue by implementing their own recommendations in the client's organization.

IT consultants such as Accenture, IBM, and SAP develop practical solutions that they test and deploy for their clients. Training and organization development consultants such as DDI, Forum, and PDI develop and conduct training programs that, in effect, only make recommendations about changes in employee and managerial behavior. Organization development consultants rarely advise company management on what to do, but rather facilitate a process that enables the managers to decide for themselves. Hundreds of specialized firms that redesign and improve any business function or management system, from compensation strategies and benefit systems to lean manufacturing, often implement the changes they recommend.

A great deal of implementation work takes place in meetings, conferences, and training rooms where consultants facilitate discussions to help clients take ownership of the solution. Presenting recommendations to clients has its own set of challenges; the reader is encouraged to consult Rasiel & Friga (2001) for help with this important skill set. Because testing and administrative matters are mostly solution-specific, in this chapter we focus on the more general consulting issue of deploying change: advising clients on change management and enabling them to deploy solutions through training. We concentrate on the following topics:

- Change management
- Implementation strategies
- Skills transfer
- Measurement of customer satisfaction

Stage Four Competencies: Implementing and Deploying

Table 9.1 shows the three competencies and twelve behavioral practices associated with the implementing stage in the consulting cycle. This stage involves a number of important tasks, including two different but related opportunities to give advice. The first, when solutions are deployed by the client (not by the consultant), is advising the client on how to implement such solutions in their organization and can be a worthwhile way to add value. Second, consultants must search for the right moment at the end of an engagement to advise the client on additional issues or problems

TABLE 9.1 IMPLEMENTING COMPETENCIES AND BEHAVIORAL PRACTICES

Purpose	Stage	Tasks	Role	Outcome
Exceed Client Expectations	Implementing	• Testing • Change Management • Administration • Renewal/New Business	× Deploying	= Solution

Competencies	Practices
Testing and Refining	1. Ensures that solutions are tested before final delivery 2. Disseminates information so project teams can refine deliverables 3. Actively seeks feedback about the client's satisfaction with the consulting solution 4. Encourages people to try to exceed the client's expectations
Managing Change	5. Encourages continuous improvement in consulting work methods and processes 6. Explains any changes needed in the client's business and why the changes are necessary 7. Helps clients to manage the change process called for by the new solution 8. Ensures that people are trained in the knowledge and skills needed to use the solution
Closure and Renewal	9. Develops appropriate materials that document the solution 10. Ensures resolution of any project administrative problems with the client 11. Conducts client meetings with diplomacy and tact in a way that grows the consulting relationship 12. Helps clients to understand other business problems in their organization

that need solving. Assuming the project has been successful, such advice is often given after measuring customer satisfaction, and it is a natural way to position the consultant to bid on new consulting opportunities. In a trusted consultant relationship, this proposal opportunity is often automatic.

In addition to the *closure and renewal* competency tasks shown in the table, consultants must ensure that final expenses have been accounted for, the final invoice is submitted to the client, client feedback has been sought, and a final discussion about engagement satisfaction has been held with the client. Administration also includes updating the consultant's files to ensure that the firm's client files are current.

Finally, stage four ends with an internal review of lessons learned by the consultants on the project team with a senior manager in charge of the firm's practice area responsible for the client work. All best practices and learning from the entire engagement, including strengths and weaknesses, become part of the firm's database of knowledge, shared with colleagues for future use.

Managing Change

One useful service that consultants can provide to clients is helping them think through the barriers and drivers of change in their organization, especially when clients choose to implement solutions themselves. Our advice can add a lot of value in this challenging area. One reason implementation is so difficult is that all organizations have a natural tendency to resist change. As introduced in Chapter Eight as a topic for coaching, resistance can arise for many reasons, such as fear of disruption to routines or political disruptions, ideological differences, or high levels of anxiety (Burke, 2008; Hambrick & Cannella, 1989); here we will consider a few of the most common causes:

1. *Bureaucratic Routines.* Organizations create rules, procedures, routines, work processes, and habits that are designed to create efficiency and productivity. By increasing the stability of operations (that is, reducing variability and change), management produces more efficiency, which in turn enables employees to learn how to do things better and faster. Over time, work efficiencies become routine and predictable. Because routine and predictable work processes can lower costs, businesses often resist changing how things are done because lower costs create opportunities to lower prices. This allows companies to be more competitive and increase profit margins, thereby increasing revenue and market share. This string of logic is a business and managerial imperative, the essence of which creates resistance to change—which consultants must deal with. Even change that improves the efficiency of work processes must be presented convincingly.

2. *Political Resistance.* People often believe that they are likely to lose something of value when changes are made. Employees fear they will incur a loss of status, power, income, responsibility, or self-esteem. Managers and leaders may feel threatened by solutions that require (perhaps even demand) a change in the way their organization functions: the way it makes decisions, how it manufactures products, and how it coordinates resources. Changes may demand a new management structure and new people. In such situations, in order to maintain their power and influence, people often create unreasonable or unnecessary barriers to change, resist

by restricting access to things needed by consultants, manipulate the availability or accuracy of information, or engage in behind-the-scenes criticism of the consultant's work.

3. *Ideological Resistance.* Employees may have deeply held values that they believe will be violated by the changes and new solutions. Their objections are often intellectually honest and genuine; they may be grounded in philosophical differences tied to their belief systems and core values about what is right and just. As a result, such employee resistance will continue until their voices are heard, accommodations are made, or—in the absence of the preceding mediations—they give up hope and leave the organization.

4. *Emotional Resistance.* Employees may resist because they simply dislike any change to their routines and familiar work situation. They may not understand the changes and why they must be made. They may have an emotional reaction because they are nervous about their ability to learn the new procedures, language, equipment, or technology. Their level of anxiety may seem irrational, even blind, to the outside observer. But for such employees, resistance may be the only means by which they can handle their anxiety.

Despite so many potential philosophical, emotional, and practical change management problems, consultants still must implement their solutions, even as the solutions disturb and disorient the organization, its employees, and its management. It's only natural that some people deal with such disturbances by resisting the recommended change. When the resistance is strong enough, deployment of the consultants' solutions may be delayed, denied, or perhaps even defeated. It should be apparent that at this stage all of the technical expertise that enabled the consultants to produce a brilliant solution is of little help. Resistance is rarely a technical problem; it is usually a people problem. As we have argued from the beginning of this book, consultants' *people skills* are critical for completing successful consulting engagements.

Because change and change management lie at the heart of consulting, consultants are in fact change agents. Consultants are *catalysts of change.* They must communicate to help people understand *what* changes are needed and, most important, *why* they are needed. Consultants need to provide a picture of the future state that people can see and understand. They must show people the plan to achieve the necessary changes and provide training, counseling, and support that helps the client organization recognize and overcome its resistance. Consultants must give people the skills they need to successfully implement the solution.

Models and Concepts

The literature on managing change is replete with concepts, steps, models, anecdotes, stories, and checklists. They come from academic researchers, popular business writers, consultants, and business leaders. Recommendations about managing change range from simple short list of steps to complex, multivariate models; from practical best practices to rather abstract concepts drawn from general systems theory of organizations.

A useful review of managing change can be found in Burke (2008); he outlines the history of organization change interventions; the characteristics and requirements of evolutionary versus revolutionary change; change strategies and tactics at three levels of analysis: individual, group, and total systems change; and the role of leadership. He discusses the shift from theories drawn from the physical sciences to those drawn from the life sciences and consultants' need to understand the complexities of large-scale change management. The shift in thinking and understanding requires consultants to use different tools and techniques, and Burke concludes that although we are in our infancy in understanding how to change organizations as living, complex organisms, it is clear that real and lasting change, at any level of analysis, requires an open systems perspective and systems thinking. Consultants specializing in organizational change will find the ideas discussed by Burke to be rewarding—and even challenging. Consultants whose primary consulting service is not change management can use various models to advise their clients on how to work through the stages of change in their organization at the individual, group, and organization levels. For example, Kotter (1996), based on his research of many companies' change efforts, suggests the following steps to manage change:

1. Establish a sense of urgency.
2. Create a guiding coalition.
3. Develop a vision and strategy.
4. Communicate the change vision.
5. Empower employees for broad-based action.
6. Generate short-term wins.
7. Consolidate gains and produce more change.
8. Anchor new approaches in the culture.

Tichy and Sherman (1993), based on their work at General Electric (U.S.), formulated a three-phased model for both organizational change and changing individual employees:

1. *Awaken.* Communicate the new reality of the business environment and the need to change in order to survive.
2. *Envision.* Define, explain, and communicate the new kind of organization needed in terms of structure, culture, systems, leadership, and management practices.
3. *Rearchitect.* Redesign and deploy the new strategy, structure, systems culture, social, and political dynamics of the organization.

Bridges (1986, 2009) links organizational change to individual human transitions. This transition is a psychological process that takes a great deal of time for employees to work through and is not always a rational, logical process. Consultants must facilitate the process with sensitivity and understanding. Bridges explains how individual employees go through transitions in three phases:

1. *Ending.* A process of surrendering the past, with all of its comforts, familiarity, certainty, routines, and emotional stability.
2. *Wilderness.* A kind of "no man's land" of competing emotions, conflicting thoughts, and positive and negative feelings, reflecting both the loss of the old ways and the excitement of future benefits.
3. *New Beginnings.* Acceptance of the changes and new ways of being in role and job; learning new skills, seeing the benefits and gains, and developing greater psychological confidence.

Making Change Management Part of the Engagement

We believe that executives and managers need help in the change management process. Regardless of which models and best practices consultants use to guide their clients through the steps, if consultants personally provide these services, they can be paid for this work. It is a good practice to ensure that change management is discussed from the beginning of a consulting engagement. The issues and challenges of solution implementation can be discussed throughout the four stages of consulting, from needs assessment and the proposal on, so that by solution-deployment time the client's organization can deal with any resistance, accept the need to change, and be receptive to implementing the solution. In other words, consultants can advise their clients on how to:

- Think through the issues and challenges of deployment
- Plan the change management steps
- Get their organization ready for change
- Implement the steps in the change plan

- Be a role model and champion for change
- Help employees overcome their natural tendencies to resist change
- Measure the success of the change management process

Managing change is a crucial stage in the consulting process. Not only does it ensure the successful deployment of a solution that solves a client problem, but it is also proof of a consultant's value, skills, and abilities. This significantly raises the client's confidence and increases the likelihood of getting repeat business. As we have reinforced throughout the book, such values and competencies (in this case, managing change) lay the foundation for consultants to build long-term relationships and become trusted advisors.

Implementation Strategies

We discussed previously that stage three is the most challenging part of consulting. However, for a consulting firm, the implementation stage is strategic for long-term success. According to business strategy lore, it is better to have a poor strategy excellently implemented than to have an excellent strategy poorly implemented. This is so because a company's strategy will eventually become well known and transparent, disseminated by (of all people) consultants and academics. Given that the competition can eventually copy a company's business strategy, the only way to create a sustainable competitive advantage is to implement the strategy (be it poor or excellent) better than the competition. Companies that had excellent strategies *and* excellent implementation, such as in the airline industry (Southwest Airlines), the automobile industry (Toyota and Honda), the farm equipment industry (Komatsu), and the photographic industry (Fujitsu), had competitors (America West, General Motors, Caterpillar, and Kodak, respectively) that copied their strategies but were unable to implement them equally successfully. In general, companies that consistently executed their strategies better than their competitors have been very hard to outperform. Therefore getting the implementation strategy right is a critical success factor—and this is an area in which consultants can offer a great deal of beneficial advice.

Several practical tools are available that consultants can use to give their clients advice and support on implementation strategies. These include project management strategies, transformation mapping and activity fit, and recent work published on the principles of successful strategy execution.

Project Management Strategies

Managers and executives usually think about implementation in terms of traditional management practices. They start with long-term goals and then devise a strategy for how to achieve the goals. Then they create initiatives and projects that reflect short-term objectives, which are, in turn, delegated to specific people who are held accountable for delivering results. Project leaders create project structures (work plans) composed of specific tasks, task owners, timetables, activities, and deliverables. Individuals do their work, and the project team meets periodically to assess their progress and to judge where each individual stands in relation to project goals. The meeting addresses problems and how to take care of them; it also identifies new opportunities from the completed portion of the overall project work.

As discussed in Chapter Eight, traditional thinking about project management strategies has proven to work well. Consultants who adopt this linear, logical, analytical, deductive implementation strategy in their own work can advise their clients to use the same thinking and tools. In some situations they may need to educate their clients on this process and train them on how to use it in their clients' organizations. A second strategy for thinking about implementation is "change mapping" or "transformation mapping."

Transformation Mapping

Another tool to planning an effective implementation is what the consultants at the Capgemini consulting firm call "transformation mapping." or "T-mapping." It begins with a fact-based analysis of the client's current state, the "as-is" condition; then identifies the future state to be accomplished, the "should-be" condition. Figure 9.1 depicts typical T-maps showing the current (From) and future (To) states, categories of change, and schedules.

The transformation mapping (T-map) technique can be developed by a steering committee, a management team, or project teams responsible for implementing change. There are a number of important advantages to using it. A T-map provides focus and guidance for specific areas of work as well as ease in managing the implementation actions in sequence and in relation to one another. Accountability and control are thus enhanced. A T-map also provides an overall vision that helps everyone to see the big picture and has the benefits of being simple, visual, easy to understand,

FIGURE 9.1 TRANSFORMATION MAPPING

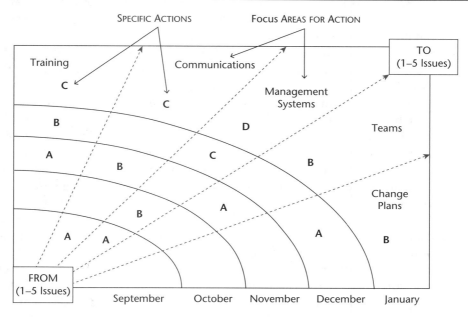

Transformation Map for New Customer Focus Strategy

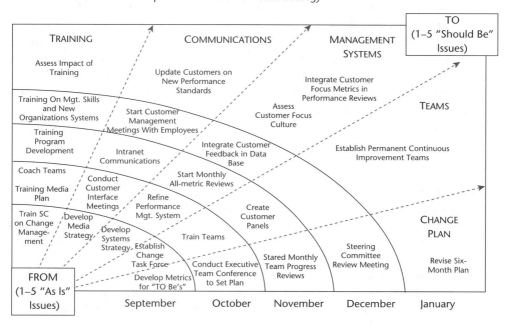

and easy to communicate. Transformation maps show a brief description of "From ("As Is") and "To" ("To Be"), the target areas for action, specific actions within each target area, and a timeline for each action. This visual picture is three-dimensional. It enables one to see an integrated set of actions *within* a target area as well as the actions *across* target areas, within a prescribed *timeline*. The idea of a set of integrated actions is consistent with the thinking of Michael Porter (2009), whose work in strategy formulation and implementation shows the importance of making sure that all of a business's strategic activities fit with each other. By extension, he means that successful implementation of a business strategy requires achieving three criteria: (1) all of the business activities contribute directly to achieving the strategy (there is nothing superfluous or wasteful); (2) the activities mutually reinforce each other, thereby achieving synergy and greater benefits; and (3) each activity is optimized. Porter's concept of "fit" and successful implementation is consistent with the thinking behind transformation mapping and has general applicability to the successful deployment of any consulting solution.

It is a relatively straightforward exercise for consultants to conduct a transformation mapping session with a client. It can serve a number of purposes. The end result is that a team from the client's company will understand the bigger picture *and* the micro requirements for the changes required by the consultant's solution. It can also be a team-building opportunity, wherein the client's implementation team develops a high level of commitment to implementing the changes required in the organization. An equally important outcome is that the implementation team takes ownership of the solution—a necessary condition for dealing with resistance and any post-implementation problems. Also, the concept of "activity fit" and use of T-mapping are consistent with the literature on the requirements of successful change (Burke, 2008).

Execution of Strategy

A third perspective on how to help clients implement solutions is from the work of Bossidy and Charan (2002). They describe what they call the building blocks of successful execution (implementation) of strategy. Figure 9.2 shows the blocks as *areas of focus and action*: (1) nine aspects of the leader's personal agenda and attention, (2) two major areas of change, and (3) four organizational systems and processes that need alignment. Successful implementation requires allying the input, content, and output of each of these areas of focus to ensure they are enabling the organization to fulfill

FIGURE 9.2 THE BUILDING BLOCKS OF SUCCESSFUL IMPLEMENTATION

LEADER'S FOCUS	CHANGE FOCUS	ORGANIZATION FOCUS
• Know Yourself • Know Your People • Know Your Industry • Follow Through • Insist on Trust • Insist in Reality • Set Clear Goals • Set Priorities • Reward Doers	• Change the Culture • Transform People's Values, Beliefs, and Behavior	• Place Right People in Right Job • Refine Performance Evaluations • Develop Succession Planning • Develop People

Source: Adapted from *EXECUTION: The Discipline of Getting Things Done*, by Larry Bossidy and Ram Charan, copyright 2002. Used by permission of Crown Business, a division of Random House, Inc.

its strategic goals. Bossidy and Charan remind us that all consultants can and should engage their clients in discussions of the substance of each of the building blocks to ensure that once consulting solutions have been developed, they can be successfully deployed, with the support of the organization's leaders, infrastructure, and change directives.

Strategy and management consultants such as McKinsey often finish their work with a presentation to senior management on strategic options and recommendations for the next steps, in what McKinsey calls the "blue book" (Rasiel, 1999). At this point, less effective consultants can simply turn over the implementation of the strategy to the client management and let them worry about change management. Or they can engage clients in a deep discussion of the keys to successful execution. Consultants who have achieved the status of *trusted advisor* will do this automatically.

With their deep knowledge of the firm, trusted advisors can provide a great deal of valuable insight and advice to their clients by helping analyze such things as

- Organizational pockets of political support and resistance
- Areas that are prone to blockages and bottlenecks
- Opinion leaders who support or prevent successful implementation
- People who are change leaders
- The drivers of and barriers to successful implementation (using a "force field" analysis) (French & Bell, 1978)

In the journey of becoming a trusted advisor, consultants take stage four very seriously and can be effective in giving clients advice on (1) how to implement their recommendations or (2) deploying the solution they have built for their client. The advice takes the form of helping a client think through implementation issues, designing a skills transfer event, or running a deployment workshop. The concepts, principles, and tools of project management, T-maps, and building blocks can be used to add value. This can be a refreshing advantage for clients who could use the help at a time when they are striving to achieve results under the pressures of politics, time, and budgets. And as we have noted, it can also be a natural extension of the service offered by a consulting firm.

Skills Transfer

Another service essential for successful implementation is designing, developing, and delivering a workshop to train client employees on how to use a solution—as well as, perhaps, managing change and various implementation strategies. Training requirements abound, as employees may have to learn a new software application, certain behavioral skills, their role in a business strategy, how to conduct a performance review or ensure compliance with new laws, or the features and benefits of a new product. To convey the requisite knowledge and skills, we need to deliver what Microsoft Consulting Services calls a "capabilities" or skills transfer event.

It is not the purpose of this book or within its scope to describe the many types of actual solutions developed by consultants. But we can examine skills transfer as the event *common to all consulting* at this stage in the consulting cycle, in which solutions are recommended and deployed. This is a *reoccurring event* in consulting, and it is an area ripe for improvement by all consultants.

In this section we review the principles behind how to organize a workshop or skills transfer event, based on the common denominator of all training: *how people learn*. From this understanding, consultants will be able to give advice to clients about how to design skills transfer or do a good job of organizing and running training sessions themselves.

Program Design

All training programs should be designed to achieve a set of objectives, which are best stated in behavioral terms. Objectives bring focus to the content to be covered and force the consultant to think about what par-

TABLE 9.2 SAMPLE BEHAVIORAL OBJECTIVES FOR A TRAINING PROGRAM ON CONSULTING

Topic	Behavioral Objectives
Process of Consulting:	Describe the stages, roles, tasks, and outcomes of the consulting process.
	Understand the merits of research methods.
Project Identification and Problem Framing:	Conduct a needs analysis.
	Define the scope of a project.
	Distinguish different risks in a project.
	Write a consulting proposal.
Client Relationship Management:	Use listening skills.
	Administer a client satisfaction metric.
Gaining Solution Acceptance:	Describe reasons why clients resist change.
	Assess the factors that make an excellent presentation.

ticipants will be able to do as result of completing the program and to design the program to ensure that this happens. Table 9.2 shows an example of topics and behavioral objectives for a skills transfer program on consulting.

Broadly speaking, consultants who design and deliver training programs use the following principles in their work:

- Programs are governed by a unifying theme (program purpose).
- Programs are organized into self-contained, discrete topics (program objectives).
- Each topic or objective is defined as specific knowledge and skills needed for successful performance (program modules).
- Modules are organized into a logical, integrated sequence.
- Each module contains:
  - A definition of the skill
  - An explanation of why it is important to learn
  - A discussion of how it fits with other skill sets in the program
  - Examples of good and bad use of the skill
  - The learning methods used to acquire the skill
  - The learning methods linked to learning styles and the experiential learning cycle (see the following section)

Finally, participants accomplish behavioral objectives by acquiring certain knowledge and practicing specific steps and techniques. Skill levels increase with practice, and, if desirable, metrics for each skill and objective can be built into the design. Measuring skill levels before, during, and after the program provides a valid way to measure the program's success.

Learning Styles

An understanding of the concept of learning styles is central to creating and delivering a skills transfer event. The concept is related to, but separate from, the traditional pedagogical typologies of teaching children and Knowles' concept of adult learning known as *andragogy* (Knowles, 1980; Knowles, Holton, & Swanson, 2005). It is different from personality profiles such as DiSC (Inscape, 2012), the Myers-Briggs Type Indicator (Myers, 1980), and NEO-PI (Costa & McCrae, 1985). It is also different from conflict management styles (Thomas & Kilmann, 1974), employee development described by Situational Leadership (Hersey, Blanchard, & Johnson 2007), and established models of motivation and social styles.

The concept of learning styles has its origins in the work of researchers Honey and Mumford (1992) in the UK and David Kolb (1984) in the US. Their models are similar but they each use distinct nomenclature. Honey and Mumford acknowledge their indebtedness to Kolb's model of experiential learning, which shows that we can understand how people learn on two dimensions: Active—Passive versus Feelings—Concepts. Figure 9.3 shows Kolb's two dimensions of learning that combine to form four learning styles: *accommodator, diverger, assimilator,* and *converger.*

Kolb's well-validated instrument (the Learning Styles Inventory) measures people's learning preferences and learning styles. Because each of us learns, to varying degrees, by *feeling, watching, thinking,* and *doing,* we

FIGURE 9.3 LEARNING DIMENSIONS AND STYLES

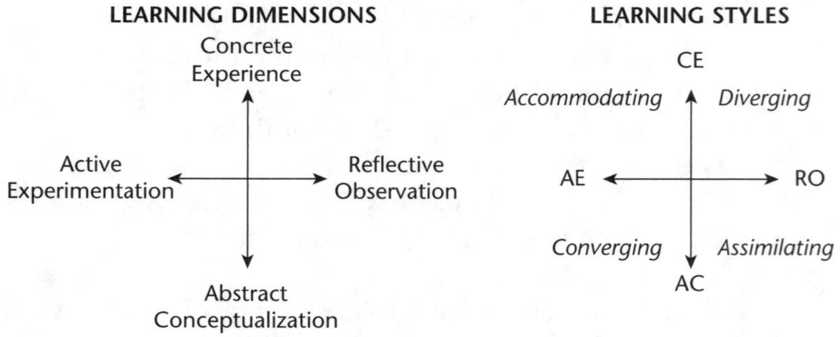

Source: Adapted from D. Kolb, *Learning Style Inventory,* 2008, with permission from Hay Group.

can construct a skills transfer (training) event with methods that use each style of learning, and thereby enhance learning in a training program.

In general, different learning styles have different characteristics that draw from the two basic active-passive and feeling-thinking dimensions. Kolb has found that certain styles gravitate toward certain careers. Furthermore, problem solving and decision making can be enhanced with a group that has a mix of learning styles. In consulting it is a best practice to diversify learning styles among the consultants on a team. This improves the group dynamics, problem framing, analysis, and discussion, and ultimately it produces better results.

Most skills transfer is conducted in group training sessions. There is ample evidence that in all training sessions there will be a mix of learning styles among the trainees in the room. Therefore, although it would be impractical to customize the skills transfer process and method to each individual, it is possible to design training events to maximize the learning for the *whole group* by using a wide range of learning methods. Mixing learning methods appeals to the motivations, preferences, and needs of the different styles of learning of the people in the skills transfer session; this makes the training much more effective. Table 9.3 shows the link between learning modes and styles and the many different kinds of learning methods that can be used during skills transfer. Training and skills transfer is an

TABLE 9.3 TRAINING METHODS BY LEARNING MODES AND STYLES

Learning Styles and Modes	Training Methods
Accommodator Combines learning by concrete experience (feeling) and active experimentation (doing)	Case examples Case discussion Role plays Experiential learning Trials
Diverger Combines learning by concrete experience (feeling) and reflective observation (watching)	Brainstorming Team learning Lecturing Sampling Site visits
Assimilator Combines learning by learning by reflective observation (watching) and abstract conceptualization (thinking)	Modeling Reading Documentation Lectures Data analysis
Converger Combines learning by abstract conceptualization (thinking) and active experimentation (doing)	Simulations Model building Role plays Scenario debates

important aspect of change management. When training people, the consultant is adding new knowledge and new skills and changing the client's behavior so the trainees can use the solution being deployed. The design and delivery of change management (training) events can be significantly enhanced if consultants take into consideration some instructional design principles related to learning styles.

During stage four when we are trying to deploy solutions effectively, remember the fact that different people have different learning preferences has many implications. First, consultants must realize that trainees' motivation to learn and the effectiveness of how they learn is directly related to their style of learning. Second, in a group of trainees there will be a range of learning preferences. Third, not only do trainees have learning preferences, but they also prefer training methods and techniques that fit their learning style. Fourth, because people's learning styles differ, it follows that a skills transfer must include a wide range of learning techniques and methods.

Broadly speaking, change management is a strategic time for consultants when they can use skills transfer events tactically to demonstrate additional value and service. Exhibit 9.1 shows a set of well-established

---

Exhibit 9.1 Learning Principles for Use in Skills Transfer

- For group learning, mix the learning methods.
- Not everyone learns the same way as the instructor.
- Motivation to learn rises and falls around the experiential learning cycle.
- Ask learners how they prefer to learn.
- Teach as well as coach (tell, guide, question, facilitate).
- Use learners' senses: feeling, watching, thinking, doing.
- Periodically ask about learners' progress.
- Develop skills from existing capabilities.
- Work from familiar to unfamiliar material.
- Build from simple to more complex.
- Never knowingly embarrass learners; be tactful.
- Realize that questions are as powerful as answers.
- Expect progress, not perfection.
- Provide positive feedback often (catch learners doing something right).
- Remember: Failing less is a positive improvement!

learning principles to add such value, if consultants want to design and deliver outstanding training.

Experiential Learning Cycle

An important concept underlying learning and change is the *experiential learning cycle* (Osland, Turner, Kolb, & Rubin, 2010). This concept defines effective learning as a process involving four steps: experience, concept, generalization, and application. To be effective, all skills transfer events should have modules designed and delivered using the four steps. When skills transfer events are designed with the four steps built into each module, a complete spectrum of learning styles is used. For example, a training event can be designed in the following way:

1. Give the trainees something to experience using a role play, simulation, presentation, or case discussion that actively reaches their emotions.
2. Draw out concepts from the trainees' experience in step 1 with questions that require them to reflect on what they learned from the experience. Enable them to conceptualize the experience.
3. Take the concepts that the trainees share and make generalizations to similar situations they may find in other business organizations—especially, if possible, their own.
4. Give the trainees the opportunity to apply the concepts directly to their own roles and responsibilities by asking them how they would use their skills, insights, and concepts to improve their own work.
5. Finish the learning module by asking the trainees to practice using the concepts and skills in some aspect of their own role and job.

In summary, a skillful consultant will be able to advise clients that skills transfer is an important application of change management and that learning styles play a critical role in making the event effective. The consultant may simply advise the client to use the principles and methods for different styles of learning during the training, or they may take those principles and methods into consideration if the scope of the work includes the consultant's designing and delivering the training. Finally, the principles of learning can be applied to any kind of skills transfer event, even to one that is strictly a presentation of findings with recommendations. Although presentations seem to appeal only to the intellect, such an event can be designed to be interactive and experiential, using techniques to engage the audience with questions, dramatizations, examples, various media, and humor.

Measuring Customer Satisfaction

Clients start judging the effectiveness of our consulting from the first moment they meet us, and they keep doing so right up to the last handshake. Savvy consultants know that it is important to constantly assess clients' perception of value and to be conscious of these judgments throughout the four stages of a consulting engagement.

We discussed expectations in Chapter Five, and it should now be abundantly clear why conversations about managing expectations throughout the consulting engagement are so important. Assessing and managing expectations cannot and should not be left to the end. A continuous, conscious, and deliberate alertness is needed to ensure that expectations are aligned. Only then will we be able to make needed adjustments and when we measure customer satisfaction, know if we exceeded them. Thus, we must keep asking ourselves:

- To what extent have we achieved the expectations set forth in the proposal?
- What issues or problems, if any, remain unresolved?
- How can we measure the client's level of satisfaction with our service?

David Maister (1993) has helped us to understand what clients want from their consultants throughout the cycle. They expect four basic and important things: availability, affability, ability, and (based on the consulting experience of this author) accountability. Those consultants who really understand these four expectations and discipline themselves to live by them will increase customer satisfaction levels; build solid, long-term client relationships; and, in all likelihood, acquire more business.

Availability

The first high-priority expectation, availability, is strange and somewhat paradoxical in the consulting context. Although consultants naturally assume that their expertise is the thing that clients prize the most, it turns out this is not necessarily true. What clients *really* want is their consultants to be available to them. They want their consultants to be accessible and present when they are needed. This stems from the fact that clients are under pressure and feel exposed; they feel vulnerable to the political threats in their organization. Consequently, what clients cherish is the ability to pick up the telephone or send an e-mail to "speak" directly with the consultant to deal with an immediate problem. They do not want to wait until the consultant finds time to get back to them; they most assuredly do not want to get a recorded menu of options, only to be asked to leave a voice message or call the consultant's assistant. What they want is to be able to speak with the consultant immediately! However, because clients also live in the real world and know that consultants are not always immediately available, they will live with a level of availability that is less than their ideal. With this in mind, it is an excellent consulting practice to find a way to let every client know:

- Where you are
- How you can be reached
- When you can be reached

Giving clients information about where the consultant can be reached is a relatively easy thing to do, but with a busy consulting schedule it is easy to overlook and forget. Professionalism means, in part, empathizing with one's client's personal circumstances and organizational situation. Effective consultants make an effort to give every active client that information, especially when the consultant is on international trips. Clients usually do not call unless they have an emergency, but they require the comfort of assurance that, should an emergency arise (and these are, by definition, unexpected), the consultant can be reached. If Maister is right and it means that much to clients, consultants should make a great effort to be available to them.

Affability

Clients want to work with people whom they enjoy working with and can trust. Being enjoyable to work with means being a warm and friendly person with a sense of humor, being honest, being serious-minded when that's called for, and being able to focus on the client rather than only on oneself. The enjoyability factor is related to being at ease and relaxed around the client. This includes being able to put others at ease and to relieve interpersonal tension with "small talk" to break the ice and help people relax. Being warm and friendly comes from being pleasant, having a positive attitude, looking people in the eye, smiling, and keeping a conversation going with a natural rhythm. It is reflected in our style in conversation, how we explore ideas and debate issues, and our ease of discussion. Affability means that when we communicate we convey that we take the work very seriously and have a passion for it, yet do not take ourselves too seriously.

As important as affability is, clients may or may not trust someone just on the basis of their friendliness. Trust is not a function of our sense of humor or pleasantness. Those attributes help, but the sources of trust are credibility, integrity, reliability, authenticity, truthfulness, and social intelligence (our ability to act appropriately in the context of the client's situation and organization).

Trust increases when what we say is *credible*—grounded in facts, reason, logic, expertise, and experience. The essence of *integrity* is to not be one way with people to their face and another way behind their back. It comes from operating from an internal set of positive values and principles so that our private, inner self is the same as our public self. This is what having "character" means. Clients often have a good sense of our integrity and seek (even unconsciously) to judge whether we have character or not. *Reliability* follows from integrity; it means being consistent in our words and deeds and never breaking a promise or an agreement, whether verbally or in writing. *Authenticity* comes from being honest with ourselves and, when needed, sharing with clients our strengths and weaknesses, our capabilities and shortcomings. Authentic behavior also means putting into words the positive and negative experiences we are having with clients as we work with them (Block, 1981). Effective consultants develop strong *social skills*, communicating with emotional intelligence in ways that make it easy to work with them as they share their experience authentically and give advice, without being arrogant or self-centered.

Affability, then, is a collection of personal character attributes and behaviors that constitute our style of working with people. They add up to our personality. At this juncture, take a moment to reflect on your personality. Ask yourself:

- Do I have a consulting personality?
- Do I think I have an affable personality?
- Just how affable am I?
- What have people told me about my personality?
- How does my personality match with my self-concept?
- What areas of my personality need improving?

Ability

Clients want their consultants to be experts. They expect their consultants will be able to perform all of the tasks, responsibilities, and accountabilities put before them. They expect their consultant's expertise to be grounded in broad and deep experience and to be current. They expect a consultant's ability to be appropriate to the problem at hand and for the consultant to give 100 percent of that ability to solving the client's problem.

All consultants have expertise in one area or another. Winning business usually occurs when a consultant's expertise and preparation meet an opportunity. However, it is a mistake to assume that expertise is all that is needed to win business. The client is buying both rational and emotional qualities in a consultant. Ability and expertise are expected, but must be communicated in the following way:

- Demonstrate the breadth and depth of expertise.
- Talk about your expertise passionately without bragging.
- Sense the right time to share knowledge and opinions.
- Connect experience and expertise to the client's problem.
- Balance sharing with careful listening and questioning.

Accountability

Clients expect consultants to be responsible for achieving results and to hold themselves personally accountable for:

- Proposal terms, specifications, and conditions
- How they work in their organization
- Keeping them informed of issues and progress
- Admitting to any problems the consultant has caused
- Being adaptable and flexible
- Keeping their word
- Producing agreed-upon solutions

In a client environment that is undergoing a lot of change, negative politics, or high turnover, clients feel vulnerable and look for consultants who can stabilize things and reduce uncertainty. Clients enjoy working with consultants who can reduce both their workload and their stress. When clients see a high level of personal accountability in a consultant, their confidence level rises, they offer more projects, and they want a long-term relationship.

These four factors of client satisfaction indicate that clients want qualities that are both rational and emotional, both technical and human. They want hard and soft skills: trust, reliability, ownership, accountability, integrity, affability, *and* solid, relevant expertise. Effective consultants understand these dimensions and develop an ability to communicate and demonstrate these attributes accordingly.

Actions When Clients Are Unhappy

What should consultants do if the client is not satisfied? The best answer is simple: "Fix it!" When this situation occurs, it does not necessarily mean the consultant should return fees (unless the situation is an unmitigated disaster). Simply say to the client that you are *willing to do whatever is necessary to make the situation better.* This may mean re-doing or amending a deliverable, redressing various specific problems, or repairing certain relationships. At this juncture, consultants must be thinking about how to improve the client's perception of the work on two dimensions: *what* was done (content) and *how* it was done (process). Problems with both dimensions are obviously more serious. At this point, the consultant's reputation (and possibly the consulting firm's reputation) is at stake. Future business is at risk. All of the goodwill accumulated with many people over a long period of time may be in jeopardy. Therefore, it is critical that consultants do what is practical, prudent, and necessary to solve the problem. Moreover, this may mean doing it for free. If the client is unhappy, and the consultant is obviously at fault, *do not try to negotiate payment to fix the problem. Just fix it.* When things go wrong it is important to keep our eyes on the big picture and focus on the long term. Think of fixing the problem as an investment in the future; a business development expense for future revenue. Therein lies the power of thinking and behaving as a trusted advisor.

When consultants envision themselves as a trusted advisor, they think differently; the conversation changes; attitudes and behavior are modified. If consultants are focused only on short-term gain and maximizing income, it will be frustrating to perform the corrective work. Inevitably, this will show up as negative feelings and attitudes in the client-consultant relationship. Highly effective consultants put the client first and at the center of their work. When things have not turned out as expected, effective consultants do *not* blame the client (*even* if there is some culpability). They "eat humble pie," do what is in the best interest of the client, and do what is right.

Satisfaction Assessment Metrics

Now, at the end of stage four in the consulting process, we have one last opportunity to assess the client's level of satisfaction with our entire consulting effort. There are a number of ways this can be done:

- Face-to-face, in the context of a final status review and administrative closure meetings
- With end users as they provide feedback on solution efficacy
- By assessing the degree of acceptance amongst management of the consultant's solutions and recommendations
- By administering surveys at the end of a consulting engagement

Table 9.4 is an example of the range of questions and issues that can be discussed in meetings with clients or included on a feedback survey questionnaire. Completing survey questionnaires usually requires members of the client organization to rate pertinent engagement issues on a five-point Likert (1967) scale. For example, each item might be rated on a scale from *Poor* to *Excellent* or from *Never* to *Very Frequently*. The

TABLE 9.4 FEEDBACK QUESTIONNAIRE TO ASSESS CLIENT'S PERCEPTIONS

Item	Description
1. Business orientation	Consultant(s) understood the business issues which drove this assignment; s/he maintained a business perspective.
2. Problem definition	Consultant(s) was quick to see the problem and appreciate the issues to be addressed.
3. Development of solutions	Consultant(s) was resourceful in finding a solution; s/he was innovative.
4. Acceptance of solution	Consultant(s) was very convincing in getting acceptance of the solution.
5. Technical ability	I have confidence in the consultant's technical ability.
6. Human relations	Consultant(s) maintained good working relationships with me and my staff; s/he was a pleasure to work with.
7. Personal discipline	Consultant(s) was disciplined in the way s/he worked (such as meetings, urgency, keeping commitments, reliability)
8. Project or assignment management	Consultant(s) worked to a clear project schedule, met deadlines, managed or coordinated team members well, took action to recover from any slippage, and kept me informed of progress.
9. Assignment completion	The assignment was completed satisfactorily; at completion there were no loose ends.
10. Capabilities transfer	Consultant(s) successfully transferred knowledge and skills to those on our team that s/he worked with.
11. Value for money	The assignment represented value for money.
12. Meeting expectations	The assignment met my expectations.
13. Satisfaction	I would use your company's assistance again (if not, please explain).
14. Follow-up	I would like your company's management to contact me, so we can discuss any other issues that need to be addressed.

questionnaire may also include a section of open-ended questions where the client can make written comments to elaborate on, for example, the strengths and weaknesses of the whole project, any aspect of the consulting process, or on any individual consultant.

One question always arises: what to do with the questionnaire data and the summary findings once the survey is finished. A best practice is to *share a summary* of the survey results with the people who provided the data. This could include members of the project team, members of client management (especially those directly affected by the work), the client project leader, consulting firm management, and, when relevant and practical, the client's end users. Sharing the summary expresses interest in the client's views of the feedback and provides closure to the project as a whole.

In training and development consulting, consultants may use different metrics than those used in other kinds of consulting. Figure 9.4 shows a "learning assessment" survey that provides feedback from training participants on the effectiveness of a training delivery. The questions are written as behavioral statements to provide insight into consultants' specific behavior, rather than measuring broad attitudes and abstract qualities. In addition, some training assessments include questions tied directly to the training program *objectives*, so the consultant sees the extent to which the client believes those objectives were achieved.

It is a good practice to keep surveys and questionnaires short, even those administered electronically, as this increases the likelihood of a good response rate. In workshops it is common to get 100-percent response rates from participants. A 40 to 50 percent response rate is considered good in all other contexts.

Consultants are human; we love good news, and it is hard to read about any aspects of service that the client did not like. Yet learning about negative perceptions is the only way to know how well we have performed and where there is room for improvement. Often, in face-to-face meetings, clients provide mostly positive feedback, and although this is nice to hear, it may be of moderate value. Surveys, on the other hand, have the advantage of anonymity, so that client feedback may be more balanced, both positive and negative; both constructive and air-clearing. Effective consultants take the bad with the good and try to learn from both.

Finally, a best practice is to review the customer satisfaction survey at the beginning of an engagement with the entire consulting team, to let them know what will be measured at the end. This helps ensure that all parties will strive to do their very best on all of the dimensions throughout the four stages of the consulting cycle.

FIGURE 9.4 LEARNING ASSESSMENT METRIC FOR CONSULTING TRAINING

<u>**Name(Optional):**</u> _____ **Date:** _____

<u>Overall the workshop was</u> *(please check one):*

1. Excellent ___
2. Above Average ___
3. Average ___
4. Below Average ___
5. Poor ___

<u>**Workshop Focus and Content**</u> *(Circle the number that most closely matches your opinion)*

	Agree		Not Sure		Disagree
The workshop focus was about right:	1	2	3	4	5
Session time was utilized well:	1	2	3	4	5
The content covered can be used in my job:	1	2	3	4	5
I would recommend this program to others:	1	2	3	4	5

The content was Too much ___ About right ___ Too light ___

The speed of the program was: Too fast ___ About right ___ Too slow ___

<u>**Workshop Leader's Effectiveness**</u>

	Agree		Not Sure		Disagree
Had a thorough knowledge of the subject:	1	2	3	4	5
Held my attention:	1	2	3	4	5
Encouraged interaction/discussion:	1	2	3	4	5
Was open to differences of opinion:	1	2	3	4	5

Any other comments about this training?

Conclusion

The competencies in stage four include testing solutions before implementation, refining them during deployment, and post-implementation administrative functions such as documentation, billing, assessing customer satisfaction, and discussing new business opportunities. In addition to this work, at this point in the cycle consultants can provide three basic types of services as part of their original proposal:

- Presenting recommendations
- Providing advice on managing change
- Conducting skills transfer workshops

In this chapter we avoided discussing the largely technical aspects of implementing particular solutions and administrative functions, in favor of focusing on two areas often underdeveloped in many consulting firms: managing change and skills transfer. Each is intended to help the client take ownership of solutions. Each has its own set of skills and key success factors that enhance a consultant's added value.

With these areas well developed, after the project launch the team leader can then hold everyone accountable to do their best. Such accountability will certainly contribute to helping team members become trusted consultants.

Firms not specialized in organization learning consulting would do well to develop stronger competencies in change management and really good capabilities transfer, as a way to create a differential advantage. By developing these organizational learning services, all firms will gain insight into how to ensure that their consulting engagement ends on a high note, based not only on the quality of the solutions produced but also on how well the consulting was conducted from start to finish.

The manner in which we help clients take ownership of solutions says a lot about the quality of our consulting and the lasting effect of our advice. It will reflect how well we have gained the client's trust and their acknowledgment that we produced a solid return on investment.

PART THREE

THE BIGGER PICTURE

CHAPTER TEN

IMPROVING CONSULTING AS A PROFESSIONAL PRACTICE

Marvin Bower, a long-time leader of McKinsey and influential force in the consulting industry, believed professionalism could be achieved by codifying the firm's own "up or out" culture, indoctrinating their employees accordingly, and positively shaping society's acceptance of the industry's professional standing. This, he and his colleagues believed, would be sufficient and comparable to their primary example of professionalism—law firms. From the beginning, consultants fought the concept of an outside state regulatory licensing entity or an industry association setting rules that impinged on their independent governance and practice. Industry firms relied on their cultures and analytical techniques to establish their professional standing. Despite a fifty-year effort to codify firm cultures, define processes, and improve analytic techniques, as well as communicate the global growth and economic importance of management consulting, by the end of the twentieth century consulting still had not achieved the professional status long accorded law in the United States and accounting in Great Britain (McKenna, 2006).

But the premise of this book is that consulting does, in fact, have its own set of professional factors—steps, ethics, rules, standards, values, and skills—that are independent of any particular firm's culture and technology. The factors can be applied to any application of consulting and augment a firm's own proprietary processes and analytical tools. This suggests that achieving professional status is not out of reach. There are two requirements: (1) individuals need clear behavioral definitions of the factors needed for professional development, certification of a person having acquired requisite knowledge, and demonstrated "apprenticeship" experience with an established consulting firm; and (2) firms need mechanisms to regulate entry and unify minimum knowledge and skills for generic practice, and a way to self-regulate professional performance. Perhaps McKinsey used the mechanism of codifying its culture to establish itself as the industry standard and to create differential advantage over its competitors (Peters & Waterman, 1981). But one firm cannot accomplish that in what is essentially a knowledge industry; this requires more collaboration than McKinsey may have been willing to undertake at the time.

Whatever mechanisms are invented and established to achieve professional status, they must accommodate the ever-growing areas of consulting application, similar to the professions of accounting, law, and medicine. This chapter provides a perspective on a way to achieve such accommodation. We describe generic building blocks needed to stabilize and standardize professional preparation yet allow for new areas of consulting to be practiced. This perspective is intended not so much as a complete treatment of the question of professionalism as an introduction to its potential.

We begin with an introduction to the current reality of consulting practice and then argue that, as an adjunct to the consulting processes and skills explicated in the preceding chapters, consultants must demonstrate four building blocks of capabilities to achieve professional rank: business focus, interpersonal skills, technical capability, and effective leadership.

A Reality Check About Consulting

Corporate managers who hire consultants have a wide range of perceptions about the value of consultants. They often believe consultants do not know enough about their organization to be of real value. Managers may believe consultants are used too often, tell them things they already know, cost too much, are often arrogant, have low emotional intelligence, circumvent the hierarchy inappropriately, have too much power—and are unavoidable.

Powerful client managers may resent consultants demanding time, pointing out flaws and organizational problems. They may see consultants as intruders who are paid a lot of money to ask awkward questions—and then, after offering recommendations or building solutions, leave the managers to implement them! There are often hidden resentments among client managers and employees who may be looking for ways to sabotage consultants.

Consulting can also foster negative organizational politics. Managers are afraid of consultants because they can make them feel inadequate, foolish, ignorant, or out of control. Managers fear consultants because they fantasize that the changes consultants recommend will put them out of a job. They do not trust consultants who parachute in, stir things up, make fancy presentations, recommend changes, and then disappear. As a result, managers tend to hold back information, obstruct, or mislead.

I have heard clients say they believe their new IT systems suffer from a toxic mix of arriving late; being hard to use, unfamiliar, or confusing; or missing certain key features. New systems seem oversold and underdelivered. Consultants resemble a "bull in a china shop."

In some respects such negative perceptions are no different from the way society feels about lawyers or doctors—until they need one to get them out of trouble. Perhaps more needs to be said by the consulting industry of the benefits they provide and the good work they do. But a concerted effort to rebrand consulting will not be enough. It needs entry requirements and apprenticeship similar to those of the established professions.

Standards of entry into consulting are almost nonexistent. An MBA degree is believed to be essential, but in some firms even that requirement is wavering. There is a trend toward hiring people who bring in-depth knowledge with other degrees or have a broader, nonbusiness perspective. Such technical, engineering, or liberal arts hires are then trained by the consulting firm in their particular methods and techniques.

In general, no certified training in consulting is required to be a consultant. Some MBA programs offer courses but not concentrations or specializations in consulting. The same is true for technical colleges. Professional consulting associations that offer training have little or no policing authority over their graduates. Standards of practice among consultants are vague, irregular, and difficult to identify. It is difficult to improve professional standards and to license practitioners because the barriers to entry in consulting are low. Anyone can call him- or herself a consultant—all that's needed is some expertise to sell.

Finally, it should be said that not all consultants are experts, as many walk in with some rudimentary qualitative knowledge, quantitative skill, or a product to sell, and then learn on the job at the client's expense. And not all experts make good consultants, able to apply the many principles in this book.

Despite this litany of problems, there are many very good consultants with high levels of professional expertise. Top consulting firms in the industry—such as Booz, Accenture, McKinsey, Capgemini, and IBM—have, over many decades, established excellent reputations for training consultants, completing fine work, and producing first-class solutions. Consultants in such professional service firms are unquestionably professionals in every sense of the word. But with all the challenges facing the industry, we believe the stages, roles, competencies, and building blocks of consulting presented in this book provide a foundation for such firms to train their new consultants before adding their own particular view of professional practice.

The Need to Professionalize Consulting

Consultants are found in many fields. Perhaps most well-known are the management consultants, who offer advice and solve problems across an organization's value chain in such areas as research and development, production and operations, and marketing, as well as support functions in finance, human resources, and information technology. Business consultants usually specialize in such things as process reengineering, strategy, or training, and they often develop in-depth knowledge of certain industries. There are also consultants in the medical profession, the church, and education, and there are consultants who work as advisors to government. Even the major television and cable networks have their own consultants.

The demand for consultants is high and is a career of choice for many newly minted computer science graduates, engineers, and MBAs. It is also a wonderful second career for retiring baby boomers (people born between 1945 and 1965), who often find that, immediately after retiring from their company, they are invited to return as a consultant on a contractual basis. Additionally, it is often the only viable option for many middle-aged, experienced individuals who have been laid off, downsized, fired, or "retired." The benefits and risks of becoming an independent consultant after retirement are described in more detail in Chapter Eleven.

Is Consulting a Profession?

With so many people calling themselves consultants, it is legitimate to ask what is meant by the term. Their ubiquity raises questions about their qualifications. Are there barriers to becoming a consultant, or can anyone become one? What qualities, skills, or attributes are needed (or required) to describe oneself as a professional consultant? Would all consultants define professionalism the same way? Do all consultants adhere to the same set of professional standards? Must consultants be certified? What makes a consultant *professional?* Many of these questions remain unanswered. Yet consultants practice their work as if they were professionally certified and with implicit acceptance by their clients that they are experts whose advice can be trusted.

When we think of the term "professional," we tend to combine it with the term "expert." The term "professional expert" normally implies a combination of education, certification, and work experience. A professional expert is expected to have an advanced education leading to a graduate professional degree, such as in law, medicine, business, or the ministry. Professional experts are certified. They must pass exams and adhere to standards of practice administered by an objective third-party agency such as the American Bar Association, or the American Institute of Certified Public Accountants. Professional experts usually have direct work experience in their area of expertise. Indeed, often an apprenticeship and a period of experience in "practice" is required before a person can be certified by an authorizing agency.

Degrees, practical experience, and certification are rites of passage that indicate an individual has met certain criteria and acquired knowledge and skills and the ability needed for acceptance into a profession. Based on those rites of passage (and in some cases taking an oath of ethics), the public assumes such individuals can be trusted to have a defined set of capabilities, ethics, standards, and judgment for which they are entitled to practice for a fee.

However, even with a clear set of educational, practical, and ethical requirements, the term "professional expert" remains ambiguous. For example, the accounting field has a national institute that administers a nationwide Certified Public Accountant (CPA) examination, but the exams are administered on a state-by-state basis across the United States, thus allowing for differences in standards and thresholds for passing the exam. CPAs are licensed to practice only in the states where they have passed the exam. This is also true for lawyers. Even though individuals may be granted a state license to practice a particular profession, this does not mean they are automatically a professional *in every respect*. This certifies only that they have expertise in a particular field; that they are "technically qualified" against a set of standards. The situation is even more dubious in consulting. There is no agency that certifies a consultant's credentials, and currently there are no national or state exams. Therefore, in some sense, all consultants are suspect and practicing without a license. This is possible because consultants are expected *only* to have specialized knowledge. Their ability to apply that knowledge is given authority by the company they work for, which substitutes as a credentialing body. Professionalism in consulting thus becomes a commercial brand and a firm's reputation, and the rite of passage is the adoption of the firm's attitude and style, as well as technical knowledge and expertise.

McKinsey, one of the earliest examples of a professional service firm rendering management consulting services, believed that three components were essential for creating a professional practice (adapted from Burke, 2008):

1. *Unquestioned Respectability.* Consultants must spend a great deal of time getting educated and earning credentials of social standing.
2. *Professional Exposure.* Consultants should write articles and books and make speeches and presentations to professional organizations.
3. *Reputation.* Consultants must developing a strong reputation in their areas of expertise and demonstrate obvious competence in their work.

The success of McKinsey over the years suggests that drawing on those components in the form of best practices makes sense, especially in the context of establishing a consulting industry–based set of standards.

Professional Practice as Service

But, at its heart, professionalism is not only about competencies; it is also about service attitude—how competencies are performed and whether the person genuinely cares. This is what distinguishes the technician from the professional (Maister, 1997). The concept of service attitude suggests an important basis of competitive differentiation among firms offering very similar practice areas. Interestingly, for all professional service firms (that is, consulting firms) this implies that *how* they do things—the quality of client relationships and thus their "human service skills"—is just as important as their technical expertise. In other words, even though service deliverables may have the look and function of a product (such as a software program, a new organizational design, or team-building training), consulting is ultimately and most importantly a human service profession, rendering solutions to human problems experienced by people in social organizations. Promoting and confirming such attitudes and perspective ought to be part of the credentialing process.

Codification of Consulting Practice

Although the now-ubiquitous field of IT consulting is relatively new, management and strategy consulting is almost one hundred years old. The leading consulting firms require rigorous in-firm training in their methods and have high standards of professional conduct. Yet despite this internal rigor, there are few, if any, generally accepted professional standards of practice across practice areas between firms. Consulting firms certainly have well-established principles, concepts, and models (that is, best practices that enable firms to differentiate themselves) that they use *within* their firms. But they have not collaborated across and *between the firms* sufficiently to codify their work into state or national standards of practice that could form the basis of study and examination.

In 1929 the founders of the leading consulting firms at the time formed the Association of Consulting Management Engineers (ACME) which was later renamed as the Association of Management Consulting Firms (AMCF). They remain in the forefront of promoting excellence and integrity in the profession today but do not offer a certification credential to management consultants. Presently, credentialing is conducted by private, commercially oriented institutions, which have emerged to bring the practice of consulting into a unified code of conduct, knowledge, ethics, and practice. These institutions certify that their graduates have achieved a prescribed set of standards; however, they *do not grant a license* to practice consulting. It is possible to gain a consulting credential from, for example, the Institute of Management Consultants, USA (based in Washington, DC) or at the International Council of Management Consultants Institutes (ICMCI) to become a Certified Management Consultant (CMC). According to their websites the competencies needed for certification at those organizations were developed internationally and have a degree of international recognition. ICMCI claims that their candidates may be certified if they:

- Demonstrate three or more years of experience in full-time consulting (varies by country)
- Meet the Institute's independent criteria as an owner or employee of a firm in independent practice or as an internal organizational consultant
- Provide evidence that demonstrates client satisfaction in challenging engagements
- Produce descriptions of five client engagements, including problems addressed, solutions provided, and results achieved

- Successfully pass an interview by a panel of senior consultants on methods, approaches, and competencies used in a range of consulting disciplines
- Pass written and oral ethics examinations and declare adherence to a rigorous code of ethics
- Show commitment to continuing professional education
- Demonstrate that the certification has not expired (after a three-year term, renewal is required)

Although such requirements are very good and represent an excellent way to establish standards of practice, three criticisms can be made. First, most clients who hire a consultant do not require a CMC credential; they probably are not even aware that such a credential exists. CMC has very limited recognition among clients, and at this juncture it remains in the "nice to have" category. Other factors—such as experience, degrees, reputation, and employers—play a much bigger role in selection decisions. Second, consulting credibility is as much about attitude (demeanor and style) as it is about expertise (experience and passing CMC exams). Attitude and expertise are equally important, of course, but the former is much harder to assesses, measure, and change than the latter. Third, CMC is for profit and this creates a potential conflict of interest and dubious objectivity.

If codification among consulting firms and the for-profit institutes were to be broadened into the public domain, it could be taken up by a state agency or university graduate schools of business as a specialization in their MBA programs, which would have the effect of establishing consulting as an object of study, research, teaching, and examination. This would help to accelerate recognition of consulting as a profession.

Ethical Problems and Issues

Because the consulting profession is still developing and there are varied standards of practice, the consulting industry must be alert to malpractice, and clients must be vigilant in spotting ethical violations. Ethical issues include the following:

- Baiting clients with one consultant, then switching to another
- Making decisions about the retention of a client employee
- Offering gifts in exchange for future business
- Charging senior consultant fees for a junior's work

- Disclosing competitor information
- Making recommendations based on personal gain or bias
- Masquerading as a customer to obtain confidential data

Consultants need to learn from experience and remember the recent problems in the accounting industry in which highly reputable firms violated ethical practices with suspicious conflicts of interest across their auditing, tax, and management consulting services lines of business—for example, the problems at Arthur Andersen that led to devolving their IT consulting business to create Accenture. Arthur Andersen, is, of course, the firm that audited Enron, whose own illegal activities ultimately brought down Arthur Andersen itself. Another example is American Express firing a consulting firm for doing a "bait and switch" by charging senior consulting rates while using junior employees.

The consulting industry needs a clear set of ethical standards, education, examination, assessment, and sanctioning processes administered by a nonprofit institution, such as graduate schools of business or a national institute. Such entities would oversee the entire issue and bring both rigor and objectivity to the administration of the process of certifying consultants. The consulting industry must have a way to either approve or reject applications for membership in a guild of professionals whose work has such an enormous and serious impact on business and people.

Professional Capabilities of Consultants

Consulting is as much an art as it is a science. First, in the real world of consulting, very busy professionals follow the consulting stages sequentially *and* in part concurrently, trying to maintain some sense of clarity, order, and logic. Second, they apply the science of their particular, often proprietary analytical technologies, such as BCG's portfolio analysis and cycle time reduction; Monitor's five forces, Mercer's value migration, Stern Stewart's economic value added, McKinsey's seven S's and MECE process, and Booz's PERT analysis (Biswell & Twitchell, 2002; Rasiel, 1999). Consultants endeavor to keep things organized while trying to manage often irrational people in their own ranks and among clients. The messiness of consulting sometimes tests the cool objectivity of even the best-trained professionals.

It can be argued that consultants already have many built-in requirements of professionalism in their work. As practitioners they usually have degrees and specialized training; they must produce solutions that work,

FIGURE 10.1 INTERDEPENDENT FEATURES OF CONSULTING

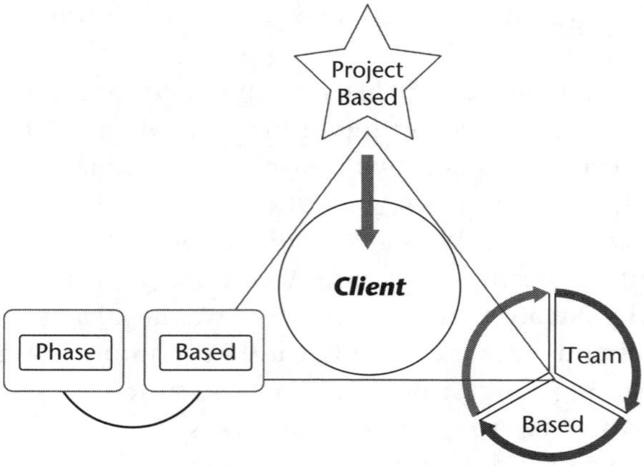

and, given the often proprietary, confidential nature of their consulting, they must work within a strict code of ethics with clients. In the broadest sense, consultants must live up to the principles and tenets in our defini- tion of "professional consultant": *one who can be trusted to use standard consulting methods and procedures; who gives advice, and who produces solutions on behalf of clients.*

Figure 10.1 depicts consulting as organized on three, interdependent features (or bases), organized around the client. Obviously, professional requirements and practices vary between consulting applications (that is, strategy consulting is done differently from benefits and organization development consulting) and vary within a consulting firm by organization level and responsibility. Ultimately though, despite its messiness and varia- tion across applications, all consulting is project-, phase-, and team-based.

Part Two of this book describes the many steps, inner logic, and actions needed to derive synergy from the features in Figure 10.1 and advocates a careful managing of their interdependence for professional performance. IT consultants, for example, use these interdependences, managing proj- ects in a logical, systematic manner to unbundled, integrate, modify, or maintain IT systems. IT project teams progress through the stages of the consulting cycle, working closely with clients and applying team skills in a "scrum" process to solve client problems. The work must be done systemati- cally because IT is in a perpetual state of evolution. Interacting with clients, IT consultants give advice and work on both the means and ends of infor- mation technology and business performance: they must constantly acquire new knowledge and skills of the hardware and software used in their consulting practice. Such continuous training and development is, of course, another important aspect of professionalism.

Project Based. Most consultants work on a project basis, which means they must have expertise in all aspects of good project management—or at least have the skills discussed in detail in Chapter Six.

Team Based. This may be challenging for independent consultants who prefer to act as subcontractors, performing a specific piece of work within a set time period and for a predetermined amount of money. In virtually all consulting situations, however, the work is done by a team of consultants drawn from (1) a consulting company's full-time employees, (2) third-party subcontractors, and/or (3) individuals from the client company. Team skills and capabilities are therefore very important, as discussed in detail in Chapters Seven and Eight.

Phase Based. As discussed in Chapter Five, a consulting engagement involves a series of phases of work, described in the consulting proposal and launched sequentially:

1. Data gathering and research
2. Design and development
3. Testing and prototyping
4. Deployment of solutions
5. Maintenance and some form of continuous improvement services

As these phases progress, the scope of the consulting may change; this may require negotiations with the client to ensure that any new work is paid for by the client. Generally, the only exception to this is when the consultant has made a mistake and must fix a problem without charging the client.

The Building Blocks of Professional Consulting. Are there professional capabilities that apply to all forms of consulting, which, if acquired, would improve practice and professional standing? The answer is yes. These can be thought of as building blocks of knowledge, skills, and attitudes that are the foundation of professionalism and independent of any firm's culture. Although consulting firms have their own way of fulfilling each building block, the blocks apply to all firms and to individual, private consultants. Collectively, the five components shown in Table 10.1 form the building blocks needed by all consultants who wish to represent themselves as professionals. Each component provides areas for personal training and development. Taken together and combined with one's particular field of consulting, they encompass the set of requirements for working

TABLE 10.1 BUILDING BLOCKS OF PROFESSIONAL CONSULTING

Component	Competency	Skills Sets
1. Clients' Business Focus	Needs analysis framing Navigating politics Managing change	Macro-contextual thinking Strategic planning Organizational performance Understanding clients' business context Micro-economics of business
2. Business Management	Developing proposals Project resource planning Closure and renewal	Business development (selling skills) Proposal and contracts Project management Administrative procedures and requirements Understanding economics of own firm
3. Technical Requirements	Launching projects Producing deliverables Testing and refining	Diagnostic and support tools Analytical techniques Methods and protocols Documentation Coaching clients to use the (technology) solution
4. Interpersonal Attributes	Managing expectations Team performance	Having a good rapport Being at ease around people Active listening Emotional intelligence Effective questioning Building relationships of trust Team building and group dynamics
5. Effective Leadership	Enrolling others	Creating appropriate change Inspiring people Exercising power and influence Using language clients understand Rational decision making Creative problem solving

with clients and for building and managing the consulting firm as a business. We will explore each of these in more detail.

Building Block One: Client's Business Focus

One perennial complaint about consultants is that they do not have a strong enough business focus. This means that consultants can be exceptional in their expertise but lack a fundamental understanding of how business works as a total system. In strategy consulting, for example, the requirements of implementation are often secondary to formulating a great strategy. Organization development consultants may be too focused on one team or department without addressing the organization as a whole. This frustrates clients. The problem lies in the fact that consultants become myopic in their work, focusing on the use and application of their technical expertise to solve the "technical problem" at hand. Although this may seem to make sense for a typical consultant, in most situations *clients* are hoping for a solution that will make their *business* more competitive, not just one that will solve a particular problem. This is particularly true for senior-level clients who are focused on how the business runs *as a whole*—how the various parts of the organization integrate and fit together using, say, technology to run the business more efficiently and effectively as a whole system. In IT consulting, the elegance of a technical solution is of less concern than its practical help in making the business faster, bigger, better, or cheaper.

Developing a holistic business understanding of the client's business is essential in consulting. Understanding the fit and linkages among business strategy, goals, tactics, work processes, task routines, systems, culture, people, property, plant, and equipment is essential to building solutions that fit the organization to make it more stable and adaptive (see Chapter Two).

Professional consultants must take a *systems view* to understand the business, always considering the larger context and realizing that their work in *one* part of the client's business has implications for the functioning of the larger organization.

Included in a systems view is considering the client's personal, organizational goals and agenda; thinking seriously about the client's *organizational position and role*. Consultants must try to understand how their activities fit into their client's set of business objectives and personal career aspirations. They need to think empathetically, trying to see how their work fits into the bigger picture and contributes to (helps or hinders) the client's personal success in the organization.

Developing a business focus does not require understanding client companies to the extent that the clients understand their own organizations. It simply requires looking up, out, and beyond to see what is going on around the consultant's specific assignment in the organization. Table 10.2 presents the actions professional consultants should take in order to know the client's business.

In summary, keeping a business focus enables consultants to

- See new ways to improve operations
- See new consulting opportunities
- Help clients develop high levels of trust in the consultant's perspective and point of view

TABLE 10.2 HOW TO KNOW A CLIENT'S BUSINESS

People	Assess the players to see who is for or against, helping or hindering the current project.
	Identify the opinion leaders who may be helpful at any stage of the consulting process.
	Learn about employees and managers who are coming and going.
Culture	Develop a realistic perspective on what it will take for the client to be successful.
	Identify and describe the client's organizational culture.
	Follow developments in the organization's internal press and local media.
	Read the client's annual report and related investor publications and reports.
	Make sense of the client's organizational structure.
	Show interest in the client's immediate set of working relationships (on a 360-degree basis) and try to understand the strengths and weaknesses of those relationships.
Business	Understand the major external issues and trends affecting the client's business.
	Understand how the company makes money.
	Learn about the actual nature of the company's products and services.
	Buy and use the client's products.
	Become conversant with the company's current performance and business results.
Leaders	Understand the client's political dynamics.
	Study how the client's leaders and managers make decisions.

- Demonstrate an ability to put specifics into context
- Discuss the broader implications of any particular solution for the client's business goals and objectives

This business focus is how external consultants can really add value. They can see things the client cannot. Consultants see things with a fresh perspective, drawing on their experience to explain things that the client may find inexplicable and confusing. Professional consultants simplify complexity.

Building Block Two: Business Management

The use of the phrase "business management" in this section is different from the business perspectives just described—that is, having a "business focus" on the client's business. The skills represented by this building block are those needed by consultants to ensure that they pay attention to their *own* business—*as a business*; to assess whether their firm is making a profit as it is supposed to. For both sole practitioner consultants and those who work in consulting firms, this is a very important issue. All consultants must pay attention to their own business management issues. This includes having knowledge and skills regarding new business revenue development opportunities, proposal and contract writing, project management, administrative requirements, billing, and getting invoices paid.

Business Revenue Development

Business development skills include finding prospects, marketing, presenting one's skills and abilities, and turning prospects into client contracts. Key skills in business development include but are not limited to:

- Writing cases of previous consulting (successful) assignments
- Designing and conducting direct marketing activities
- Maintaining a website that describes the services offered
- Attending professional meetings of various kinds to become visible and to develop contacts
- Getting involved in professional association projects
- Writing articles and books on consulting-related topics
- Speaking at meetings that relate to one's consulting service
- Building a broad personal network to gain industry referrals
- Publishing articles in target market journals, newspapers, and magazines
- Working with the sales force, early in the sales process
- Researching and preparing as fully as possible before meeting with a prospect
- Developing a game plan or clear agenda for client meetings

Proposal and Contracts

As discussed in Chapter Five, proposal and contract documents establish what the consultant will do for the client and how the work will be done. The proposal development process is a task in itself. It may involve some or all of the following activities, depending on the policies and practices of the consulting firm:

- Working with several people who contribute to writing the proposal
- Producing a detailed project plan so a realistic schedule and profitable fee structures can be established
- Setting a deadline for delivery of solutions to the client

- Going through iterations of rewriting to get the proposal just right
- Presenting the proposal before a client panel
- Handling any and all questions about the proposal
- Dealing with any resistance that emerges from the client about any aspect of the proposal
- Getting signatures on the proposal if it constitutes a contract

In most cases, a separate document is prepared once the client has accepted the proposal. This is the official and legally binding contract between the parties. A *letter of intent* is sometimes a preliminary agreement that binds the parties before a formal contract is signed. In a competitive bidding situation, it is a good idea to have such a letter prepared to establish in writing that an agreement has been made and that both parties have agreed to work together on the assignment at a point in the near future. The proposal is often the first deliverable and therefore can profoundly influence the client's perceptions of the quality of a consultant's service. An unprofessional proposal with mistakes and poor logic sends negative signals to the client about the consultant's future performance and standards of work.

Project Management

The detailed project *work plan* prepared during the proposal development process is an internal document used to set up the project phases, resources, and process; it is *not* sent to the client. Many companies have adopted project management software to make this step easier. It can be easily set up on Microsoft's Excel or Project programs. The plan and how it is developed sets the standards for future work by focusing on such things as the importance of professionalism, timeliness, quality, metrics, customer satisfaction, meetings, scope of work, and commitment to the project.

The project manager is responsible for selecting and organizing a project team of people who collectively have the right knowledge, skills, and experience to do the work. This may not be easy in a busy consulting firm, where resources can be scarce. Nevertheless, it is important to enroll the people needed for the assignment. An astute lead consultant or project manager will present the project in such a way that consultants can see its value as:

- An interesting and challenging opportunity
- A potentially significant revenue producer

• An opportunity for other consultants to increase their "applied time" (the percentage of time for which a consultant can bill the client)

Project management can be handled through virtual communications channels, such as an internet message board, to keep everyone up to date with the project status. However, use of such efficient and productive technology is not a substitute for good face-to-face meetings. There are many valuable project activities—such as relationship building, bonding, and hands-on involvement —that cannot be done by technology alone. As good as modern video conference calls are, there are times when the team must meet face-to-face.

Project kick-off meetings, project status review meetings, technical review meetings, and general management meetings are conducted regularly throughout the engagement. These all should be seen as a time for team building and as an opportunity for strengthening client relationships.

Finally, the ultimate purpose of project management is to make sure that deliverables *are delivered* and on time. Obviously, it leaves a bad impression in clients' minds if they end up spending lots of money only to wait for the solution longer than was described in the proposal. Professional consultants always try to exceed client expectations in every way possible, especially in the quality and timeliness of solutions.

Administrative Procedures and Requirements

Although consulting is first and foremost a people business, the work also requires attention to important administrative matters. Poor administration often means poor client service. If the consultant wants more business from the client, the consultant must pay attention to all of the administrative procedures and requirements. Table 10.3 shows the various administrative tasks to be completed for a typical consulting engagement.

Please note that unless the consulting firm is a "one-person shop," the individual consultant on a team *does not* have to do all of the work associated with each of these administrative tasks. Rather, it is the duty of the lead consultant or project manager to make sure these things are done, and done correctly.

Finally, as legal entities, consulting firms must maintain a set of files and records of their business dealings. There should be individual human resources files for each consultant in the firm as well as separate legal,

TABLE 10.3 ADMINISTRATIVE TASKS

Item	Important Details
Client Files	Proposals and contracts Letters and correspondence Client profile (including all projects) Project plans Invoices
Accounting	Client invoicing Internal billing Expense receipts and accounting
Case Histories	Details of each consulting assignment written for internal use or as a marketing tool; covers problem, approach, and solution
Consultant Time Record	Record of consultant's time, broken down by time billed to clients, business development time, professional development time, and discretionary time
Leads Records	Detailed records of new business opportunities identified by the consultant in the client's organization
Solution Documentation	A complete, detailed CD or hard-copy manual that explains the solution's specifications and functionality, software protocols, code, inputs and outputs, and use

financial, and accounting files maintained by those departments, in accordance with the standards set by local and state authorities.

Building Block Three: Technical Requirements

Technical requirements refer to the technical aspects of the type of consulting performed (that is, strategy development, information technology solutions, or organization development), the use of a firm's proprietary methods and analytical techniques, and how systematic a consultant is in conducting a consulting project (that is, following and using the stages, roles, and tasks to produce the outcomes of the consulting process described throughout this book).

Each type of consulting application has its own technical requirements and every consultant develops a preferred way of doing things. If a person enters the consulting profession through a consulting firm, he or she will learn the technical aspects of the firm's consulting practice, the way the firm does business, and how they work with clients. This is commonly how new consultants learn a firm's modus operandi.

Consulting firms often try to invent proprietary methods and analytical techniques that they market as better than alternatives offered by competitors, producing better solutions, and as proven ways to get more robust results. It is the responsibility of each consultant to develop the highest level of capability in each technical area used by the firm. These include:

- Diagnostic tools
- Analytical techniques
- Methods and procedures
- Documentation
- Application development processes
- Protocols
- Service standards

Clients hire "brand name" consulting firms to, in part, gain access to the firm's methods and techniques and expect their consultants to use such tested and proven technical procedures to produce solutions. This building block ensures that consultants continuously keep up-to-date with the technical requirements associated with their consulting services and search for new and improved tools and techniques. Such methods are the way a firm improves its efficiency and effectiveness and thereby can differentiate itself from its competitors.

Building Block Four: Interpersonal Attributes

Whether consulting is concerned with building and deploying information technology systems or dealing with the cold, objective analysis of facts needed to formulate and recommend strategic business options, consulting is fundamentally about *people*. As we covered in Chapter Four, consulting is a people business. It may sound obvious, but it's important to keep in mind that *people* decide whether to engage in buying consulting services. *People* use computer systems. *People* listen to recommendations. *People* accept or reject insurance benefit packages. *People* have problems that need to be solved. *People* spend a company's money for consulting services. When consultants do not make a conscious effort to work with and through people in their business, the result is a transaction, a short-term relationship, and limited cash flow. It is the difference, for example, between the drop-off-and-pick-up transaction with our local pharmacist and the caring relationship (we would like to have) with our medical doctor. Consulting should never be about transactions. It should be about working in a way that builds long-term relationships with our clients that makes it clear we care about them. That is the nature of *professional* consulting.

Some consultants (especially, it must be said, IT consultants) are simply not very people-oriented. They must learn to become so. The skills needed for this building block are complicated and challenging, but can be learned and are essential to building rapport and relationships of trust.

Building Rapport

Often stemming from other interpersonal skills, rapport-building skills include the ability to relate well with others and to have a thoughtful, considerate conversation that builds camaraderie, disagrees respectfully, and naturally expands into areas that everyone enjoys, in which everyone contributes. The following five interpersonal skills can be learned and help to build rapport:

1. *Putting people at ease.* Consultants who are at ease with themselves find it easier to put others at ease. Skills here include the most obvious, smiling; asking easy, noncontroversial questions (that is, avoiding religion, politics, and sex); avoiding controversial statements; looking for humor in situations; commenting on nonpolitical issues such as the weather, commuting, and traffic; looking for common interests by observing and commenting on the objects, art, and family photographs in a client's office; striking a relaxed pose; and giving the conversation a natural rhythm and timing.

2. *Being at ease around people.* All of the skills of putting other people at ease apply to oneself. The key is to be yourself, be natural, and be genuine. Consider the possibility that other people really like you and enjoy listening to your point of view and stories. Silence is a natural pause in a speech. It does not have to be filled by you, even if the silence lasts a while. Also, if needed, an inner pep talk that helps you feel genuinely confident about your expertise and past successes will help you to relax and stay calm.

3. *Listening carefully.* Listening is something we do naturally—so naturally that we may ignore its importance. We rarely think about how to be a better listener. It takes training. Listening carefully, fully, with comprehension and interest has to be learned and practiced. The discussion in Chapter Four provides details about effective listening.

4. *Using emotional intelligence.* This collective term asks us to be in touch with our emotions and to control our response to our emotions in sensible ways. Skills include being socially appropriate in our behavior, given the situation and people in our presence; showing empathy for other people's situation and circumstances; labeling our own emotions to

gain control of them and using them appropriately; gaining insight into how we deal with situations—over- or underreacting; and continuously increasing our awareness of how our inner life can be better regulated with the outside world.

5. *Questioning effectively.* We all ask questions, but a good question, when it is asked for the right reason and in the correct form, is a primary way to gather information and understand a situation. Consultants need to learn the SPIN questioning strategy (see Chapter Five) and to deliberately shift between asking open, leading, and closed questions. Never ask questions that are too personal, show bias or prejudice, or are too scattered, and never be so persistent or pushy that the exchange feels like an interrogation. Questions should flow naturally as part of the conversation.

Building Relationships of Trust

The essence of good consulting is to build long-term relationships of trust in which clients share more and more of their thoughts and opinions about a wider range of business issues—even, sometimes, personal matters. If they trust the consultant with such information, there is a very good chance that the client will offer more consulting assignments, either directly or through referrals. The skills of trust building require having integrity, being reliable, being credible, and being accountable for results—good and bad.

Finally, careers in the fields of science, engineering, information systems, technology, and research often attract people who like to work independently—thinking and analyzing, manipulating data, testing hypotheses, writing papers, or writing code. Consultants who come from those fields often have impressive academic, analytical, or knowledge strengths—which makes them excellent technical experts. However, it bears repeating: technical experts must be able to communicate effectively and work as a team. For many highly technically trained individuals, learning interpersonal skills may be difficult and challenging. It requires recognizing just how important people skills are in the transition from expert to professional.

Building Block Five: Effective Leadership

In our view, "being professional" is related to "being a leader." The former was introduced earlier in this chapter; the functions and thinking characteristics of leadership can be found in Appendix C. Here we highlight particular leadership facets of importance to professional consulting: creative problem-solving and decision-making skills, political intelligence, our language, personal appearance, and teamwork.

Creative Problem-Solving Skills

When leading the client and team through the consulting cycle, there are times when we need creativity to come up with innovative and unique solutions. Creative problem solving asks individuals or a group to "think outside the box"; to brainstorm and look at a problem from many points of view. Creativity is the product of combining unlikely ideas, processes, opinions, concepts, and emotions in ways that allow for the unexpected. Creative insight may take time; it may be envisioned in dreams, in free association, in quiet moments of contemplation, and when conversation is allowed to flow as freely as possible with maximum energy. Creativity can be seen in colors, shapes, and sounds, drawing pictures, free-flow conversations, and writing, and it can be found in logical connections that were never thought of before. Project leaders must be comfortable allowing creativity to flourish as they keep in mind what is practical. By keeping the goal or outcome clearly in mind, and at the same time allowing the mind to flow wherever it wants to go—especially in a group setting—unusual and ideas and creative solutions can emerge.

Rational Decision-Making Skills

Decisions can be made on the basis of intuition, emotion, values, or logic. The central feature of McKinsey's fact-based consulting is the application of rational decision making, from creating a logical structure for the problem and developing causal hypotheses to gathering and synthesizing facts to test the assumptions, from which recommendations can be made. Situational decision making requires consultants learn how to:

1. Clarify goals
2. Identify and separate facts from assumptions
3. Analyze the facts
4. Identify alternative ways of achieve the goal
5. Assess each alternative against objective criteria
6. Choose the best alternative on the basis of the criteria, impact, achievability, and contribution to accomplish the goal(s)

As is true with creative problem solving, decisions arrived at through team-based decision-making can be superior to individual decisions, so long as the discussion is facilitated skillfully (see Chapter Seven).

Political Skills

Active consultants generally have a fear and loathing of dealing with organizational politics—to the point that many try to avoid it completely in their consulting practice. However, if consultants can develop even a small amount of confidence and skill in this area, there is a great deal to be accomplished throughout the consulting cycle. Here are some of the learnable leadership skills that can enhance a person's ability to be more politically astute:

- Acknowledging that politics can be a positive force
- Thinking strategically about organizational politics
- Thinking contextually, not just analytically
- Identifying organizational opinion leaders
- Knowing one's own values and principles
- Building a network of trust
- Understanding how to use power positively
- Being able to influence others effectively

In essence, politics is about the positive use of power and influence in a network of relationships to get things done. It is not all negative, backbiting, manipulation, and phony gamesmanship. It is, however, a game with rules, risks, and rewards, all of which can be learned. Consultants can successfully lead projects if they develop political skills.

Language Use

We are referring not to English, Spanish, or Chinese but to the technical language used in a consultant's area of expertise or specialty. It is the automatic (default) language that only fellow experts understand and nonspecialists typically do not. For example, in IT consulting it would be product language or computer software language. Professional consultants need to choose words and ideas that fit the audience and to avoid trying to impress others with obscure terms related to their expertise and knowledge. In the interest of building long-term trust relationships, it makes sense to use language that others understand. Experts can easily fall into the trap of using what they know best and are most comfortable with—with unfortunate results. For example, by using only software jargon in presenting a software development proposal to marketing and finance managers, an IT consultant is likely to frustrate the prospects, fail to connect, and ultimately lose the business.

Appearance

It is a gross mistake to assume that what the consultant likes to wear is fine with clients and that formal business attire is not cool. IBM acquired the image of a "gray flannel suit" company because in the early days its computer applications were designed to run corporate finance and accounting systems run by clients that wore gray suits. The IBM sales force successfully sold to accounting and finance employees and likewise wore gray suits, or something approximating a very conservative manager. The same principles hold true eighty years later. Most companies today have dress-down days and allow business casual clothing, and IT departments have become very informal. Naturally, consultants who work with lots of IT clients may also dress informally. But getting the client's dress code wrong can leave a bad first impression. Leaders must look the part and dress as if they are the leader. The key is to be cautious and dress up rather than down; always check with a client contact ahead of time to learn the company's dress code.

In general, keep an eye on personal grooming. As a rule, pulled-together is always better than shabby chic. When working with top management, unless told otherwise, men and women should always wear a suit with an appropriate tie or accessories. At the very least, it shows respect for the client's office and position in the company.

Teamwork Orientation

The importance of team leadership and teamwork was discussed in detail in Chapters Six and Seven. To briefly reiterate, many clients expect their consultants to work in teams, foster teamwork, and build high-performing project teams. Most consultants understand this intellectually, but only some can actually do it without any difficulty. Consultants tend to be schooled in and wedded to their area of expertise, so if their specialty is technical, they tend to ignore or avoid the people side of consulting, thereby underplaying the value of teamwork. It is hard work to lead a group of "experts" from a group of strangers to a fully-functioning team. The process takes time and is usually fraught with a mix of tension, conflict, and confusion *as well as* fun, excitement, and pride. However, a team is what consultants must become, for no one works in isolation.

Conclusion

Becoming a professional consultant is as much a state of mind as it is a matter of skills. It cannot be acquired fully by earning a degree, gaining a certification, or becoming a Microsoft Solution Provider. Certainly experience tests, broadens, and deepens our strengths and weaknesses and gives us a deeper understanding of the level of our professionalism.

The argument set forth in this chapter is that in consulting there are foundational capabilities, or building blocks, needed to become a professional, including: business, technical, interpersonal, and leadership capability. To these skill sets must be added attitudinal dimensions of striving to be one's best, caring, integrity, and ethics.

Individual consultants can use the building blocks as a framework to identify ways to improve their professionalism. Consulting firms can use them to assess their strengths and weaknesses and, through professional development and their own cultural norms, strengthen their professional reputation and in turn the level of client satisfaction.

Professionalism is vital to consulting. For fifty years the big industry players have spent a lot of time and money trying to achieve the professional status of traditional legal, medical, and accounting professional service firms. Consulting companies like Bain, Booz, IBM, SAP, and Accenture swamp the marketplace with their consultants, leverage their brands, and promote their consultants as consummate professionals. At the same time, small boutique firms and individual consultants provide specialized services as professionally as they can, often without knowing what professional standards look like.

Even though clients know the consulting industry has no defined professional standards, they hire consultants nevertheless, relying on the strengths of their brand, reputation, alumni status, and experience. As the twenty-first century matures, the industry once again faces questions about the nature of its professional standing—and offers opportunities to those who can demonstrate professionalism. The building blocks presented in this chapter, as well as the principles and practices advocated throughout the book, are offered as an initial perspective and catalyst to further professionalize the industry and individual practitioners.

CHAPTER ELEVEN

LESSONS OF EXPERIENCE

The challenge of understanding and practicing professional consulting can seem daunting. Certainly, both efforts can be confusing, complex, and both rational and emotional.

Consultants are expected to demonstrate technical expertise and, at the same time, use high levels of emotional intelligence as they work with people. Human resource consultants need to convince clients of their technical expertise; technical consultants need to demonstrate their people skills. Consultants must demonstrate an ability to use tried and tested techniques and methods and, at the same time, be flexible and open to change. Consultants are expected to grapple with the complexities of their client's organizational failure and problems that are often ambiguous and ill-defined, yet still communicate in simple, clear, and convincing language. Consultants are expected to exceed client expectations by providing solutions at lower cost while also adding value. The reality of consulting can be full of contradictions and conflicting, unreasonable expectations.

Our consulting model in Chapter Three provides a springboard for developing our professional practice, but it did not describe the realities that happen in the white space between the neat boxes. We cannot speak to *all* of the many real-world difficulties found in consulting. But we can describe some lessons garnered from many years of experience and conversations with other consultants. In this chapter we focus on:

- How to grow in professional capability
- Lessons from McKinsey
- The pain and joy of a consulting career
- Professional proficiencies in consulting
- Trends for the twenty-first century

How to Grow in Professional Capability

The journey of becoming a professional consultant never really ends. Consulting, by its very nature, involves the life of the mind and requires constant learning and development. It is also a service. That service is rendered by a person such that the *quality* of the service is directly related to the person's personality, knowledge, skills, experience, and capabilities. The professional's journey therefore is dependent on constant improvement in those areas. Highly effective, professional consultants seek out opportunities to improve, by:

- Asking for feedback from other consultants and one's supervisor throughout a consulting assignment
- Studying feedback from diagnostic surveys (see the Consulting Role Preference Indicator in Appendix A)
- Reading material that expands their knowledge
- Taking on stretch and challenging assignments, increasingly bigger in scope
- Learning from mistakes, which are inevitable in the journey
- Attending professional meetings on consulting and clients' business
- Assessing their performance of consulting assignments
- Leading people in greater numbers and with more diverse backgrounds
- Being introspective and honestly assessing their strengths and weaknesses
- Working with diverse colleagues who approach consulting in different ways

Being a professional means both (1) building knowledge about "typical" client problems and needs and (2) learning to use standard diagnostic procedures and methods to understand the true nature of a client's need. It means putting oneself to the test with colleagues and allowing people to judge one's fitness and worthiness through examinations, referenced publications, and promotions. It means keeping confidences and being intellectually honest. It means learning how to give one's best advice in the face of limited knowledge and understanding and, at the same time, doing so with the client's best interest at heart. It means taking the long-term view rather than being seduced by immediate gratification or maximizing income. Finally, professionalism means learning how to deliver on promises and to live by a set of values governed by honesty, integrity, and trustworthiness. It means never personally violating those values even in the face of the greatest temptation.

What Professionals Do. Think about other areas of life in which professionals traditionally work: medicine, the law, religious ministry, and education. Based on these professionals' education, training, examination, certification, and experience, society expects doctors, lawyers, clergy, and teachers to work at the highest standards as they use defined processes, give advice, solve problems, and achieve results for their "clients." For the field of professional consulting, expectations must be the same. Exhibit 11.1 lists some characteristics of high-performing consultants. In reality, none of us is perfect, and it is easy to find examples of people in these fields who have been less than—sometimes *far less* than—professional. That does not mean that we should not try our hardest to achieve the highest possible standards of professional conduct.

Exhibit 11.1 Characteristics of the High-Performing Consultant

- Is sought after for an informed opinion
- Is considered an expert in an area of consulting
- Can lead projects of increasing scope
- Can quickly analyze complex situations
- Uses high-level and mature judgment
- Communicates ideas and opinions clearly
- Can persuade others easily and effectively
- Is seen as a trusted advisor
- Knows how to exceed clients' expectations
- Seeks and listens to the client's point of view
- Understands the client's business
- Understands the client's customers
- Uses tested, valid processes to build solutions
- Gives advice based on both experience and expertise

"The highest possible standards of professional conduct" may seem broad and beyond the reader's personal vision; they may seem to dictate a level of conduct that is unreasonable, unnecessary, or perhaps unobtainable. However, whatever standards are used to measure professional conduct, they ought to be difficult and challenging in order to differentiate the average from the good, and the best from the great.

The imperative of achieving professional status for consulting raises questions such as these:

- What distinguishes consulting as a field of professionalism?
- In what ways is consulting the same as or different from the standard professions of lawyers and doctors?
- What are the agreed-upon standards of knowledge, skills, and practice for consulting?
- How is consulting practiced by the world's leading consulting firms?
- Who ought to administer examinations for professional certification?
- Should there be international standards of practice?

In the sections that follow, we will explore some of the answers.

Lessons from McKinsey

In many ways, consulting is still an emerging field, even though the leading consulting firms such as ADL, McKinsey, and Booz are almost one hundred years old. Since its founding in 1926, the McKinsey organization has been the source for the invention of many analytical methods and a culture that fosters highly professional conduct. Rasiel (1999) and Rasiel and Friga (2001) describe many McKinsey principles and practices of consulting that have become standard nomenclature and practice in various fields of management consulting. McKinsey's rigorous, fact-based, and issue-based form of consulting has produced outstanding results for thousands of clients around the world. Many consulting firms use or adapt McKinsey's methods even as they themselves continue to create new ways to understand and solve client problems.

As is true for many top firms, there are a number of factors that help McKinsey successfully implement their principles and practices. They hire talented staff, recruit MBAs from top business schools around the world, follow an "up or out" career principle (of which we will say more later in this chapter), ensure that senior consultants mentor junior consultants, and foster a culture of rigorous training, heavy workloads, and rapid responsibility. Many aspects of McKinsey's culture, principles, and consulting practices are explained by Rasiel (1999):

- The problem is not always the problem.
- Don't reinvent the wheel.
- No "standard" solutions.
- Don't make the facts fit the solution.
- The solution must fit the client.
- Follow the 80/20 rule.
- Don't "boil the ocean."
- Find the key drivers.
- Use the elevator test.
- Pluck the low-hanging fruit.
- Make a chart every day.
- Hit singles.
- Look at the big picture.
- Just say: "I don't know."
- Don't accept "I have no idea."

The lesson of "Don't reinvent the wheel" refers to the fact that over time client problems do resemble one another—and by using the firm's analytical techniques, it is possible to solve a broad set of problems. Analytical techniques include analysis of value added, product portfolio analysis, process redesign, and the learning curve.

Another lesson from McKinsey—"Sometimes you have to let the problem come to you"—means that when all else fails, if you make sure the facts are gathered and analysis is done, and allow for creative thinking time, the problem will eventually surface and become known. "Don't 'boil the ocean'" reminds us that not everything has to be analyzed. Set priorities, use judgment, cull the data, set practical limits on what can be done; then stop doing more data gathering and realize that when the ocean is boiled, you end up with a bucket of salt.

Because consultants learn something new every day, it is good practice to ask yourself: "What are the three most important things I learned today?" "Make a chart every day" means to convert those lessons into one or two charts that describe insights. Finally, McKinsey consultants take a step back from their busy schedules and look at the big picture by asking themselves how what is being done solves the problem and advances thinking, and whether or not it is the most important thing to be doing.

These lessons help us to be conscious of ourselves and assess the efficacy of our consulting practice. Are we being smart in the use of our time? Are we "advancing the ball"? Are we becoming mired in details and trivia instead of focusing on the vital few issues? Such lessons can enable new consultants to advance along the learning curve more quickly and more successfully as they progress through each stage of the consulting process. As with most challenges in life, however, the learning curve can be both exhilarating and painful.

The Pain and Joy of a Consulting Career

Again, a consultant's ability to produce value is as much an art as it is a science. Models, templates, and logical processes are the science of consulting. The art lies in the interplay of the science with people's temperaments, values, and personalities in any given situation. Getting the interplay right can be painful or a joy, because a consultant's work is full of *competing potencies*. It is challenging yet rewarding. Consulting can be frustrating yet intriguing, demanding yet exciting, exhausting yet intellectually stimulating. It demands a unique mix of technical, rational, factual, and logical analytical requirements, along with emotional, feeling, and people skills. Consulting is an adventure that demands excellent people with technical skills. It requires good business sense and vision. Consultants are expected to make sense out of ambiguity, simplify complexity, rationalize emotions, and inject cold logic with excitement.

Part of the joy is that consulting is a high-paying job and is never boring. It provides constant learning; stretches us intellectually; develops an aptitude for negotiating, influencing, and political skills; builds emotional stamina; and develops fortitude in the face of resistance. However, with this mix of competing potencies and positive attributes, is consulting for everyone?

Consulting Qualities and Attributes

One may well ask: *Do I have what it takes to be a consultant? Do I have the temperament and traits for a consulting career?* One long-time consultant recently remarked about life at one of the bigger firms: "It was a field-based organization. For ten years I'd get on a plane Monday morning and go to the client, and get on again Thursday evening. Friday was spent on other client work. I hardly saw my family, and I am surprised we didn't get divorced."

Consulting firms operate mostly on a tough "up or out" principle. This means that over time, in order to stay employed and get promoted, each consultant must demonstrate an ability to:

- Develop and successfully use an ever larger set of consulting skills (that is, the competences in our model)
- Grow in facts and knowledge about areas of specialty
- Function well in diverse teams
- Supervise other consultants
- Bring in revenue
- Lead engagements effectively with clients

This principle can be painful. The pressure to perform is relentless. In addition, very early in their careers, consultants must demonstrate that they can bring in new revenue. The work environment is intense and competitive, demanding a great deal of time away from home, excellent social skills, and mental stamina, during workweeks that are sixty to ninety hours long. It is not for everyone.

But for those who have the drive, there is the promise of real joy. Consulting can be the best of all possible careers, as it provides a constant source of learning and personal growth and a high level of earnings. Exhibit 11.2 shows the fundamental knowledge, skills, and attributes needed by effective consultants. Because many of these qualities are acquired in university business schools, consulting remains a top career choice for MBAs (and increasingly computer science graduates and engineers).

Exhibit 11.2 Knowledge, Skills, and Attributes of Consultants

Knowledge
- Basics of each business function
- Business and industry trends and issues
- Macro and micro economics
- Organization behavior
- Project management

Skills
- Analytical
- Computer

- Interpersonal communications (written and oral)
- Presentation (PowerPoint and the like)
- Problem solving and decision making
- Relationship management
- Research techniques and methods
- Sales
- Statistical analysis

Attributes
- Client focus
- Ability to cope well with pressure
- Creativity and innovation
- Individual initiative, self-directedness
- Team player
- Desire to influence and have impact
- Intellectual flexibility
- Physical health
- Smart, professional dress and demeanor
- Honesty and tact

Many *individual consultants* who work for themselves believe they should have started a long time ago. Now out on their own, freelancing consultants report the following benefits:

- Can earn more than when they were full-time employees
- Have the independence they always dreamed about
- Feel needed and wanted
- Derive satisfaction from projects having natural conclusions
- Apply their knowledge and expertise in interesting ways
- Are their own boss
- Are not tied to one company but a portfolio of companies
- Can tie their income directly to their individual effort
- Do not have to worry so much about organizational politics
- Are free to say "no" to work, if they choose
- Can travel as much or as little as they choose
- Are able to strike a better work/life balance

The biggest downsides and fears for self-employed consultants are: (1) not being able to sustain their income; (2) being dependent on the state of the economy; (3) having erratic cash flow; (4) feeling a bit isolated from people; (5) feeling lonely; and (6) getting tired of selling themselves all the time. Many are not able to keep their motivation alive, and they yearn for the days when they had a stable, predictable paycheck.

Salaries for Consultants

One of the joys of a consulting career is its compensation—it pays well. According to the U.S. Bureau of Labor, in 2004 the *median* annual wage and salary earnings of management consultants in the United States was $63,500. Research by the Association of Management Consultants (2004) and Notre Dame (2011) indicates that starting salaries in consulting for analysts with a bachelor's degree ranged from $40,000 to $80,000 (including bonus) and for MBAs, from $90,000 to $140,000. Recently, the median income for MBAs from the top schools was $145,000, one of the highest of any profession. Table 11.1 shows salaries in the U.S. by level and role.

When joining one of the larger firms, one can also expect to receive a signing bonus plus relocation and moving expenses, boosting the starting compensation by $5,000 to $35,000. Table 11.2 shows research by Prospects (2010) and Top-consultant (2011) indicating that consulting

TABLE 11.1 TYPICAL CONSULTING SALARIES BY ORGANIZATIONAL LEVEL

Research Associate (no bachelor's degree)	$40,000 to $80,000
First-Year Analyst (bachelor's)	$55,000 to $80,000
Second-Year Analyst (bachelor's)	$60,000 to $120,000
Management Consultant (MBA)	$80,000 to $170,000
Senior Consultant (MBA plus two to five years' experience)	$280,000 + bonus
Junior Partner (MBA/Ph.D. plus five or more years' experience)	$450,000 + bonus
Partner (MBA/Ph.D. plus five to twenty years' experience)	$600,000 + bonus

TABLE 11.2 CONSULTING SALARIES IN THE UK, 2011

Position	UK Starting Salaries
Junior Consultant/Consultant	£37,000+ (US$55,000+)
Senior Consultant	£55,000 (US$83,000+)
Managing Consultant	£68,000 (US$102,000+)
Principal Consultant	£93,000 (US$130,000+)
Partner	£125,000 (US$188,000+)

salaries in the UK are lower, on average, than in the United States but still high-paying salaries for the UK and, by extension, for Europe. UK firms include one-off signing bonuses (called a "golden hello" in the UK) and an overall package that can include car allowances, private health care insurance, pension, life insurance, on-site gyms, childcare, and season tickets.

Of course, many factors affect earnings, including one's negotiating skills, years of experience, geographical location, level of education, size of employer, and area of expertise. In general, the private, corporate sector pays higher than the public sector and not-for-profit organizations.

Finally, although the life and work style of consulting is not for everyone, it can be an excellent way to gain a lot of responsibility and experience very quickly, while learning a great deal about an industry and how to work with people. These can arm the consultant with an impressive range of skills, knowledge, and experience—excellent attributes that can be used in any company, government agency, or one's own business.

Professional Proficiencies in Consulting

Experience clearly demonstrates that cutting across the entire cycle of consulting stages and roles, the three core proficiencies of negotiating, influencing, and political skills are needed by practitioners to make it all work. Figure 11.1 shows the proficiencies as mutually reinforcing and overlapping.

These proficiencies give consultants the ability to access various sources and uses of political power to get work accomplished within a team and the client's organization, to influence the thinking and behavior of all consulting stakeholders, and to negotiate positive outcomes with everyone by applying emotional intelligence, resolving tension and conflict, and making mutually acceptable decisions.

Negotiating Skills

Negotiating skills are used at every stage of consulting, from proposals to changes in scope and from team responsibilities to deployment schedules. In complex organizations and complex team situations, it is vital that consultants recognize that they are working with people who have different interests and needs from their own. It is always in the best interest of consultants to search for solutions that foster healthy long-term relationships and to negotiate in good faith, avoiding aggressive, negative power

FIGURE 11.1 PROFESSIONAL CONSULTING PROFICIENCIES

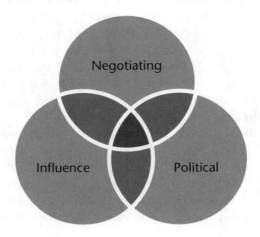

tactics in favor of a "win-win" common vision and aspiration. This is the essence of what Fisher and Ury (1981) call "getting to yes."

Effective negotiating requires being able to see the world from the other team member's point of view, understanding the needs and constraints of the other side, and being willing to "give and take" in order to satisfy both sides. The negotiation process is easier if consultants use GAINS:

- Plan *goals* and an *agenda*
- Discuss mutual *interests* and *needs*
- Agree on optional *solutions*

We have found GAINS to be a simple and useful way to improve consultants' confidence and outcomes when negotiating.

Influencing Skills

Consultants *must* by definition be influential; indeed, of the three skills, this is the one that consultants want the most. Every meeting at every stage in consulting offers a chance to exercise it. Influencing is a communications power that draws on various sources of personal and social power to change events, circumstances, and people. Paradoxically, consultants can be more influential if they allow themselves to *be influenced* (Carnegie, 1981). Influencing tactics include:

- Clarifying the benefits for others
- Strengthening one's argument
- Describing exciting possibilities that can be realized with agreement
- Strengthening long-term relationships
- Showing admiration for team members
- Providing direction when there may be none

Consultants and project leaders can master any or all of these tactics. Being influential requires knowing other people's needs and wants, being self-conscious and deliberate about using personal energy to affect other people, developing flexible thoughts and attitudes to move smoothly in or out of conversations, being clear about goals, and, as with negotiating, striving to produce mutually acceptable results.

Political Skills

As discussed in Chapter Eight, fundamentally, political savvy is a measure of how intelligently a consultant (project leader) exercises power and influence to get things done, both within a team and with an ever-expanding network of relationships. It requires using the knowledge and insights gained from those relationships to achieve objectives in a way that produces benefits to both parties in a political transaction. Many people do not like politics; they think of it as negative, manipulative, deceitful, and bad. Such attitudes restrict people's ability to discover ways to use politics to accomplish consulting goals. The fact is, all organizations are political by nature, and consultants cannot avoid the dynamics of this reality. Consultants have a choice; they can choose to avoid the political game and only watch it from the sidelines, or they can embrace it and play the game to make things happen. Politically savvy consultants choose to participate in the political game by learning its rules, taking some risks, getting to know what works, and building alliances of trust. From this experience, within their teams and with their clients, consultants and project team leaders can then exercise political influence intelligently to achieve goals as the cycle progresses.

Although each of these three proficiencies takes work and effort to master, consultants can attain them by being trained and developed, measured, and rewarded as they progress in their careers. One of the lessons of experience is that, in addition to the many other skills required of the roles and tasks in the consulting model, these proficiencies must be developed in order to effectively orchestrate the whole process. The reader is encouraged to make them a part of any personal development strategy.

Trends for the Twenty-First Century

In the preface to this book, we described the essential nature of consulting and the central place of importance practitioners have in the health and effectiveness of business and industry:

> Consulting is also a strategic endeavor that enables people and organizations to better adapt to the changing conditions of their environment. The questions consultants face are often complex and challenging, involving matters at the very heart of an organization's vision and purpose. As such, consultants solve problems in organizational processes and workflows, governance structure, organizational culture, the skills and capabilities of people, management systems and administrative procedures, policies and practices, as well as business strategy. Consulting is therefore a vital and an incredibly important responsibility with thousands of people in an organization often affected by the consultant's work.

Beginning a hundred years ago as an extension of normal managerial responsibility—identifying and solving organizational problems—consulting has become an independent industry with its own methods, operating principles, and values. Every day thousands of consultants around the world apply their intelligence to business and governmental issues using an evolving, robust collection of analytical techniques and methods. At close to $400 billion in annual revenues, this global endeavor is recognized as a source of entrepreneurial activity and a favored career. Consulting in the twenty-first century will continue to grow and expand.

Future Trends and Issues. There are predictable trends that are sure to shape the future of consulting—and there are some speculations that are a matter of possibility. First, the predictable trends:

1. *Employment growth will continue to rise.* According to the United States Bureau of Labor, employment for management consultants (that is, all forms of consulting) is expected to grow faster than the average of all occupations over the next five years. This is likely to be true in large international consulting firms as well as smaller specialized firms, such as in biotechnology, health care, information technology, human resources, engineering, and marketing.

2. *Industry growth will continue.* A number of key factors are driving consulting industry growth: the forces of globalization, the rise of state capitalism, intensive competition, the growth of international business, as

well as the speed and intensity of change driven by technological innovation. As the drivers create commercial opportunities, consulting firms will expand in number and size. The industry will also experience consolidation, because the cost of capital used to merge and acquire competitors is less than the cost of organic growth.

3. *Globalization will create opportunities.* As the economies of the world become more integrated with each other due to technological innovation and the desire to trade, the resulting complexity will produce an exponential growth in problems to be solved—and the intellectual firepower to solve them. Consultants are ideally suited to exploit such complexity.

4. *Sustainability initiatives will create opportunities.* As society demands more accountability from companies to do less harm to the environment, consulting firms will specialize in this area and will both benefit from its growth and influence the form of that growth.

5. *Technology will create opportunities.* IT consultants will continue to shape company business models as IT fundamentally changes how information is accessed and used for commercial purposes. IT will continue to alter how each business function operates and how they integrate with each other. The result will be opportunities for all types of consulting.

Speculations about trends for consultants and the consulting industry in the twenty-first century include the following:

1. *Demand for professional standing will increase.* University business schools will lead the effort to teach consulting as a subspecialty of business management (similar to law and medical school education, each with their own subspecialties). In business schools, consulting will be seen as an integrating discipline similar to the role played by courses on strategy and business policy. This will lead to a coalescing of principles and practices drawn from across business school curricula that, in turn, will create a "certification exam" to establish a minimum threshold of consulting knowledge, skill, and attributes for professional practice.

The Association to Advance Collegiate Schools of Business (AACSB) will work with the top consulting firms to establish professional standards, policies, and practices. Results of this work will be incorporated in business school education.

2. *Client expectation for credentials will rise.* Clients will use credentialing as one of their criteria when selecting consultants. It will not be the primary criterion, but one added factor in their decisions, much as an advanced degree or an MBA is today. Consulting firms will respond to this expectation by including professional credentialing in their hiring and as part of their internal professional development strategy.

3. *Profit margin pressure will intensify for consulting firms.* In a knowledge industry like consulting, an oligopoly is not possible with suppliers available worldwide. Therefore clients will demand lower fees as the number of competitors in the industry grows. Brand names will become globalized but commoditized, making it harder to charge premium prices. Firms' margins will be under downward pressure as clients expect high value at lower cost. Brand will be less of a factor in clients' buying decisions.

4. *Clients will demand more partner relationships.* Clients will be focused more on the best way to solve their problems, less on who does the consulting. This will lead to consulting firms' joining with other (competitor) firms to win and deliver consulting, forming temporary, tactical alliances for certain engagements. Horizontal industry collaboration will become normal. The trend of becoming a "one-stop shop" firm will decline, seen as a too-expensive business model.

5. *Risk/reward sharing will become more common.* The pressure to win and sustain client loyalty will make consulting firms strike deals where they bear some of the risk of consulting losses. Losses will be defined as cost overruns or not achieving a (specified FBBC) business benefit. Value pricing will be used more frequently by consulting firms to offset profit, cost, and revenue pressures. The demand for excellent skills in negotiating changes to an original proposal will increase for consultants.

6. *Consulting firms will reduce operating expenses.* Consulting firms will focus intensely on lowering their operating cost structure. The rising cost of health care and the breakthrough Voluntary Employee Benefits Association (VEBA) Trust (between the United Auto Workers and General Motors, to offset GM's huge legacy pension and retirement benefits) will demand that consulting firms shift from defined benefits to defined contribution plans, using technology to conduct more of the consulting work, using client employees in more aspects of the consulting, substituting certain benefits for higher salaries, and making compensation more variable by increasing the bonus portion of total compensation.

Conclusion

This explication of the fabric of consulting is designed not to be the end, or a completed picture, but rather a staging ground for more research and thinking about how to make consulting a stronger professional service. This is important as the industry grows around the world, consulting firms expand, more people make consulting a career choice, and pragmatic questions are raised about the degree of professionalism found among individual consultants. With this in mind, this chapter has examined some important lessons from our experience and pondered the future of our industry.

This book has articulated the journey of becoming a trusted consultant. That vision remains constant, but the path there can take many twists and turns. Armed with the concepts and techniques in this book, an ordinary consultant can chart a course to becoming a great one.

Whether working as an individual freelance consultant or in a firm of consultants, readers will find there are many professionally satisfying rewards from being involved in the process. We have seen all that the process includes: formulating hypotheses about the client's problem; collecting, reviewing, and analyzing information; designing and developing deliverables; making recommendations; and assisting clients with the changes required of solutions. We hope and trust this effort has helped the reader understand what consulting is all about—its undergirding values and principles that govern practice, and competencies that guide application.

At the end of a hard day, when the team is up against impossible odds and tough client expectations, a review of a pertinent chapter may provide solace and insight. It may provide some help. It will certainly produce comfortable sleep. Then, after a good night's rest and some strong coffee the next morning, the team will be ready.

Carpe diem!

THE CONSULTING ROLE PREFERENCE INDICATOR

In this appendix we present the Consulting Role Preference Indicator (CRPI), a diagnostic instrument invented by the author and used in different parts of the world to help consultants assess their current use of the four roles in the consulting model presented in this book. This version is organized as a "self-rater" to be completed by the reader. If other people were asked to rate you, a small language modification would be required in the questionnaire, from "I" to "H/She."

The Use of Competencies

There are many consulting companies devoted to competency-based training and organizational development. They help their clients to improve the quality and capability of their managerial and leadership talent by defining a set of standard behaviors that constitute best practices for the organization. These benchmarks are then embedded in various human resource systems and applied in such things as the design of management development systems, succession planning, leadership training, and performance management systems.

In leadership development, for example, a typical situation is a company's hiring of a management consulting firm to complete a multirater, leadership development assignment. Usually, the firm starts by developing a set of leadership "best practices" (that is, behavioral competencies) for their organization. Working closely with the client, the consulting firm then designs an employee survey instrument and a survey process using those competencies. The survey process usually follows these steps: a questionnaire is distributed to employees asking them to rate their leaders on the defined competencies. The anonymous surveys are conducted on a 360-degree basis (that is, obtaining self, supervisor, peers, and direct report input); once completed, they are collected and summarized into feedback reports for individual managers and group profiles, for whole departments or business functions. Often the leaders receive their feedback reports and group profiles during leadership development conferences. Over time, the client organization gains a picture of its overall leadership competency profile of strengths and weaknesses, and can identify leadership competencies for which additional training and development are needed.

As with any research process, the multirater survey feedback process for leadership development is imperfect. But the competency approach to organizational change has become an important way for organizations to bring a higher degree of objectivity, science, and measurement to their management and leadership development.

The CRPI can be used in a similar manner as the leadership development example, to help individual consultants or consulting firms assess their strengths and weakness across the four roles. Some consultants prefer to work in certain phases of consulting and not in others. This narrowness is often related to their experience, when and where they were successful, what came easily to them, or what fit naturally with their way of thinking and working. As a result, in order to advance in their career and be of greater value to their consulting firm, they can use the CRPI to assess and broaden their consulting skill set.

Consulting firms, on the other hand, can incorporate the CRPI into their existing team feedback, peer reviews, and partner-supervisory assessments. It can be used as a coaching tool for a firm's professional development activities. This appendix offers a validated set of consulting competencies that is applicable to any kind of consulting. The reader is encouraged to do a self-diagnosis and to develop a profile.

Development of the Consulting Role Preference Indicator

In 2001 a research project was conducted to answer the question: what differentiates high-performing consultants from low performers? The initial findings identified sixty-four behavioral practices. These were submitted to twenty business consultants conducting a range of consulting applications to assess their validity in the real world of consulting. Based on their assessment and subsequent feedback about the wording, ordering, applicability, and validity of each practice, a template of competencies was developed and vigorously refined. In its final form, forty-eight practices were organized into the following twelve consulting competencies, which are discussed in the chapters in Part Two of this book, "Applying the Model."

1. Needs analysis/problem framing
2. Managing expectations
3. Developing proposals
4. Project resource planning
5. Enrolling others
6. Launching work
7. Producing deliverables
8. Team performance
9. Navigating politics
10. Testing and refining
11. Managing change
12. Closure and renewal

The CRPI instrument is intended to indicate and profile one's preferences for each of the twelve competencies and four consulting roles. If done with input from one's manager, colleagues, and team members, it is possible to look at gaps in perception between oneself and one's colleagues, along with high and low ratings based on the frequency of one's use of the consulting behaviors and roles.

The value of 360-degree feedback for professional growth and development cannot be overstated. Using the CRPI for such multirater survey research is an excellent way for individual consultants to gain insight into their strengths and weakness and to make decisions about areas needing improvement. Because it is a common practice in many parts of the world for consulting firms to include their clients in "customer satisfaction" surveying, whenever feasible and practical it would be equally useful to ask clients to complete the CRPI on each member of a consulting team. Eventually a database of scores could be developed, along with a norm base for all consultants in a consulting firm. Then individual consultants would be able to compare themselves statistically against other consultants in the norm base, and the firm could make more strategic investments in its professional development, based on the results. In this manner, the CRPI can be a powerful tool for improving professional practice by individual consultants, consulting teams, practice areas within a firm, or, for that matter, the entire firm.

Of course, just performing a competency does not mean the work is being done well or effectively—it simply means the consultant is performing the behavior, perhaps without regard to alternative ways that the quality or effectiveness of the behavior could be improved. So the CRPI is a starting point for measuring, assessing, and understanding one's consulting effectiveness. Ideally, it will suggest as many questions as it answers.

The CRPI has been used with both new and experienced consultants in the United States and Europe for over ten years. With some minor modifications, the practices have withstood the examination and criticism of those consultants, and having learned from this scrutiny, the competencies and practices are offered here as a benchmark. If the reader has any suggestions for change and improvement, please contact me (see About the Author).

Finally, the competencies in the CRPI can be viewed as a template that undergirds the four stages of the consulting process discussed throughout the book. The template is a link between theory and practice, intended to encourage the reader and user to contemplate what is required to become, first, a very good consultant, and then a trusted advisor. Individuals with no consulting experience who wish to take the questionnaire can answer the questions based on whether they would *automatically* think to behave this way in a consulting situation. If they would not think of doing it, they should self-rate as a "one."

Consulting Role Preference Indicator

Self-Rating *Instructions:* On the following pages you are asked to rate forty-eight work practices that are used in consulting.

- For each work practice, please consider how well you think the behavior describes you in consulting situations that you have worked in.
- Base your answer to each statement on what best describes you in your work—that is, how you *actually* behave, *not* how you would *like* to behave or *should* behave.
- For each question, record your answer on the *Profile Score Sheet* at the end of the CRPI. Enter the rating number that most closely matches your actual behavior, based on this frequency scale

Rating		Frequency
1	0–19% of the time	Almost Never
2	20–39% of the time	Occasionally
3	40–59% of the time	Average Amount
4	60–79% of the time	Frequently
5	80–100 % of the time	Every Time

Please answer *every* question.

1. I rapidly identify the major forces driving the client's business.
2. I seek agreement with clients on engagement roles, deliverables, timing, fees, risks, and constraints.
3. I understand the client's strategy, plans, and goals.
4. I convert broad proposals into specific work plans, schedules, and task flow charts.
5. I communicate the project vision, plan, and strategy with enthusiasm and passion.
6. I demonstrate an understanding of the overall project requirements.
7. I ensure orderly progress is made on data gathering, analysis, and assembly and development of deliverables.
8. I set challenging but realistic team goals.
9. I balance advocacy and diplomacy with clients to win support.
10. I ensure that solutions are tested before final delivery.
11. I encourage continuous improvement in consulting work methods and processes.
12. I develop appropriate materials that document the solution.
13. I have a basic grasp of the client's present business and how the client makes money.
14. I work with clients to develop a strategy for producing a solution to their problems.
15. I draw conclusions and make recommendations from an analysis of client data and information.
16. I use planning documents to communicate people's roles and responsibilities.
17. I generate excitement about a shared vision and common goals among consultants.
18. I conduct effective meetings with all relevant parties to launch consulting projects.
19. I make decisions in the face of ambiguity and time constraints.
20. I build people's confidence in their work with useful feedback and help.
21. I understand how stakeholders in the client's organization use their power and influence.
22. I give information so project teams can refine deliverables.
23. I explain any changes needed in the client's business and why the changes are necessary.
24. I ensure that any project administrative problems with the client are resolved.
25. I gather, organize, and systematically analyze data about client needs.

(Continued)

26. I manage the client's expectations about the scope of the work.
27. I prepare comprehensive proposals that summarize how the solution will be produced.
28. I assemble a consulting team for the work, when needed.
29. I listen carefully to the point of view and needs of the client and other consultants.
30. I use influence in a way that builds trust to gain the support of others.
31. I hold individual consultants accountable for agreed-upon goals.
32. I encourage team-based decision making when solving problems.
33. I draw on informal contacts and networks of people to get things done.
34. I actively seek feedback about the client's satisfaction with the consulting solution.
35. I help clients to manage the change process needed by the new solution.
36. I conduct client meetings with diplomacy and tact in a way that grows the consulting relationship.
37. I ask questions to frame and clarify issues that identify the real problems and needs.
38. I test the client's and my own assumptions to ensure that they are valid.
39. I identify actions that reduce risks to ensure project success.
40. I ensure that team members have clearly delegated goals, roles, and responsibilities.
41. I encourage the examination of differing views in order to build a consensus.
42. I ensure that everyone is heard, respected, and valued.
43. I seek constructive feedback about the effectiveness of deliverables as they are developed.
44. I ask team members for their self-assessment of progress toward goals.
45. I avoid taking credit for successful initiatives begun by others.
46. I encourage people to try to exceed the client's expectations.
47. I ensure that people are trained in the knowledge and skills needed to use the solution.
48. I help clients to understand other business problems in their organization.

Profile Score Sheet

Enter the score you assign to each statement in the space provided below. Please answer every question. Use the following rating scale:

1: Almost Never   2: Occasionally   3: Average Amount   4: Frequently   5: Every Time

1.	2.	3.	4.	5.	6.	7.	8.	9.	10.	11.	12.
13.	14.	15.	16.	17.	18.	19.	20.	21.	22.	23.	24.
25.	26.	27.	28.	29.	30.	31.	32.	33.	34.	35.	36.
37.	38.	39.	40.	41.	42.	43.	44.	45.	46.	47.	48.

Column Total:

Profile Scale Number:	1	2	3	4	5	6	7	8	9	10	11	12

Instructions:

1. Add your scores in each column and enter the total in the Column Total row.
2. Post the column totals on the **Profile Scale Number** row.
3. Create a profile by drawing a graph with a line that connects your scores.
4. Identify your strengths and areas for improvement:
   - In which competencies do you have the highest and lowest score?
   - Which of your competencies need improving and why?
   - In which specific practices of the forty-eight do you need to improve?
   - How can you become a better consultant?

(Continued)

TABLE A.1 CRPI PROFILE

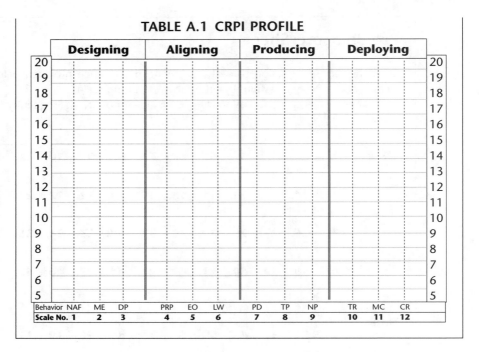

Behavior	NAF	ME	DP	PRP	EO	LW	PD	TP	NP	TR	MC	CR
Scale No.	1	2	3	4	5	6	7	8	9	10	11	12

Consulting Roles Description

This section provides a description of each role. Having assessed your role preference, read the description of that role to deepen your understanding of what the role requires, keeping in mind that each role combines two primary behaviors in each stage of the consulting cycle:

- Designing Role: Scoping and Planning Behavior
- Aligning Role: Planning and Mobilizing Behavior
- Producing Role: Mobilizing and Developing Behavior
- Deploying Role: Developing and Scoping Behavior

Roles that you scored high on can be refined and improved; your low-scoring roles are the ones that need more attention in your professional development. Elements of the role descriptions and the behavioral practices of each of the twelve consulting competencies offer specific areas for attention and improvement.

Designing Role

This consulting role combines *scoping* and *planning* behaviors. A consultant with this preference is good at needs assessment and problem framing when analyzing and diagnosing client situations. This person is able to assess and define the boundaries of possible solutions to client problems and convert them into proposals that describe project methods, approaches, goals, and plans. This role combines creativity, sometimes bold visions, and the discipline to put together the architecture or picture that describes and defines a unique solution. This consultant often sees what others have not yet seen in the environment, understands how to identify specific client needs, carefully assesses the practical business potential, and describes how to convert this insight into practical client work using systematic methods and processes. Good at asking questions and carefully listening, this role enjoys leading brainstorming sessions that may produce inventions, unique breakthroughs, and creative solutions.

Aligning Role

This consulting role combines *planning* and *mobilizing* behavior. A consultant with this preference enjoys working with people and values the process of getting agreement and shared vision on plans, project goals, and deliverables. This person actively seeks to work with other people to build commitment and to help people get involved with the work. Building people's trust is seen as important to motivation and creating a positive work climate. This role demands strong interpersonal skills, teamwork, team building, and lots of discussion to ensure that everyone has been heard. This person is often skillful at producing win-win outcomes when negotiating issues and items such as project timing, resources, and deliverables. This role demands a consultant who is patient yet enthusiastic, assertive, and supportive, and who makes sure that project team members have a clear set of roles and responsibilities in relationship to the plan. The role seeks to influence people through empathy, emotional intelligence, persuasion, finding common ground, developing a shared understanding, and commitment to project goals.

Producing Role

This consulting role combines *mobilizing* and *developing* behaviors. A consultant with this preference has a strong desire for action and producing results through practical problem solving and decision making. The role fosters collaboration, enthusiasm, and lots of team communications. This consultant is comfortable using metrics and controls to ensure that things are progressing and on track, and is usually very well organized and has good time management habits. Regular meetings emphasize status reviews, issue identification, and problem resolution of both a technical and interpersonal nature. This role prefers to use existing, tried and tested procedures and tools but is open to using them in new ways to adapt to new client circumstances. Comfortable with moderate risk taking, this consulting role enjoys coaching people and seeing that results are achieved. Gathering and using political intelligence and using the influence from organizational opinion leaders is seen as crucial in getting things completed on time.

Deploying Role

This consulting role combines *developing* and *scoping* behaviors. A consultant with this role preference likes to ensure that tasks are completed and enjoys seeing how implemented solutions affect client performance. This role is comfortable with making practical changes and adaptations in solutions and with experimentation to see whether something actually works in the client environment. This person likes to accumulate lessons from experience and to build intellectual capital that can be leveraged for use in future projects. Risk taking tends to be moderate and incremental. This role relies on established processes and work methods to implement change while also encouraging learning and testing norms to see whether things can be improved. The role fosters the use of best practices and encourages their use in the consulting practice. Past implementation experience is a valued source of learning that this role uses to set up and run new consulting assignments. The deployer therefore often seeks and finds new business opportunities. The role demands a consultant who enjoys the process of change management and helping clients with the changes required by the solution that is being implemented.

GUIDELINES FOR SUCCESSFUL CONSULTING

In Part One of this book we covered how good consultants add value to the consultant-client relationship by simplifying complexity. This appendix applies that principle to this book by simplifying the practice of professional consulting into a set of clear guidelines or rules whose central purpose is to assist in the journey of becoming a trusted advisor.

Table B.1 lists principles and guidelines drawn from professional consulting experience, organized in the four stages in our consulting cycle. They are useable by all consultants regardless of their area of consulting practice, professional experience, or organizational rank. Experienced, successful consultants will be familiar with most of the guidelines, as they are a natural way to think about how to work, and they are conceptually simple. However, as simple as the guidelines appear, their use and implementation can be difficult, even for experienced consultants.

The sixteen guidelines are meant to be a starting point for individuals to think about and critically reflect on their consulting values, attitudes, and behavior. Experience shows that the likelihood of professional success increases through such reflection and assessment, so long as actions are taken to put the principles into practice.

For new consultants the guidelines may be hard to understand in practice. Though abstract and perhaps seeming obvious, the guidelines provide a context for consulting problem solving and decision making. They guide a firm's policies and are targets for individual professional

TABLE B.1 GUIDELINES FOR PROFESSIONAL CONSULTING

Developing	1. The client buys *you* first, then your expertise.
	2. Most new business comes from existing clients.
	3. We are in a people business, regardless of our technology.
	4. Describe how you can help clients do business faster, bigger, better (quality), and/or cheaper.
Mobilizing	5. Teamwork is not optional.
	6. Be present and listen actively.
	7. Each consultant is responsible for finding new business.
	8. Profitability is driven by application and realization.
Building	9. Integrity forges long-term client relationships.
	10. Having a "*can do*" attitude is a critical success factor.
	11. Combine IQ with EQ to enhance political intelligence.
	12. Contribute to the client's career success.
Implementing	13. The goal is to become a trusted consultant.
	14. Put the customer first, even if it risks revenue.
	15. Continuous improvement is a critical success factor.
	16. Live the consulting cycle (four stages, forty-eight practices).

development. In order to show why they are important and useful, in the following sections, we provide more detail about putting the guidelines into practice.

Developing Stage Guidelines

∘ The client buys you first, then your expertise. Brands such as Accenture, Bain, Mercer, and DDI carry a great deal of weight in the customer's mind. Customers expect the "branded" consultants to have the expertise relevant to their problem. However, the marquee value of the brand only gets the consultant in the door. What is more important is whether the client thinks there is a fit between the company culture and the consultant's style and language. The client will quickly judge whether or not the consultant can work well with employees while applying their expertise, will be easy to work with, and can communicate effectively using language that is understandable. If the customer's assessment of fit and expertise is positive, the consultant has cleared a major hurdle to being hired.

∘ *Most new business comes from existing clients.* Consultants spend a great deal of time in their client's organization, during which they become aware of many new problems. Over time, consultants see many things, discuss many organizational issues, and gain insight into the client's people, processes, operations, products, services, and culture. Astute consultants seek to turn such insights into new business opportunities. This does not mean making a hard sell of one's services; rather, it means using insights to communicate a serious interest in the client's business and personal success. Winning new business from an existing client is not guaranteed, but it is very likely, given that people like to work with people they know and people they trust. Consequently, over time, consulting firms find that most of their new business does come from existing customers.

○ *We are in a people business, regardless of our technology.* Expert consultants tend to believe that it is solely their technical expertise that clients seek. As a result, they tend to make their expertise the driver of their customer relationships. As an extension of guideline number one, it is crucial that all consultants (especially technical, scientific, and engineering consultants) realize that people buy from people; customers buy based as much on their perception of the quality of the relationship as on the technical qualities. Therefore it is crucial that consultants hone their ability to form and build professional relationships. This is accomplished by listening effectively, being friendly, managing tension and disagreements, acting with humility, not arrogance, moderating discussions with seriousness and humor, and learning to be interested in people. Consultants must learn to be open and transparent, share experiences honestly, and be honest about the scope and depth of their technical competence. By extension, the way in which consultants manage such relationships reflects on their consulting firm's brand and reputation.

○ *Describe how you can help customers do business faster, bigger, better, and/ or cheaper.* In today's global and highly competitive business environment, all business organizations need to be faster, bigger, better (quality), and/ or cheaper (FBBC) to achieve a sustainable competitive advantage. Consultants must discuss and demonstrate in concrete, practical ways exactly how their solutions achieve those business outcomes. This is true for all forms of consulting, large and small, in all organizational functions and at all organizational levels. When the focus of the consultant's communication is on those four outcomes, the consultant is forced to empathize with the customer's problems; to speak the customer's language; to think in business terms, not just technical terms; and to demonstrate a serious interest in the customer's long-term business and organizational success. It is a mark of professionalism when consultants demonstrate a range of interest, broader knowledge, and competence that embraces helping clients to be faster, bigger, better, and/or cheaper.

Mobilizing Stage Guidelines

◦ *Teamwork is not optional.* Business organizations today operate on the basis of teamwork, cross-functional projects, multilevel task forces, and various committees. In addition, systems (contextual) thinking tells us that in business organizations (that is, functions, roles, management, operations, and administrative procedures) everything is connected to everything else. No one works in isolation. Managers expect suppliers to work with them as a team and want customers to be long-term partners. This means that to be successful, all consultants must learn to be role models for excellent teamwork, demonstrating to clients the skills and competencies of joining, collaborating, and building team effectiveness. Project leaders must understand the drivers of individual behavior, the positive and negative behavior of group dynamics, and the stages of group behavior that people go through on their journey of becoming a high-performing team. This can be a challenge when the client organization has norms and culture different from those of the consultant's own firm. It is harder still when technical consultants prefer to do their work in isolation from people and may find it stressful when working with other people. But forging relationships with clients, working closely with other consultants to produce deliverables, and finding creative solutions to unique problems all demand effective teamwork. It is not optional.

◦ *Be present and listen actively.* The world is a very busy and noisy place, and consultants and clients have sophisticated communications technology in their hands to stay constantly in touch with friends and colleagues. The net effect is that a new generation of employees has entered the workforce used to multitasking at the expense of real human engagement. Increasingly, even as people more frequently communicate remotely, including video and telephone conferencing, they are losing the skills (and perhaps the interest) to listen effectively in person. As a consequence, consultants who multitask in the same room as their clients risk offending the clients, who feel insulted by what they consider rude behavior. When a consultant is distracted by a cell phone or computer, the consultant cannot be fully present and engaged with the client. When the consultant is thinking about something other than what the client is talking about, the consultant is not fully present. Important things can be missed. Such behavior is contrary to trust building and teamwork; it is symptomatic of arrogance and selfishness. Effective consultants understand the potential risk of insulting clients, so they work hard to give them 100 percent of their attention, every time, without exception. Successful consultants develop the skills of first deciding in their mind to be fully present and then demanding of themselves intellectual integrity by actively listening to and engaging in what the client is expressing.

○ *Each consultant is responsible for finding new business.* While engaged in client work, consultants see and hear about many client problems beyond their immediate engagement. It is every consultant's responsibility to bring that awareness and insight back to their firm for consideration and, possibly, a proposal. Similarly, independent, self-employed consultants need to consider submitting new business proposals that address the problems they have become aware of in their client setting. All consultants must look for new business, even if they will not carry out the consulting assignment themselves. Even consultants with limited client contact, such as junior consultants or software application developers, have a responsibility to think about how they may continue to improve the client's business. This is a corollary to the earlier guideline that most new business comes from existing customers. When all consultants on a project acknowledge and accept their personal responsibility to look out for new business opportunities, then new business will follow.

○ *Profitability is driven by application and realization.* Realization lies in the firm's management policies, systems, and procedures that effectively and efficiently win new business, produce deliverables, bill clients, and bank the money. It is a measure of success in this regard when a consulting firm (or an individual) has more proposals won than it can immediately deploy and a backlog of work accumulates. The larger the backlog of pending business, the greater the firm's ability to hire new consultants, pay existing consultants more money, and invest in and expand the firm. The ratio of business won to business lost must be positive, and the financial structure of new business must produce a profit. Application rates (sometimes called chargeability or utilization rates) must be sufficient to justify the fixed cost of a consultant, contribute to overhead, and yield a profit to the firm. Firms usually set target application rates for all their consultants (the rates vary by the consultant's rank, experience and role) and expect their consultants to achieve those targets. A well-managed firm ensures that application and realization issues are carefully controlled, thereby ensuring profitability.

Building Stage Guidelines

○ *Integrity forges long-term client relationships.* Because most new business should be coming from existing clients, it follows that consultants ought to run their business with rules and procedures that create long-term relationships with their clients. Such relationships are built with integrity. For consultants, integrity means ensuring complete consistency between one's spoken word and one's behavior. Therefore, throughout the entire consulting process, consultants must be alert to the expectations they are setting, their spoken intentions, and communications that set standards of work and behavior. Broken integrity is very difficult to restore. It breaks trust—the most fundamental psychological tenet of human relationships—with its obvious negative effect on forging long-term, profitable client relationships. Being a role model for integrity within one's own firm and with clients is central to being professional and vital for success.

  ◦ *Having a "can do" attitude is a critical success factor.* Client organizations are complex, often confusing, and full of unexpected events. Simultaneously, consultants are usually amplifying all of these factors by driving some sort of change. The amount, direction, and intensity of change often leads employees to resist the consultant's work. When faced with this natural resistance, consultants still need to get things done and produce deliverables. They must have a "can do" attitude, rather than capitulating or complaining about client resistance. This means consultants must determine what is possible, choose alternative paths, devise new strategies, explain vision and values, and communicate with influence in ways that gets people to act and move the client's organization forward. After all, consultants get paid for adding value and being catalysts for change. To be successful, change agents must be willing to tackle resistance, facilitate learning, and lead. Such positive, action-oriented attitudes and behavior are critical for effective consulting.

  ◦ *Combine IQ with EQ to enhance political intelligence.* Clients hire consultants for their fit, expertise, and intellectual ability, expecting them to bring rigor to the problem-solving and decision-making process that leads to a solution. Such competencies are necessary for solving complex organizational problems that are both rational and emotional. Sometimes in consulting, emotional factors affect decisions more than objective analysis. That is when consultants must use their emotional intelligence. The emotional intelligence quotient (EQ) is a set of human relations skills that enables a consultant to respond appropriately in all situations, but especially when emotional stresses and pressures increase. This is important because some client organizations are notoriously high-pressure and political environments, with client managers putting a lot of pressure on consultants to deliver. In such difficult situations, a combination of intellectual and emotional intelligence is needed to navigate the subtle nuances of power and influence. It is crucial that consultants have the mental and emotional resources to choose how to deal with emotional situations rather than react automatically and say or do the wrong thing.

○ *Contribute to the client's career success.* A client is not necessarily an organization or a whole business entity. It is usually a single representative person—the individual in the client's organization who has primary responsibility for the success of the consulting engagement. Effective consultants are cognizant of that client's role and career needs. Clients want to be successful, to be perceived positively; to get a promotion, get an increase in pay, enjoy a successful career in the organization; and to keep their boss happy. Having hired a consultant, the client may also be feeling quite exposed and vulnerable, hoping that the project goes well. With this in mind, successful consultants may change priorities, make concessions, share political matters, put in extra work, and so on to make sure their client looks good inside the organization. By helping their clients to be perceived positively by upper management and perhaps advance in their careers, consultants are more likely to get repeat business, forge long-term relationships, and become a trusted advisor.

Implementing Stage Guidelines

○ *The goal is to become a trusted consultant.* The benefits of achieving the status of trusted advisor or trusted consultant are so significant that it should be every consultant's goal to become one. The keys to achieving this goal are being trustworthy, working with integrity, expanding one's knowledge and understanding of the client's business, and working to develop a professional yet friendly relationship with the client. The trusted consultant relationship yields benefits: clients focusing less on price and more on the value delivered by the consultant, expanded business opportunities, readily provided referrals, and professional satisfaction.

○ *Put the customer first, even if it risks revenue.* Clients always expect more for less. Consultants are often under pressure to do "a little bit extra" for clients. Because even a small amount of additional client work means time and money, consultants periodically face the dilemma of whether or not to charge for the extra work. This is a judgment call and never easy. If the consultant judges that the extras or changes in scope are substantial, then the fee should be renegotiated (in fact, clients may be surprised if the consultant does *not* raise this). Anything else is discretionary and should be done pro bono because it is in the best interest of the client and of doing quality work. It is simply the right thing to do. For example, working late to get something done on time (or ahead of time) pays dividends and is usually worth doing. At the same time, consultants should not intentionally expand the time spent on the work in order to charge more money; that is unethical.

○ *Continuous improvement is a critical success factor.* Continuous improvement is vital for consultants and critical for professional growth. As self-proclaimed experts, though, this may be difficult for some, because it requires consultants to admit that there is something they do not already know. It requires expanding their expertise and being open to learning new things. If they avoid this, they run the risk of ignoring client data, important issues, and analysis in order to deploy existing, ready-made solutions over and over again. This can be seen as an ethical issue when consultants promote themselves as having, say, ten years of experience, when in fact they only have one year's worth of experience, repeated ten times over. There is little value in that. Continuous improvement lies at the heart of professionalism to ensure a competitive advantage for the consultant and giving the client the very best service.

○ *Live the consulting cycle.* The cycle of consulting is a fully integrated process requiring four stages, four roles, twelve competencies, and forty-eight practices. For clarity of presentation, we have organized the competencies and practices into a linear sequence by each stage and role. In practice, however, the cycle is dynamic and interactive; knowledge and skills used in one stage can be used in any other stage to one degree or another. Certain stages require an emphasis on certain business and technical competencies. But all the stages require excellent interpersonal skills, an ability to influence people, the exercise of leadership, and good organization of time and resources. Throughout the cycle, consultants must be able to establish clear goals, formulate a strategy, decide on activities, establish responsibilities, delegate work, and follow established procedures and protocols—all while remaining creative and innovative as they live the cycle and get the work done.

THE LEADERSHIP ROLE OF CONSULTANTS

Consulting is a leadership responsibility, and successful consultants need to understand the way in which this is exercised throughout a project.

Even though leadership is a very big topic (see, for example, Bennis, 2009; Buckingham & Clifton, 2001; Drucker, 2008; Goleman, 1998, 2000; Hill, 2003; Roberts, 1990) and beyond the scope of this book, it is valuable to discuss at least the rudiments of what it is, how it works, and why it is important in consulting. First, by "leader" we do not mean the person who is head of a national consulting practice or the managing partner or president of a firm. That is leadership as a noun, by position. We mean leadership as a set of functions that parallel the four roles in our consulting model.

Leadership Thinking for Consultants

In the arena of consulting, leadership encompasses these actions:

1. Setting direction with a vision and a strategy designed in conjunction with the client
2. Rallying people's commitment to the engagement and motivating project team members

3. Ensuring that the results produced are consistent with project plans and client needs

4. Establishing changes in the client's organization and people in a way that solves the client's problem.

When individual consultants perform these functions, they are acting as a leader. Details of this work may include the following:

- Framing and reframing the client's problem
- Providing thought leadership during discussions
- Defining tasks and how they will be performed
- Orchestrating and running meetings
- Congratulating people for good work
- Admitting mistakes and making amends
- Communicating the vision for the engagement
- Taking initiative to resolve any conflicts
- Representing their firm's interests to the client
- Coaching people to help them learn

Thinking as a leader also includes these mental skills: (1) using two distinct types of thinking, (2) realizing that a consulting project is a set of integrated activities, (3) understanding the link between leading and managing, and (4) using principles to guide decisions and actions. These serve to strengthen consultants' leadership capability.

Types of Thinking

During *each* stage of the cycle it is important and helpful for consultants and project leaders to use two kinds of thinking: analytical and contextual. *Analytical thinking* occurs when we examine a situation or problem by taking it apart, breaking it down into its components, looking at the parts, generating data, comparing and contrasting data, and drawing rational and logical conclusions from what we have found. *Contextual thinking*, on the other hand, is looking at the client's situation or problem in terms of the environment in which it exists. In this bigger picture or larger context reside issues, data, trends, patterns of behavior, facts, perceptions, purposes, intentions, and connections that help to explain how and why the client's problem is affected (or caused) by something in the company environment.

Taken all together, the insights produced by contextual and analytical thinking help consultant-leaders to understand the full complement of factors affecting a client's general situation and specific problem. Based on this, they can then decide on a set of project activities to tackle and solve the problem.

Consulting Activities and Strategy

A well-designed consulting project is a *set of integrated activities* that is orchestrated into a strategy. *Generic* activities might include, for example, writing proposals, doing research, developing software, building a prototype, conducting various project meetings, making presentations, and writing reports. Within each of these are more specific activities and detailed tasks, all of which must add up to a coherent whole. Crafting and executing these activities is the essence of a consulting strategy. Porter's (2009) research on strategy helps us realize that to be successful, consulting activities require meeting three criteria:

- Each activity must contribute directly to the project purpose and goals.
- All activities must mutually reinforce each other.
- Each activity must be optimized.

These criteria and conditions apply to all consulting projects and engagements, and it is the responsibility of engagement leaders, project leaders, and individual consultants to ensure that all project activities are clear and meet the criteria. Project leaders and team members must use analytical and contextual thinking to define the activities and integrate them into a coherent plan.

For those interested in starting a consulting business and leading a consulting firm, this same process of actions and thinking is needed to formulate the firm's vision and mission and to craft a strategy with a set of activities that represent the unique way the firm and its consultants deliver services to its target markets and clients.

Leading and Managing

Throughout this book we have frequently used the term "leader" rather than "manager" to describe the skills needed by consultants. This is deliberate. In the literature on leadership, leadership is associated with creating, stimulating, and fostering change, whereas management is about establishing stability and order and controlling complexity (Kotter, 1990). To be successful, a consultant must be a leader *and* a manager. As consultants, we certainly manage our complex projects with proposals, budgets, plans, and performance coaching, but we cannot control our clients. Consultants must *lead* clients to adopt the changes we are recommending, and we must *lead* our team members through the steps and challenges of becoming a high-performing consulting team.

APPENDIX D

CONSULTING CASE APPLICATIONS

The following cases are based on real situations; identifying details have been altered for reasons of confidentiality. The cases illustrate the work as represented by the consulting framework and the complete consulting cycle. Included are cases representing training, executive coaching, and organizational development consulting. They are not presented or intended to describe the only way to conduct consulting, but as examples of how the framework can be used in the real world of consulting.

CASE 1. TRAINING: STRATEGIC LEADERSHIP IN MANUFACTURING

Step	Case Overview
Develop	*An RFP competitive bid situation in which a chemical company needed to train its manufacturing managers to be more strategic in their thinking and decision making.* Consultants met with their manufacturing council representative to understand the need and to develop a proposal; the proposal was presented to the council by two consultants and the business was won.
Mobilize	Conducted a structured interview with a wide range of managers in worldwide manufacturing operations, studied internal manufacturing initiatives, and worked closely with manufacturing council representatives.
Build	Set up a design committee that included manufacturing managers from several sites; reviewed the priorities, objectives, and design; and tested content ideas, concepts, tools, and techniques of the training program with the committee. Visited the company's leading manufacturing sites, benchmarked best practices, and developed cases of best-in-class manufacturing. Produced participant manuals, training aids, handouts, a PowerPoint slide presentation, and a strategy guide.
Implement	Conducted a pilot program that included the design committee as participants, thoroughly debriefed the pilot, made revisions, and rolled out the program to the company.

CASE 2. EXECUTIVE COACHING

Step	Case Overview
Develop	*An RFP competitive bid situation in which the company's head of human resources (HR) met with several executive coaches to choose the one with the best fit.* The consultant attended a joint meeting with the senior executive client, the client's manager, and the head of human resources. The problem was identified as a lack of teamwork, poor interpersonal skills, and deteriorating relations with colleagues.
Mobilize	Met with the senior executive (the client) to gain a deeper understanding of the client's situation, expectations, and timetable, and to check whether the client was comfortable with the coach. Subsequent positive feedback from the head of HR started six months of coaching.
Build	Through careful questioning and listening, a rapport was built so the senior executive could feel safe and confident in sharing personal thoughts and feelings. Trust and coaching effectiveness were established and verified, and 360-degree data and diagnostics produced patterns of behavior and indicators of priority areas for change and improvement.
Implement	Confidentiality was maintained throughout the coaching process. A developmental strategy was established and followed. Changes in mental outlook and interpersonal behavior led to new priorities in the executive's role and specific business outcomes. Positive feedback and changes in perception led to a substantial promotion for the executive.

CASE 3. ORGANIZATIONAL DEVELOPMENT: CROSS-COMPANY CONFERENCES

Step	Case Overview
Develop	*A competitive interview and bid situation in which a global professional services firm sought to foster greater collaboration across its disparate operating business units, with the objective of forging a network of colleagues that could share ways to develop incremental client revenue.* Several meetings with the design committee led to a proposal and the consultant's acceptance to do the work.
Mobilize	Worked very closely with the design committee to create a unique and tailored conference design. Interviewed presidents of operating units and company chairperson to encourage participation and engender support. Validated conference design with presidents of the operating units.
Build	Gave the conference an industry focus. Carefully selected senior managers from across the business units with responsibility for revenue growth in that industry to attend the conference. Interviewed each participant before their conference attendance. Ensured that modules and speakers had industry expertise; used company confidential material; involved respected company executives as presenters. Produced manuals, presentations, and conference handouts.
Implement	Consultant provided strong facilitation to ensure that the conference achieved its objectives, kept to its timetable, engendered good discussion, got full participation, built collegiality, tested assumptions, synthesized ideas, and developed next steps and an action plan. Rolled out subsequent conferences in different industries; this led to additional cross-company training and development programs. Produced incremental revenues for the company.

DIAGNOSTIC PROCEDURES AND INSTRUMENTS FOR CONSULTING TEAMS

Edgar Schein, a leading researcher and writer in the field of organizational psychology, defines a group as: "A psychological group is any number of people who 1) interact with one another, 2) are psychologically aware of one another, and 3) perceive themselves to be a group" (1980, p. 145).

Group members must develop a consensus on a broad set of both internal and external tasks (Schein, 1980). In general, these tasks include the following:

○ *External:* Core mission, functions, and tasks vis-à-vis the environment; specific goals; basic means for accomplishing the goals; criteria used to measure results; and remedial or repair strategies if goals are not met.

○ *Internal:* Common language and conceptual systems to work together, including space and time; group boundaries and criteria for inclusion; criteria for allocating power, status, and authority; criteria for intimacy and friendship; criteria for allocating rewards and punishments; and concepts for managing the unmanageable—ideology and religion.

Properties of Groups

Malcolm Knowles (Knowles, Holton, & Swanson, 2005), an important pioneer in our understanding of adult learning and what he calls "andragogy," provides an insightful overview of the properties of groups that drive group behavior and affect group performance. He defines a group as having the following qualities and properties:

Definable Membership—Two or more people identify themselves by name or type.

Group Consciousness—Members think of themselves as a group, have a "collective perception of unity"—a conscious identification with one another.

Sense of Shared Purpose—Members have the same goals or ideals.

Interdependence—Members need the help of one another to accomplish the purposes for which they joined the group.

Interaction—Members communicate with one another, influence one another, and react to one another.

Unitary Manner—The group behaves as a single organism.

The definition and properties of a group are starting points in understanding the factors that affect group dynamics. This also aids in understanding both the helpful and the disruptive behavior of members that affect group performance.

Factors Affecting Group Performance

Groups are *complex systems* in motion, with many moving parts, involving multiple factors at the group, individual, and behavioral levels. The nature and quality of a factor at one level affects conditions and circumstances at other levels of the group. Adapted from Knowles (1972), these factors can be used to assess a group's effectiveness and make decisions about actions needed to improve group performance.

Commitment, loyalty, and performance increase or decline with the presence or absence of the following factors:

Group-Level Factors:

- Group is highly valued by outsiders.
- Goals are clear and compelling.
- Issues driving conformity are important.
- Group organization is appropriate to the tasks.
- Resources (economic, material, legal, intellectual, and so on) are available.

Membership-Level Factors:

- Individuals find being a member attractive.
- Individual needs are satisfied.
- Individuals feel acceptance and security.
- Individuals are clear about their goals and roles.

Group Behavior Factors:

- Agreement is sought about:
  - Group activities, tasks, and goals
  - Means to achieve group task and goals
  - Health of members' interaction with one another
  - Quality of leadership
- Members are congenial.
- Everyone participates in group decisions.
- Energy is mobilized around group activities.
- Members coordinate in a manner required by group tasks.
- Processes are appropriate to group goals and tasks.
- Stages of team development are managed.
- There is unanimity about conformance to group norms.

The presence or absence of these factors is important to consider when trying to understand the drivers of group dynamics and performance.

Context of Group Dynamics

Peter Block (2000) explains that groups exist within a larger organizational context as an integrating mechanism. It is important to understand that relationship if we are to understand how and why a group is operating in a particular way: "Small groups are the vehicle for integrating activity in organizations. Two people can be a group—or forty. Small group discovery is one step more complex than individual discovery, for it encompasses the interaction among people" (Block, 2000, p. 201).

Block identifies the following set of factors within a group that members and the project leader can use to examine a group's effectiveness.

- Attitudes about the project
- Attitudes about the consultant
- Authority and power impact

- Goals and objectives
- Conflict management process
- Decision-making process
- Domination of one or more members
- Evaluation of performance
- Gender roles and discrimination
- Leadership style strengths and weaknesses
- Norms for individual behavior
- Resource management
- Subgroup relationships
- Support between members
- Status differences between members

Block also believes that understanding the strengths and weaknesses of the group (project) leader's style is important to team effectiveness. He cautions, however, that problems with the leader's style may be overstated and can be used as an excuse by individual members to avoid taking personal responsibility for group problems.

The preceding properties and factors are general principles and norms that help consultants and project leaders to identify and form judgments about the merits of individual and group behavior. The next section describes specific behavioral and group psychology issues that can help or hinder the growth and maturity of a group. Practical actions are suggested to overcome problems and find ways to move a consulting group forward to become a team.

Group Member Behavior and Team Development

Project leaders can discuss the presence or absence of the following behavior with team members to ascertain what behavior needs to change that will produce better teamwork.

BEHAVIOR THAT HELPS OR HINDERS PROJECT TEAM DEVELOPMENT

Helps Team Progress	Hinders Team Progress
Avoiding the "hinders" behaviors	Fight-or-flight as responses
Encouraging	Resisting change
Mediating	Lots of errors and mistakes
Sense of humor	Rudeness with clients
Relieving tension	Confusion
Sharing	Absence from team activities
Focus on group process	Withdrawing from team activities
Demonstrating personal integrity	Hostility or defensive arguing
Honest but diplomatic speech	Excessive excuses
Active listening	Deflection of personal responsibility
Being emotionally intelligent	Disagreements becoming personal
Being "present" in group activities	Not helping one another
Setting and role modeling standards	Carelessness about quality of results
Following others' lead	Not honoring commitments
Generating energy	Special pleading
Testing assumptions	Blocking progress
	Dominating
	Seeking excessive recognition
	Inappropriate language

Team Problems and Solutions

Project leaders can diagnose (1) task skills and competencies, (2) relationship of group members, (3) resources and equipment, and (4) the team leader. Although there are technical matters that cause problems in consulting, the most difficult matters to resolve are usually "people issues." The following table provides the characteristics of each type of problem and suggested solutions to improve consulting team performance.

Type of Problem	Characteristics	Solutions Steps
Skills and Competencies	<ul><li>Lots of errors and mistakes</li><li>Equipment not used properly</li><li>Misunderstandings</li><li>Confusion</li><li>Process cannot be performed with new capabilities</li></ul>	<ul><li>Provide training and practice.</li><li>Issue metrics that show progress in performance.</li><li>Educate on relevant topics.</li><li>Encourage team members to help each other.</li></ul>
Relationships of Team Members	<ul><li>Absence and withdrawal from team activities</li><li>Hostility toward others</li><li>Excuses and deflection of personal responsibility</li><li>Disagreements becoming personal</li><li>Inability to reach agreement</li><li>Failure to help one another</li><li>Carelessness about quality and achieving agreed-upon results</li><li>Not honoring commitments</li></ul>	<ul><li>Use a diagnostic instrument to measure the team's views on key team attributes (goals, roles, responsibilities, processes, and so on).</li><li>Discuss the feedback.</li><li>Facilitate an open discussion of issues between contending members.</li><li>Surface underlying tensions and conflict.</li><li>Search for practical and mutually agreeable solutions.</li><li>Keep the team's purpose and shared vision in mind.</li></ul>
Resources and Equipment	<ul><li>Tools and equipment that do not work</li><li>Administrative systems and documents that are not user friendly</li></ul>	<ul><li>Repair or replace tools and equipment.</li><li>Reengineer processes, procedures, and documents.</li></ul>

(Continued)

Type of Problem	Characteristics	Solutions Steps
Leadership of the Team	• Team processes that are not clear and well defined • Unclear goals and agenda • Meetings poorly handled • Unclear communications • Little useful feedback to people • Lack of personal enthusiasm and commitment • Lack of confidence in role • Inability to make decisions in a timely manner • Lack of understanding of people • Not serving as a thought leader	• Conduct an open discussion of effective team leadership. • Seek help from team members. • Get some training; do some reading. • Practice and take risks with one's own opinions and decisions. • Be clear about team values, including learning the culture. • Become introspective to understand oneself better. • Rotate the leadership role to study how others do it effectively. • Develop one's own style.

Resolving team problems always demands confronting reality. Most of the hard work of team building comes from admitting what is *really* going on and using an effective process to discuss the issues openly and realistically, to produce a practical consensus on actions that all agree will improve team work.

Steps in Team-Building Interventions

Traditionally, organization development (OD) consultants focus on improving the performance of work groups and building stronger teams. Over the years they have developed a rigorous set of steps, values, and tools to be successful in this work. The following ten guidelines are suggested by a leading authority in this type of consulting (Block, 2000). Anyone who wants to do this work (known as *action science*) successfully should not pursue it lightly without study, careful planning, and help.

1. *Purpose and Values.* Present and discuss why the session is being held, what it will focus on, and the expected outcome. The discussion should identify the underlying values of teamwork such as integrity, honesty, confidentiality, collaboration, learning, improvement, openness, mutual respect, and trust.

2. *Ground Rules.* Establish the behavioral rules that will make the session a positive, productive one. The rules may include such things as: no one is left out; what is said here stays here; team time is for team time (not e-mails or mobile phones); let people finish a thought; no interruptions; listen actively; deal with reality; keep track of all key issues; do not hold back; and no personal attacks.

3. *Generate Data.* It is very useful to have some information available that explains behavioral patterns, habits, group dynamics, communication issues, and behavior that helps or hinders teamwork. The information may be a mix of feedback from the client, a summary of anonymous input from each group member in the form of a survey questionnaire, or the results of brainstorming by the group regarding its effectiveness as a team.

4. *Discuss Group Issues.* It is generally easier for a group to talk about team-level issues, barriers, and problems, rather than focusing on the behavior of individual members. Use group data and feedback to "warm things up" or to "break the ice" so that people feel safe talking about the group issues. Avoid focusing on individual team members (if relevant) until the group norms are well established and things can be discussed in a constructive, supportive way.

5. *Individual Problems.* If it becomes clear that the team's effectiveness is tied to a problem with individual members, at some point this must be raised and dealt with in a constructive manner. Keep the discussion focused on the person's behavior, not generalities about personality or attitude. Keep the discussion focused on the future to prevent the group from dwelling on criticisms of the past. Coach the team on how to coach someone who needs to change and be more effective. Help the person in question to acknowledge the negative behavior and to feel safe about change and improvement. A team leader's mindful understanding of resistance and defense mechanisms can be useful during these discussions.

(Continued)

6. *Support Everyone.* Team building is not about embarrassing or punishing anyone. It is about building a consensus on the benefits that can accrue from the active interdependence of individuals. The message should be that everyone is needed for the team to be a team, that each person was selected for a purpose, that both expertise and style are important for success. It is a group of equals, with no prima donnas. If one or two people are preventing effective collaboration, this must be discussed by the team and changes must be made, keeping in mind the purpose, goals, and values established at the beginning of the team-building session. A consulting team always comprises individuals with specific and sometimes unique knowledge and skills. Individual uniqueness must be valued as much as those things that individuals have in common with the whole team. At the same time, as much as individual expertise is valued, mutual support also must be a group value; group members need to willingly and spontaneously make an effort to help other members. Accordingly, individual team members both hold themselves accountable for their own role and are willingly help others without expecting credit for doing so. This mutual support is essential, and its presence is a good measure of whether the team is working effectively.

7. *Action Plan.* If the team is to improve, it must take action. Changes may be required for the group as a whole as well as by individuals. Action plans should be simple and concentrate on a few issues. Action plans should be *specific, measurable, achievable, realistic,* and *time-bound* (SMART). To build commitment, discuss the follow-up process that holds individuals and the team accountable for the agreed-upon changes and improvements.

8. *Accountability.* For teamwork to be effective, it is absolutely essential that individual members keep their word and do what they say they will do. This is the essence of accountability. When a person does *not* keep his or her word, the person has lost integrity and must be held accountable by being coached. This coaching communication should be done first in private. But with repeated occurrences, it should be discussed in public when the team next meets. Integrity is regained when the person declares to the coach (or team) that accountability will be upheld in the future, so long as the person's action is consistent with that declaration. Discussion of accountability ought to be part of the team's open forum.

9. *Debriefing.* When the team-building session has reached its conclusion (which may in fact require several sessions), it is a good practice to have a final discussion about how the session or sessions went. Discuss the strengths and weaknesses of the team-building effort and identify things that need to be done the next time that will strengthen future meetings. This serves to reinforce the values of feedback, openness, change, and dealing with the reality of the team's behavior. Debriefings may also surface people's behavior that helped or hindered the team-building process itself, which were not seen or discussed during the retreat.

10. *Follow-up.* Immediately following the team-building session, distribute any information that pertains to the team's action plans and individual commitments. At the next scheduled team meeting, be prepared to share evidence that shows whether the team is making progress. Periodically put "team-building issues" on the agenda of regular team meetings. If the problems identified in the retreat recur, or if another problem occurs, another retreat may be in order. If the same problems persist after several retreats, an OD consultant may be required, or a change in team membership or leadership may be in order.

BIBLIOGRAPHY AND RESOURCES

Bibliography

Advice for consultants. (2011, June 4). *Economist*, p. 74.

Bennis, W. (2009). *On becoming a leader*. New York: Basic Books.

Bennis, W., & Nanus, B. (2003). *Leaders*. New York: Harper & Row.

Berlew, D., & Harrison, R. (1979). *Positive power and influence program*. Plymouth, MA: Situation Management Systems, Inc.

Biswell, S., & Twitchell, D. (2002). *Management consulting*. New York: Wiley.

Blanchard, K., & Johnson, S. (1982). *The one minute manager*. New York: William Morrow.

Block, P. (1981; 2000). *Flawless consulting*. San Diego, CA: University Associates.

Block, P. (2001). *The flawless consulting field book & companion*. San Francisco: Pfeiffer Wiley.

Bossidy, L., & Charan, R. (2002). *Execution: The discipline of getting things done*. New York: Crown Business.

Bridges, W. (1986). Managing organizational transitions. *Organization Dynamics, 15*(1), 24–33.

Bridges, W. (2009). *Transitions: making sense of life's changes*. Reading, MA: Addison-Wesley.

Briggs, K., & Myers, I. (1943). *Myers-Briggs type indicator*. Palo Alto, CA: Consulting Psychology Press.

Bryman, A., & Bell, E. (2003). *Business research methods*. New York: Oxford University Press.

Buckingham, M., & Clifton, D. (2001). *Now, discover your strengths*. New York: Free Press.

Buckingham, M., & Coffman, C. (1999). *First, break all the rules.* New York: Simon & Schuster.

Burke, W. (2008). *Organization change: Theory and practice* (2nd ed.). Thousand Oaks, CA: SAGE.

Business of consulting. (2011, November 17). *Financial Times Special Report,* 2–8.

Careers-in-Business. (2011). *Consulting facts and trends.* Retrieved from http://careers-in-business.com/consulting/mcfacts.htm

Carnegie, D. (1981). *How to win friends and influence people* (rev. ed.). New York: Simon & Schuster.

Charan, R., & Tichy, N. (2002). *Every business is a growth business.* New York: Random House.

Conger, J. (1998). How gen X managers manage. *Strategy & Business,* Q1.

Costa, L., & McCrae, R. (1985). NEO-Personality Indicator. *Psychological Assessment Resources.* Odessa, FL.

Covey, S. R. (1992). *Principle centered leadership.* New York: Simon & Schuster.

Dawkins, R. (2009). *The greatest show on earth: the evidence for evolution.* New York: Free Press, pp. 9–18.

Delaney, G., & Purba, S. (2003). *IT consulting in tough times: 12 keys to a thriving practice.* Berkeley, CA: Osborne/McGraw-Hill.

Deming, W. E. (1986). *Out of the crisis.* Cambridge, MA: MIT Press, 23–96.

DePree, M. (1989). *Leadership is an art.* New York: Bantam Doubleday Dell.

Drucker, P. (1964). *Managing for results.* New York: Harper & Row.

Drucker, P. (1993). *The practice of management.* New York: HarperBusiness.

Drucker, P. (2002). *The effective executive.* New York: Harper & Row.

Drucker, P. (2008). *Management: Tasks, responsibilities, practices* (rev. ed.). New York: Harper & Row.

Eldred, J. (2000). *Mastering organizational politics and power.* Course at University of Pennsylvania, PA.

Fisher, R., Ury, W., & Patton, B. (1991). *Getting to yes: Negotiating agreement without giving in* (2nd ed.). New York: Penguin Books.

Francis, D., & Young, D. (1979). *Improving work groups.* San Diego, CA: University Associates, 62–67.

French, J., & Raven, B. (1959). The bases of social power. In D. Cartwright (Ed.), *Studies in social power* (pp. 150–167). Ann Arbor: University of Michigan, Institute for Social Research.

French, W., & Bell, C. (1978). *Organization development.* Englewood Cliffs, NJ: Prentice-Hall, 78.

Gardner, J. (1990). *On leadership.* New York: Free Press.

Gilligan, C. (1993). *In a different voice.* Boston, MA: Harvard University Press.

Goleman, D. (1998, November-December). What makes a leader? *Harvard Business Review.*

Goleman, D. (2000, March-April). Leadership that gets results. *Harvard Business Review.*

Goleman, D. (2006a). *Emotional intelligence.* New York: Bantam Books.

Goleman, D. (2006b). *Working with emotional intelligence.* New York: Bantam Books.

Gray, J. (1993). *Men are from Mars, women are from Venus.* New York: HarperCollins.

Hackman, J. R., & Oldham, G. (1980). *Work design.* Reading, MA: Addison Wesley.

Hambrick, D., & Cannella, A. (1989). Strategy implementation as substance and selling. *Academy of Management Executive, 3*(4), 278–285.

Hanan, H., Cribbin, J., et al. (1973). *Consultative selling.* New York: AMACOM, American Management Association.

Heiman, S., & Sanchez, D. (1998). *The new strategic selling.* New York: Warner Business Books.

Hersey, P., Blanchard, K., & Johnson, D. (2007). *Management of organizational behavior* (8th ed.). Upper Saddle River, NJ: Pearson.

Herzberg, F. (1968, January-February). One more time: How do you motivate employees? *Harvard Business Review.*

Hill, L. (2003). *Becoming a manager.* Boston, MA: Harvard Business School Press.

Honey, P., & Mumford, A. (1982). *Manual of learning styles.* London: Peter Honey.

Ibisworld. (2012). *Global management consultants market research report.* Retrieved from http://www.ibisworld.com/industry/global/global-management-consultants.html

Inscape. (2012). Everything DiSC. Minneapolis, MN.

Johnson, B. (1982). *Private consulting.* Upper Saddle River, NJ: Prentice Hall.

Kassandra Project: Freedom against disinformation. (n.d.). Retrieved from kassandra-project.wordpress.com/2007/12/24/killer-corporations-grow-rate-from-2005-to-2007

Katzenbach, J., & Smith, D. (2003) *The wisdom of teams.* New York: HarperCollins.

Kilmann, R. (2004). *Beyond the quick fix.* San Francisco: Jossey-Bass.

Knowles, M. (1972). *Introduction to group dynamics.* Chicago, IL: Follett Publishing, pp. 40–64.

Knowles, M. (1980). *The modern practice of adult learning.* Wilton, CT: Association Press.

Knowles, M., Holton, E., & Swanson, R. (2005). *The adult learner* (6th ed.). Burlington, MA: Elsevier.

Kohlberg, L. (1981). *Essays on moral development: The philosophy of moral development* (Vol. 1). New York: Harper & Row.

Kolb, D. (1984). *Experiential learning: Experience as the source of learning and development.* Upper Saddle River, NJ: Prentice Hall.

Kolb, D. (2008). *Learning styles inventory.* Boston, MA: Hay McBer.

Kotter, J. (1982). *The general managers.* New York: Free Press.

Kotter, J. (1988). *The leadership factor.* New York: Free Press.

Kotter, J. (1990, May–June). What leaders really do. *Harvard Business Review.*

Kotter, J. (1996). *Leading change.* Boston: Harvard Business School.

Kouzes, J. M., & Posner, B. Z. (2012). *The leadership challenge* (5th ed.). San Francisco: Jossey-Bass.

Kreitner, R. (2009). *Management* (11th ed.). New York: Houghton Mifflin.

Laid off lawyers, cast off consultants. (2010, January 23). *Economist,* p. 64.

Langdon, K., & Bruce, A. (2000). *Project management.* New York: Dorling Kindersley.

Lehmann, D. (1989). *Market research and analysis* (3rd ed.). New York: Richard Irwin.

Lencioni, P. (2002). *The five dysfunctions of a team.* San Francisco: Jossey-Bass.

Lewin, K. (1946). Action research and minority problems. *Journal of Social Issues 2*(4), 34–46.

Likert, R. (1967). *The human organization.* New York: McGraw-Hill.

Machiavelli, N. (1952). *The prince.* New York: The New American Library.

Maister, D. (1993). *Managing the professional service firm.* New York: Free Press.

Maister, D. (1997). *True professionalism.* New York: Free Press.

Maister, D., Green, C., & Galford, R. (2000). *The trusted advisor.* New York: Free Press.

Maslow, A. (2009). In R. Kreitner, *Management* (11th ed.). New York: Houghton Mifflin.

McClelland, D. C. (1992). In R. D. London, *Psychology.* UK: Gross, Hodder, & Stoughton.

McKenna, C. (1995). The origins of modern consulting. *Business and Economic History, 24* (1), 51–58.

McKenna, C. (2006). *The world's newest profession.* New York: Cambridge University Press.

Miller, R., & Heiman, S. (1988). *Strategic selling.* New York: Grand Central Publishing.

Mintzberg, H. (1980). *The nature of managerial work.* Upper Saddle River, NJ: Prentice Hall.

Moosbruker, J. (1995). Developing high performing teams. In L. Butler, A. Litwin, & R. Ritvo (Eds.), *Managing in the age of change* (pp. 46–55). New York: NTL/Irwin.

Myers, I. B., with Myers, P. B. (1980, 1995). *Gifts differing: Understanding personality type.* Mountain View, CA: Davies-Black Publishing.

Nadler, D., et al. (1995). *Discontinuous change, leading organizational transformation.* San Francisco: Jossey-Bass.

Nadler, D., & Tushman, M. (1997). *Competing by design: The power of organizational architecture.* New York: Oxford University Press.

Niedereichholz, C., & Niedereichholz, J. (2006). *Consulting insight.* Germany: Bides Books.

O'Connell, F. (1994). *How to run successful projects.* Upper Saddle River, NJ: Prentice Hall.

Osland, J., Turner, M., Kolb, D., & Rubin, I. (2010). *Organizational behavior reader.* Upper Saddle River, NJ: Prentice Hall.

Pande, P., & Holpp, L. (2002). *What is six sigma?* New York: McGraw-Hill.

Peters, T. (1985). *A passion for excellence.* New York: Random House.

Peters, T., & Waterman, H. (1981). *In search of excellence.* New York: HarperBusiness.

Phillips, K., & Shaw, P. (1998). *A consultancy approach for trainers and developers.* Aldershot, UK: Gower Press.

Plunkett, J. (2009). *Plunkett's consulting industry almanac.* Houston, TX: Plunkett Research.

Plunkett, J. (2011). *Plunkett's consulting industry almanac.* Houston, TX: Plunkett Research.

Plunkett, J. (2012). *Plunkett's consulting industry almanac.* Houston, TX: Plunkett Research. Retrieved from http://www.plunkettresearch.com/consulting-market-research/industry-trends

Porter, M. (2009, March). What is strategy? *Harvard Business Review.*

Power, F. C., Higgins, A., & Kohlberg, L. (1991). *Lawrence Kohlberg's approach to moral education.* New York: Columbia University Press.

Prospects. (2011). *Management consultant conditions and salary.* Retrieved from http://www.prospects.ac.uk/management_consultant_salary.htm

Rackham, N. (1988). *SPIN selling.* New York: McGraw-Hill.

Rasiel, E. M. (1999). *The McKinsey way.* New York: McGraw-Hill.

Rasiel, E. M., & Friga, P. N. (2002). *The McKinsey mind.* New York: McGraw-Hill.

Roberts, W. (1990). *Leadership secrets of Attila the Hun.* New York: Warner Books.

Roland Berger calls off tie-up bid. (2010, November 22). *Financial Times,* p. 15.

Sayles, L. (1989). *Leadership: What effective managers really do . . .* New York: McGraw-Hill.

Schein, E. (1980). *Organizational psychology.* Upper Saddle River, NJ: Prentice Hall.

Schein, E. (2001). Groups and intergroup relationships. In W. Natemeyer & T. McMahon (Eds.), *Classics of organizational behavior* (3rd ed.). Long Grove, IL: Waveland Press.

Schermerhorn, J., Hunt, J., et al. (2010). *Organizational behavior* (11th ed.). Hoboken, NJ: Wiley.

Schmidt, W., & Tannenbaum, R. (1960, November-December). Management of differences. *Harvard Business Review.*

Schonberger, R. J. (2010). *World class manufacturing: The next decade.* New York: Free Press.

Sekaran, U. (2003). *Research methods for business* (2nd ed.). Hoboken, NJ: Wiley.

Skinner, B. F. (1992). In R. Gross, *Psychology.* London, UK: Hodder & Stoughton.

Stringer, R. (2002). *Leadership and organizational climate* (OD Series). Upper Saddle River, NJ: Prentice Hall.

Tannen, D. (1996). *Gender and discourse.* New York: Oxford University Press.

The visible hand. Special report on state capitalism. (2012, January 21). *Economist,* pp. 2–18.

Tichy, N. (1983). *Managing strategic change.* New York: Wiley.

Tichy, N., & DeVanna, M. (1986). *The transformational leader.* New York: Wiley.

Tichy, N., & Sherman, S. (1993). *Control your destiny or someone else will.* New York: Doubleday.

Thomas, K. W., & Kilmann, R. H. (1974). *The Thomas-Kilmann conflict mode instrument.* Tuxedo, NY: Xicom.

Top-consultant. (2011). The consulting industry: Six predictions of likely trends in 2011. Retrieved from http://www.consultant-ews.com/article

Top-consultant. (2011). *2011/2012 salary benchmarking report: A comprehensive study of remuneration in management Consulting.* Retrieved from http://www.top-consultant.com/salary_survey.asp

Tuckman, B. W. (1965). Developing sequence in small groups. *Psychological Bulletin, 63,* 384–99.

Ulrich, D. (1997). *Human resource champions.* Boston: Harvard Business School Press.

Ulrich, D., & Brockbank, W. (2005). *The HR value proposition.* Boston: Harvard Business School Press.

University of Notre Dame (2011). *Management consulting: Skills and talents required.* (See careers website in Websites section.)

U.S. Department of Labor. (2006, February). *Occupational outlook handbook, 2006* (7th ed.).

Verlander, E. G. (1986). *Executive education programs in the United States.* Doctoral dissertation, Columbia University, New York.

Verlander, E. G. (1999). *Executive coaching.* In F. Ashby (Ed.), *Effective leadership programs.* Alexandria, VA: American Society for Training & Development.

Verlander, E. G., & Evans, M. (2007). Strategies for improving employee retention. *Clinical Leadership & Management Review, 21*(2).

Vroom, V. (2007). In R. Kreitner, *Management*. New York: Houghton Mifflin.

Warner, J., & Robertson, P. (2000). *So you want to be a consultant*. Frenchs Forest, NSW, Australia: Prentice-Hall—Pearson Education.

Weiss, A. (2009). *Million dollar consulting*. New York: McGraw-Hill.

Whiteley, R. C. (1991). *The customer driven company*. Reading, PA: Addison-Wesley.

Resources: Websites

www.consultant-news.com
www.Vault.com
www.consultingcentral.com
www.plunkettresearch.com
www.mba-channel.com
www.consulting-world.org
www.kennedyinfo.com

Careers in Consulting

www.prospects.ac.uk/management_consultant_entry_requirements.htm
www.careers-in-business.com/consulting/mcskill.htm
www.fabjob.com/businessconsultant.asp
www.top-consultant.com
Association of Management Consulting Firms: http://www.ancf.org
Institute of Management Consultants USA, Inc.: http://www.incusa.org
McNamara, Carter (research methods): http://www.managementhelp.org/research/research
U.S. Office of Personnel Management: http://www.usajobs.opm.gov
kassandraproject.wordpress.com/2007/12/24/killer-corporations-grow-rate-from-2005-to-2007

ABOUT THE AUTHOR

Edward Verlander is chairman of Verlander, Wang & Co., LLC, an international management consulting firm. He and his colleagues deliver services in strategy, organization change, leadership development, and executive coaching. Clients are worldwide and include the Fortune 500, numerous European technology companies, and, most recently, the public and private education sectors in China.

Before going into private consulting practice in 1993, Dr. Verlander was with Harbridge House consultants and Goldman Sachs & Co., where he provided management and organizational consulting services. Previously he was a senior associate in strategic planning at the British firm Lex

Electronics, Inc., managed management education for SCM Corporation, and was associate director of executive programs at Columbia University.

Dr. Verlander has been an editor for the *Journal of Management Development* and has published many articles on executive education, executive coaching, and management development, including "Strategies for Improving Employee Retention" in 2007. He taught in executive education programs at the Columbia Business School and is currently an adjunct professor in the MBA programs at Stony Brook and Long Island Universities.

Born in England, Dr. Verlander now lives in New York. He earned a B.Sc., an MBA degree from the University of Connecticut, and master's and doctoral degrees from Columbia, and completed the Executive Program at the Columbia Business School.

He can be reached at:

E-mail: egverlander@gmail.com
Website: www.egverlander.com

INDEX

Page references followed by *fig* indicate an illustrated figure: followed by *t* indicate a table; followed by *e* indicate an exhibit.